W9-DCY-820

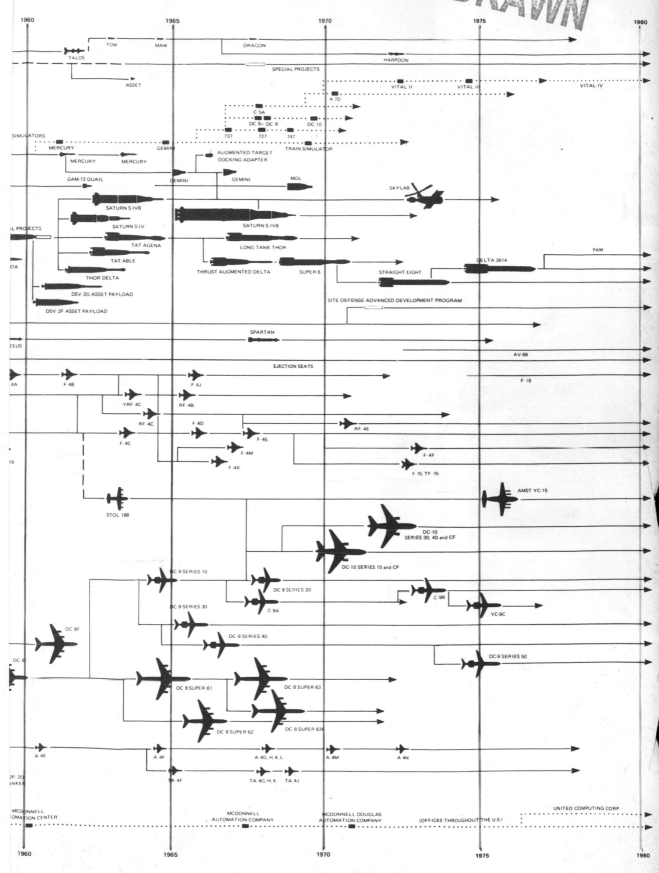

The
MCDONNELL
DOUGLAS
Story

DEDICATED TO

My wonderful and understanding wife Mary Sue Lusk Ingells, and to our favorite feline TAM O'SHANTER.

The

MCDONNELL DOUGLAS

Story

Douglas J. Ingells

AERO PUBLISHERS, INC.
329 West Aviation Road, Fallbrook, CA 92028

ISBN-8168-4995-1
Library of Congress No. 79-54064

Library of Congress Cataloging in Publication Data

Ingells, Douglas J. 1918-
 The McDonnell Douglas Story.
 Includes index.
 1. McDonnell Douglas Corporation. I. Title.
HD9711.U63M324   338.7'62'910973   79-54064
ISBN 0-8168-4995-1

Printed and Published in the United States by Aero Publishers, Inc.

Preface

IT IS GENERALLY acknowledged by historians that the Wright Brothers invented, patented and flew the first successful, controlled, man-carrying, power-driven, heavier-than-air flying machine.

That epic event occurred on December 17, 1903 on the windswept sands of Kill Devil Hill near Kitty Hawk, North Carolina. The first flight, with Orville Wright at the controls, lasted only 57 seconds; but in that short span of time history was written: The aeroplane was born. The world for better or worse, at peace or at war, would never be the same again.

Yet, oddly enough, the first flight did not generate a great deal of public interest. The event was considered headline news by only few of the nation's newspapers. Even the Wright Brothers' hometown papers carried just small items about the first flight, and these appeared on the inside pages.

Recognition and acceptance of the flying machine did not come until five years later during the 1908 trials of the *Wright Flyer,* the military aeroplane the Wrights had built for sale to the U.S. Army. Those trials were held on the parade grounds at Fort Myer, Virginia.

The flights during that two week test period had convinced the United States Army observers that the aeroplane showed military promise. Major Squier summed it up when he said, "If Mr. Wright should never again enter an aeroplane, his work at Fort Myer will have secured him a lasting place in history as the man who showed the world that mechanical flight was an assured success."

In June 1909, Orville returned to Fort Myer with a machine basically the same as the 1908 model, and the Wright Flyer successfully passed all the tests, exceeding most of the requirements. The Signal Corps bought the machine for $30,000, including a bonus for bettering the specified speed. The United States Army became the first in the world to have a military aeroplane.

Other nations were soon to follow. Wilbur Wright, while Orville was at Fort Myer in 1908, was demonstrating another Wright machine to the French, English, Italian, and German governments. All were so impressed with the plane's performance that negotiations were started immediately for the purchase of Wright aeroplanes and patent rights for their manufacture in Europe. With such generated interest it was not difficult for the Wrights to secure financial backing for organizing a company to build flying machines.

The Wright Co. was formed with a paid-in value of $200,000 in capital stock on November 22, 1909. Its offices were located on Fifth Avenue in New York City with a modern factory building in Dayton, Ohio. By summer of 1911, the company was geared to the production of about two planes a month. It marked the beginning of the aircraft manufacturing industry in the United States.

Today, the airframe manufacturers, aircraft engine companies, aircraft component manufacturers—electronic and hydraulic accessories—have grown into a sprawling, complex, industrial giant employing millions of workers from all walks of life, with orders totaling billions and billions of dollars for the design, development, and manufacture of such things as tiny transistors sending back signals from Mars; manned space laboratories orbiting the earth; lunar landing vehicles; rockets and missiles; supersonic fighters and bombers; and giant airliners whose wide-bodied fuselages are longer than the distance flown by the Wright machine at Kitty Hawk.

Among these aerospace companies is the McDonnell Douglas Corporation, an outgrowth of the merger in 1967 of the McDonnell Company of St. Louis, Missouri, and the Douglas Aircraft Company of Santa Monica, California. Headquarters for the corporation (MDC) are located in St. Louis. McDonnell Douglas has facilities located in Missouri, California, Oklahoma, Florida, Michigan, Canada and elsewhere engaged in many diversified activities.

In the following pages the reader will meet the two men who founded this aerospace conglemorate—James Smith McDonnell and Donald Wills Douglas—and the tens of thousands of "teammates" who have contributed so much to the advancement of the airplane and the conquest of space.

Introduction

THIS BOOK was actually born more than thirty-five years ago in the final days of World War II when the author, then a correspondant for *Air Force Magazine,* official Journal of the USAF, was given an assignment to interview Mr. Donald W. Douglas, Sr. I had never met Mr. Douglas and I was a little uneasy in my GI uniform. Especially when good old "Rocky" Rocklen, then head of public relations for the Douglas Aircraft Company and Mr. Douglas' right-hand man, said — "Okay, Ingells, go on in, he's waiting. . . "

The company's headquarters were in Santa Monica at that time. I "went in." Mr. Douglas' office was unpretentious, but there were a lot of aircraft pictures on the walls as well as photos of "heroes of the air." I looked around but didn't see anyone else in the room. My nervousness didn't improve any.

After about ten minutes (maybe less, but it seemed ages) I heard a voice. "Come on over Sergeant, have a seat."

There he was. He had been going through some papers in a lower drawer in his desk. The head popped up. He stood up. He came toward me, hand extended— "What can I do for you?"

You could tell by the firm handshake that he was a strong-willed man. Furthermore, I've always felt that it wouldn't have made any difference if I had been representing *Time* magazine or wearing my sergeant's uniform, the greeting would have been the same. Mr. Douglas is like that. We have had many interviews since. It is the culmination of those talks that inspired this book—*The McDonnell Douglas Story.*

It really began in 1957-58 when I wrote a very long article, entitled "Of Men and Planes"—by Donald W. Douglas as told to Douglas J. Ingells for the old *Flying and Popular Aviation* magazine. Out of that came the gist of material which went into a book about the fabulous Douglas DC-3. Much of it was prime source material, and much of it is included in this book. Of course, things have changed much since then, including the company name.

When the Douglas Aircraft Company merged with the McDonnell Company to form the McDonnell Douglas Corporation in 1967, things changed for me, too. I had known Mr. Douglas. But what was Mr. James Smith McDonnell like? I had never met "Mr. Mac" and I was told he was a pretty tough guy to get to for an interview. Fortunately, however, a meeting was arranged by Dick Davis, head P.R. man in St. Louis. The first thing I knew I was in Mr. Mac's office sitting across the desk as he rattled off a bunch of questions namely concerning *Who is this guy Doug Ingells?*

I remember one question well. He said, reading my dossier which he had before him, "So you knew Orville Wright! Did you know Wilbur?."

He was testing me.

"Not very well," I replied. "Wilbur died in 1912 seven years before I was born ."

He grinned and said, "Why don't you come out to the house to dinner tomorrow night, and we can talk some more."

James Smith McDonnell, Mr. Mac, founder of the McDonnell Aircraft Corporation in 1939, Chairman of The Board of the McDonnell Douglas Corporation.

Donald Wills Douglas, founder Douglas Aircraft Company. Honorary Chairman of the Board McDonnell Douglas Corporation.

I went out to his home the next evening and we had a delightful talk; many mutual friends, many wonderful events and moments recalled. He said to come back anytime and wished me luck on the book venture.

About eighteen months later—after the manuscript was well along—Mr. Mac wrote me a letter and said he'd like to talk to me. It was Christmas time, and that week I spent more than 22 hours talking with him about the McDonnell Douglas Corporation. The McDonnell side of the story unveiled itself. Much of it came from the one source who should know it better than anyone else—Mr Mac himself.

For his part, there was only one insistence—"Make sure you give all the credit to our TEAMMATES. They are the people that keep things going."

It is true, he is a tough boss. He runs a tight ship. But he is sincere in giving credit where credit is due and he means it when he praises the tens of thousands of teammates who make up the McDonnell Douglas Corporation. In this book you will meet many of them.

It is my hope that Mr. Douglas and Mr. McDonnell will be as proud of this book as I am of having the privilege of knowing them and the many people in their organization who have contributed so much to America's effort in the conquest of space.

After all, this is really THEIR story.

Douglas J. Ingells

Acknowledgements

THERE are so many people I am indebted to for assistance in the writing of this book that to name them all would fill a telephone directory. However, there are several I would like to recognize personally for all they have done to make this book possible.

One in particular is Dick Davis, Corporate Vice President of External Relations, Mc-Donnell Douglas Corporation in St. Louis. Dick, perhaps more than anyone else, paved the way for me to have access to many interviews with key personnel, company files and photographs. He has always been very obliging in putting up with my many requests which must have tried his patience. I hope he likes the finished product.

Then there is Gordon LeBert, also from the External Relations offices in St. Louis, who so graciously gave me permission to use a great deal of material from his own historical files on the McDonnell Aircraft Company. Furthermore, I'm appreciative of his help in insuring the technical accuracy of all details, and for the many hours he spent proofing the final manuscript.

To Ray Towne, Director of External Relations, Douglas Aircraft Company in Long Beach, I want to express a very special thanks for a longtime friendship and his assistance in so may areas of research and writing. If it had not been for Ray's encouragements, I most certainly would never have completed the manuscript. His "Where is it?" kept me going even when the word machine had stopped.

There are so many more: Jack Cooke, Chuck Chappell, Tim Tyler, Rae McGinnis, Marie Kuehner and Elaine Bendal, all from the External Relations Department in Long Beach.

Two others spent many hours helping me obtain photographs and data. They are Harry Calkins at Long Beach, and my longtime friend Walt Cleveland at the Huntington Beach facility who made it so easy for me to tell that side of the story.

Then, there is my publisher, Ernie Gentle and his wife Joy, whose hospitality, friendship and understanding when things got "rough" came through with flying colors.

To all who helped, I am most grateful and appreciative.

Douglas J. Ingells

Photo Credits

Table Of Contents

CHAPTER

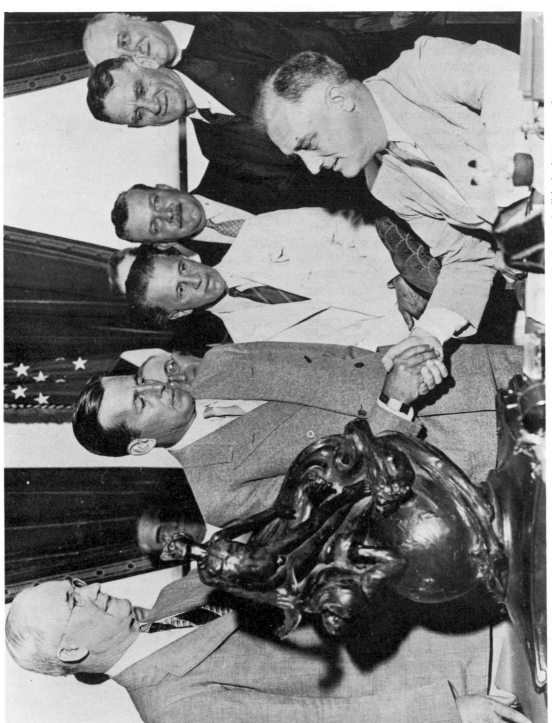

Don Douglas, 16 years after he started his own company in Santa Monica to build airplanes, receives coveted Collier Trophy, aviation's highest award, from President Roosevelt for design of DC-2 airliner.

Chapter One

Man In Santa Monica

WHEN THE FIRST U. S. military aeroplane was tested at Fort Myer, Virginia in 1908 with Orville Wright at the controls, among the spectators was a sandy haired youth of sixteen who would soon enter the U. S. Naval Academy at Annapolis, Maryland. His name was Donald Wills Douglas.

Born in Brooklyn, New York, April 6, 1892, the son of William E. and Dorothy (Locker) Douglas, the youth was more interested in ships of the sea than ships of the air. Albeit, in the not too distant future his ideas would change the shape of wings to come. But in his early childhood, Don Douglas was fascinated by ships. Indeed, they were all around him.

His father, Bill Douglas, an assistant bank cashier, oftentimes would take his son down to the big Brooklyn Navy Yard. It was a splendid sight to see the great naval vessels, and there were even times when they "went aboard" to explore the cruisers, destroyers, submarines, even the big battlewagons, America's "first line of defense" before the advent of airpower. Perhaps that is why young Douglas studied hard at Trinity Chapel School in New York City, made good grades, and passed the necessary examinations to win an appointment to the United States Naval Academy at Annapolis. Too, he was following in the footsteps of his older brother, Harold, who had entered the service school two years before. There may

have been some brotherly advice involved. But the sea, the bountiful, beautiful and boistrous sea, beckoned. It still does. Don Douglas, in his mid-eighties as this is written, is an ardent yachtsman. But his fame and fortune were made building skycraft, not seacraft. Young Don wanted wings.

There is a story that Douglas started building model airplanes while at the Academy, launched one from the dorm window one day, and it clipped the plumed hat off a passing admiral. Hogwash! Douglas, himself, has always denied the incident. In the first place, he probably didn't have the time. When he wasn't buried in bookwork, Naval history and strategy, math and military mannerisms, he was playing the rough and tumble game of lacrosse as a member of the varsity in 1911. It is likely about the same time his interest in aeroplanes was again fired up.

On January 19, 1911, a civilian pilot, Eugene Ely, in one of Glenn Curtiss' pusher biplanes, took off from the Presidio in San Francisco and flew out to sea, landing on a specially constructed platform aboard the U.S. Cruiser *Pennsylvania*. A short time later Ely took off from shipboard and flew back to his starting point. Ely's feat marked the beginning of the aircraft carrier, and from that day forward Naval Aviation was here to stay. And it is probably true that lectures, pro

"Don't bother me, boy," Martin repeated, "Now, if your name happened to be Donald W. Douglas . . ."

The bothersome one drew up his shoulders, "I am Donald W. Douglas." Martin hired him, then and there.

At Martin for only about a year, Douglas resigned and accepted a position in Washington, D.C. as chief civilian aeronautical engineer for the Army's Aviation Section of the Signal Corps. Douglas suggested ideas that never got beyond the wastebasket. He designed planes that never got off the drawing boards. The Army simply wasn't ready for his advanced thinking. Finally, fed up with the red tape, he left and went back to work for Martin, whose plant had moved to Cleveland, Ohio.

Martin assigned him to design a bomber that would dwarf any previously built U.S. plane. Result: The G.M.B. (Glenn Martin Bomber, designed by D.W.D., Donald W. Douglas), a huge twin-engined (two Liberty 400-horsepower engines) biplane with a wingspan of 71 feet 5 inches, a fuselage that measured 46 feet 10 inches, nose to tail, gross weight of 10,225 pounds with a crew of three, and a top speed of 113 mph. Delivered to the Army about the time of the signing of the Armistice (November 11, 1918), it was too late for World War I, but the Signal Corps, by then the Army Air Service, bought ten improved versions, the first order for a wholly-designed American combat aircraft. Don Douglas' reputation as a designer of planes was greatly enhanced by the Martin's performance.

The Great War was over. The Army wasn't much interested in any new warplane designs for the moment and things were pretty slow at Martin. But Douglas had other ideas. He believed the aeroplane had an important role in the peacetime society, and he decided to form his own company and design planes for commercial purposes, carrying passengers, flying the mail. Here was a new challenge. Douglas accepted it.

In April 1920, a few days after his 28th birthday, with less than $1,000 total assets, he quit Martin and boarded a train for Los

First Douglas office was in back room of this barber shop on Pico Boulevard in Los Angeles.

Angeles. He liked the warm California climate, and he had decided to locate there, start his own company and build aeroplanes, Douglas Aeroplanes. The going was tough.

Despite glowing praise in letters of introduction signed by Martin to influential, monied Californians, Douglas found little interest from anyone wanting to put up additional capital to start an aircraft manufacturing venture. Motion pictures, YES! Flying machines, NO!

Operating from a small office space he had rented in the back of a barbershop on Pico Boulevard, Douglas pounded the streets, day after day, trying to get financing. When he came home at night he hoed potatoes and tended other vegetables in a garden behind his small dwelling so the family wouldn't starve.

A friend, Bill Henry, who once had worked for Martin as a public relations man and was now a sportswriter for a Los Angeles paper, came to the rescue. Henry introduced Douglas to a millionaire sportsman and flying enthusiast, David R. Davis, who had confided to Henry a desire he had to buy a plane and attempt a coast-to-coast, non-stop flight.

At their first meeting Douglas convinced Davis he had a design on paper that could make the 2500-mile flight from L.A. to the East Coast. Davis put up $40,000 for the project. The Davis-Douglas Company was formed.

Immediately, Douglas contacted several of his former associates at Martin, among them a draftsman, James H. "Dutch" Kindleberger, who one day would become famous in his own right as a plane designer and builder, and head of the North American Aviation Corporation. Another Douglas recruit was Eric Springer, Martin's chief test pilot. Upon their arrival, work was started on the coast-to-coast plane in the loft of the Koll Lumber Mill near the Southern Pacific railroad station in the center of Los Angeles. Tools were borrowed from the shop downstairs. As the different sections of the plane were fabricated, they were lowered by block and tackle to a waiting truck, and hauled away to the Goodyear Blimp hanger on the outskirts of the city. There, in a shed Douglas had rented, final assembly took place.

One year later the plane was completed. It was a biplane with a wingspan of 56 feet, fuselage length of 35 feet and a height of 13 feet, resting on a conventional type undercarriage, two main wheels and a tail-wheel. Of wooden frame construction, it was fabric-covered and powered by a single 400 horsepower Liberty engine. A unique feature was a large "spinner"—a cone-shaped nose piece for the propeller to streamline the airflow.

According to Douglas, the plane was designed for a cruising speed of 85 mph with a

Work on first Douglas plane was done in loft of old lumber mill in center of Los Angeles. In rear cockpit is Don Douglas, with moustache. Plane was named the *Cloudster*.

After the *Cloudster,* Douglas Company moved to this factory, an abandoned movie studio on Wilshire Boulevard near Santa Monica. Plane is Army O-2 observation aircraft. Company remained in this location until 1928 when name was changed to Douglas Aircraft Company and headquarters moved into new factory adjacent to Clover Field in Santa Monica, where for more than 40 years Douglas would turn out thousands of planes for Army, Navy, Marines, Coast Guard and the airlines of the world.

range of 2800 miles. They gave it a name—the *Cloudster.*

Since the Goodyear location was too small, the machine was towed to March Field, the Army airfield at Riverside, California, where arrangements had been made with the military for its initial test flight. Eric Springer was the pilot, and on February 24, 1921 everything was in readiness for the *Cloudster* to try her wings.

Just before the start, Davis' pretty niece, Jane Pearsall, wielded an "illegal" bottle of champagne (It was the height of Prohibition) in an appropriate christening ceremony.

On its first attempt, the *Cloudster* never got off the ground. Springer, running out of takeoff distance, ground-looped the ship and came to a stop in a farmer's adjacent field. Fortunately, there was no damage to the plane, but the irate farmer, reportedly sued Douglas for $55, an inauspicious beginning.

Springer tried again, and this time the *Cloudster* took off, circled the field for about

half an hour, and landed gracefully. There were subsequent test flights, one of which set a new Pacific Coast altitude record when it climbed to 19,160 feet. But the real test was yet to come—the transcontinental non-stop attempt.

On June 27, 1921, in the chilly dawn at March Field, Springer, with Davis as a passenger, took off in the *Cloudster* and pointed the plane's nose eastward. Next stop, Curtiss Field, Long Island.

By noon they had hurdled the Western range of mountains, and were zipping along over the Arizona desert near Yuma. At 3:35 P.M. they were over El Paso, Texas. Shortly, the faithful Liberty engine sputtered, then quit altogether, and they were forced down at Fort Bliss, Texas.

Before they could get the plane repaired and fly it back to California for a second attempt, the coveted goal was snatched from their grasp. Two Army Lieutenants, Oakley G. Kelley and John A. Macready, in a single-engine, Fokker T-2 monoplane, had spanned the continent, non-stop, from Roosevelt Field, Long Island, to Rockwell Field, San Diego— 2,520 miles—in 26 hours and 50 minutes. The challenge and claim to fame gone, Davis sold the *Cloudster*, and his interest in the Davis-Douglas Company.

Although the *Cloudster* failed in its attempt to fly coast-to-coast, it set another record of a kind. The plane was the first in history to lift more than its own weight in payload. The *Cloudster* also made history of another sort when it was sold a second time to T. Claude Ryan, who rebuilt it as a twelve passenger closed cabin aircraft, and used it as the flagship of his San Diego to Los Angeles airline, one of the first scheduled passenger lines in the country. Even Don Douglas, when he had built the *Cloudster*, didn't know that he had built his first commercial airliner.

Now the head of his own company—The Douglas Company—the one-time Annapolis midshipman took a train to Washington, D.C. and hounded Navy Department gold braid to look at plans for a new torpedo-bomber created basically around the *Cloudster* design. The Navy was impressed, and Douglas came back to L.A. with an order to build three of the planes.

There was only one big hitch: he didn't

have a place to build the planes, or money enough to buy materials. This time he found another "angel" in the person of Harry B. Chandler, publisher of the Los Angeles *Times.* Chandler and some friends put up $15,000, the amount Douglas said he needed, and the Douglas Company facility moved into new quarters in Santa Monica. The building was a one time motion picture studio on the corner of Wilshire Boulevard and 24th Street. It would be the main production facility until 1929 when it was moved to Clover Field in southwest Santa Monica. This site would be headquarters for Douglas for almost forty years. Almost continuously through those years, it would be turning out aircraft of one kind or another for the Army, Navy, Air Force, Marines, the scheduled airlines, NACA (National Advisory Committee for Aeronautics) and private fliers; from planes of wood and cloth and glue, powered with piston engines, to needle-nosed metallic experimental supersonic research planes run by rocket power.

Back there in the early twenties, however, in the rehabilitated old movie studio, things were nip and tuck to fulfill the order for the trio of Navy torpedo planes. Douglas has confessed many times that he wished he had asked for more capital to start with, but it was

The Cloudster, first wholly Douglas-designed, Douglas-built aircraft. It was first airplane ever to carry a useful load exceeding its own weight.

The *Cloudster*, rebuilt as airliner, pioneered scheduled air transportation in California. Ironically, almost a decade before the DC-1—first of a long line of Douglas Commercial airliners was born —the *Cloudster* could carry more passengers than the DC-1, and it had only one engine.

Navy DT-Torpedo bomber, which Douglas sold to Navy and got contract to build three planes. It marked beginning of long association with Navy.

against his Scotch ancestral frugality and pride. He was determined to make do with what he had.

There were times when the force of 20 loyal workers sacrificed their paydays. Wives often helped to sew on the fabric covering for fuselages and wings. Sometimes, Douglas had to beg and borrow for credit to get the necessary tools and materials. But they got the job done, and the DT's (Douglas Torpedo planes) were finished on time. The Navy was so impressed with their performance that in the fall of 1924, Douglas Aircraft got an order for 38 more. Things were looking up.

By 1924, Douglas was building several different types of planes: the Navy DT's, a highly successful and economical single-engine biplane, the M-1 mail plane for the Post Office Department, and some observation ships (0-2s) for the Army.

There was also a very secret project in progress, the design and development of the DWC's (Douglas World Cruisers) for the Army Air Service in the midst of planning for a round-the-world flight to demonstrate the value of flying and its impact on all nations. The contract called for five planes (DWC's) patterned very much after the DT's and the mailplanes, but with special design features which enabled them to be quickly converted from landplanes to seaplanes.

The prototype of the DWC was delivered in December 1923 to the Army pilots at Langley Field in Virginia, where it was also subjected to rigid tests. Passing with flying colors, the first DWC was used for training specially selected crews for the globe-girdling flight.

Meanwhile, the four remaining DWC's were completed at the Santa Monica plant, and preparations were underway for the planes to be flown to Seattle, Washington, which had been designated as the starting point for the world flight. On St. Patrick's Day (1924), all four planes took off from Clover Field, Santa Monica, at five minute intervals, for the hop to Seattle.

Each had a name selected by mutual agreement among the respective flight crews, who had decided to christen their winged machines after American cities to better acquaint our world neighbors with the United States. Thus, on April 6, 1924—coincidentally, Don Douglas' 32nd birthday—we find the four DWCs, the *Seattle, Chicago, New Orleans,* and *Boston,* equipped with pontoons instead of wheels, rocking gently in the waters of Puget Sound. Their two-man flight crews were eagerly awaiting the official starting signal. Everything was in readiness. It was 8:47 a.m. that April morning in hazy weather when the first plane was airborne. The others quickly followed the *Chicago* into the air and the four planes headed westward for Prince Rupert Island, 605 miles distant.

Flying in rain, sleet and snow, the worst

When going was tough to meet Navy deadline for Torpedo bombers, wives of Douglas plant workers pitched in to help. It was probably first instance of women on the assembly line in the aircraft manufacturing industry— grandmothers perhaps of "Rosie the Riveters" of World War II fame.

Douglas M-2 mailplane. According to a Western Air Express news release in 1930: "The first Douglas Mailplane ever built (April 1926) is still in service. It has flown the equivalent of ten times around the world, has earned a gross revenue of over $500,000, has never been damaged and has never been one minute off schedule." True or not, the M-2s served the still young Air Mail Service well.

Douglas O-2 Observation plane built under Army contract, the first time the company did business with the Air Force, then the Aviation Section of the Army Signal Corps. Today, 50 years later, McDonnell Douglas is major supplier of USAF first-line fighters, F-4s, F-15s.

Don Douglas, with his mother and officers and crew of round-the-world flight, at start of the flight on St. Patrick's Day, 1924. One of DWCs is in background.

Designer of the famous *World Cruisers*, Don Douglas looks pridefully at the "New Orleans," one of the planes that completed first aerial circumnavigation of the globe.

THE MCDONNELL DOUGLAS STORY

Douglas *World Cruiser* "Chicago," equipped with floats for overwater stretches of famous round-the-world flight in 1924. Splendid record-setting performance of the DWCs made Douglas famous as plane designer.

weather in years and bucking strong headwinds, the DWC's arrived at Prince Rupert 8 hours and 15 minutes later. It was not until six months later in the afternoon of September 23, 1924, that the fliers returned to Santa Monica to be welcomed by a crowd of 200,000 persons.

Only three planes touched down at Clover Field, the *Chicago, New Orleans* and *Boston II*, the latter being a replacement for the original *Boston* ditched in the North Atlantic. *Seattle* had crashed early in the flight near Dutch Harbor, Alaska. Luckily, there were no casualties.

Covering a total of 27,553 miles in 175 days—actual flying time, 371 hours and 11 minutes—the planes returned to Seattle on September 28, completing history's first flight around the world. The remarkable feat put U.S. military aviation in the international spotlight. All the publicity and acclaim didn't hurt Douglas, either. As builder of the planes, the Douglas Company was in a prestigious position.

The world market opened up when Norway ordered some modified versions of the Navy torpedo planes. The Norwegians were also granted permission to manufacture the airplane under license.

"First Around The World—First The World Around," later became the motto of the Douglas Aircraft Company. In the years ahead, Douglas planes would live up to the maxim with many "firsts" as they flew higher, farther and faster.

There would be a long succession of planes

that changed the world, fighters, bombers, observation planes, transports.

Their names would go down in history: XB-19, the world's largest aircraft in 1939; *Havocs* (A-20s) and *Invaders* (A-26s) of World War II fame; *Dauntless* and *Skyhawk* fighters for the Navy; the fabulous DC-3, first of the modern luxury airliners and its famous C-47 *"Gooney Bird"* military counterpart; *Skystreak*, a supersonic probe; the DC-4, first of the post-World War II four-engined airliners, followed by larger DC-6s, DC-7s (*Seven Seas*)—largest of the piston-powered airliners; a whole new family of jetliners, the DC-8 and successive stretch versions culminating with the *Stretch Eight* (63 series), largest of the jetliners until the 747 came along; the DC-9, most popular of the twin-engined jetliners.

Likewise, Douglas was the developer of a long line of missiles. The missiles had memorable names—*Aerobee, Wac Corporal, Nike Ajax, Sparrow I* and *Sparrow II, Honest John, Genie, Bird Dog, Thor, Saturn IV*, each a pioneer in the new science of rocketry. Some were important adjuncts as launch vehicles for man's leap into space.

All of this was Douglas Aircraft Company during the four decades from the World *Cruisers* of 1924 to the world of missiles of 1964. These were times of progress and profit and great growth potential.

The "good years" would last until the mid-sixties, when for the first time Douglas Aircraft Company went into a tailspin. The trouble was of a nature that the best aeronautical engineers, rocket scientists, and some of the most efficient production people in the business could do little about. The trouble was financial. The Douglas Aircraft Company was going broke.

Ironically, the company had too much business and too little capital. Was it poor management? Over-zealousness? Too many cooks in the kitchen? Too many hands in too many pies? The high cost of high flying? More likely, it was a combination of all of these things. Douglas had the orders for sleek fighters, solid-performing jetliners (the popular DC-8 and DC-9), military missiles, rocket boosters for spacecraft, and it was engaged in many other fields, including atomic energy research. But it simply couldn't put it all together in a fashion to show a profit.

The alternatives were few: close the doors, get a government loan, or merge with a dollar-strong partner.

The Cloudster after conversion to airliner, in flight. The photo is rare one of first Douglas designed aircraft in flight.

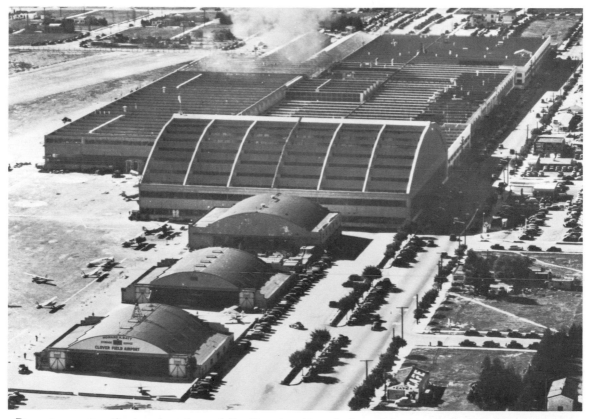

For many years, the headquarters of the Douglas Aircraft Company was located on Clover Field in Santa Monica, California.

For his dynamic leadership in aeronautics and astronautics, demonstrated by the performance of the *Gemini* spacecraft and by the *Phantom* II aircraft, McDonnell received the 1966 Collier Trophy Award on May 24, 1967 from Vice President Hubert Humphrey, on behalf of President Lyndon Johnson.

Chapter Two

The St. Louis Connection

WITH AMERICANS FIGHTING and dying in Vietnam, and another kind of "war" going on in space, the Soviets and the U.S. challenging each other in the great moon race, it was certainly no time to let an aerospace giant like Douglas Aircraft go under. The demise of Douglas could endanger American security. On the other hand, a government loan to "bail out" the financially insolvent company could be a serious blow to the American free enterprise system, another rung up the ladder of socialism. The best course, indeed, was to find a fiscally healthy partner to merge with Douglas.

Fortunately, there was an understanding benefactor waiting in the wings to come to the rescue. His name was James Smith McDonnell, Board Chairman and founder of the McDonnell Aircraft Corporation of St. Louis, Missouri. The company—renamed McDonnell Company in December 1966 — was the producer of the fabulous *Phantom* jets and builders of the *Mercury* and *Gemini* spacecraft that put the first American astronauts into space.

Perhaps it was destined that the two men—McDonnell and Douglas—should get together. Both were born under the sign of the Ram, ARIES, and astrologers tell us persons born under this influence represent a pioneering attitude, unafraid to launch new venturesome endeavors, capable of turning daydreams into realities. Both were of Scottish descent—frugal, determined, courageous, persevering, keyed to success through dedicated hard work. Both were graduates of M.I.T., likely with similar basic fundamental knowledge of aeronautical design stemming from this background. And both, each in his own way, possessed an insatiable desire to have his own company, do his own thing.

We will discuss in a later chapter how McDonnell saved the day, when on April 28, 1967 McDonnell Company and Douglas Aircraft Company merged to create McDonnell Douglas Corporation. But first, let's take a closer look at the man who put it all together to make the name McDonnell Douglas synonymous with progress in the science of aeronautics and space technology in man's quest to touch a star.

JAMES SMITH McDONNELL, JR. was born April 9, 1899, in Denver, Colorado, the son of James Smith and Susie Belle Hunter McDonnell. There were two other boys, the late Hunter McDonnell, who would become a successful New York architect, and William A. McDonnell, highly successful in the banking business. A sister, Susan McDonnell, was the fourth child. All were raised near Little Rock, Arkansas, and completed grade and high school there. Their father owned a general store in Altheimer, Arkansas.

THE MCDONNELL DOUGLAS STORY

Although "McDonnell" is an Irish spelling, the family traces its ancestry far back into Scottish lineage. In the 13th century, according to a genealogy compiled by Mrs. William McDonnell, the family spelled its name "McDonald." In the 15th century, they began to spell it "MacDonald" and in the mid 1700's it was changed again to "McDonnell!" Nobody questions that McDonnell is a Scotsman. He lives by the frugality, integrity, common sense and hard toil for which the Scots are famous.

From early childhood, he was taught that to earn money you had to work for it. There were no spending money allowances handed out to the McDonnell boys, even though their father was a prosperous cotton merchant as well as storekeeper. James Jr. earned his pocket money the hard way. He had a paper route, miles long, not blocks, and he arose at 5:30 a.m. every morning to deliver the Arkansas *Gazette* on horseback. The young predawn "Paul Revere" earned $3.50 a week!

After being graduated from Little Rock high school, James, who was the youngest of the three sons, enrolled at Princeton University in 1917. One day before the term started, he took a trolley ride to Trenton. The streetcar line ran past some open New Jersey countryside, and there in a farmer's field he espied an old rickety biplane. There was a sign that read: SKY RIDES $10! James Smith McDonnell, Jr., who one day would make millions manufacturing airplanes and space vehicles, age 18, pulled the STOP cord and jumped off the trolley.

Minutes later, with the wires of the old crate singing, the wind ruffling his hair in the open cockpit, he was getting a bird's eye view of the historic campus, and rapturously enjoying his first plane ride. In the light of future endeavors, the two $5 bills he handed over to the barnstorming pilot may well have been the best investment he ever made. By his own admission, he had been thinking previously about aviation as a career, and the first skyride certainly didn't dull that interest.

"With my country at war," he once told the author, "I tried to get into the Army Signal Corps Aviation Service, but they turned me down because of my eyes. Later, however, they changed the eye test examination, and I was accepted for flight training at Brooks Field, San Antonio, Texas, Class of 1923." He won his wings and a Second Lieutenant's

Commission in the Army Air Service Reserve the same year, along with some pretty distinguished other fledgling fliers. Among them, Hoyt S. Vandenberg and Nathan F. Twining, both of whom would become four star Generals and Chiefs of Staff of the United States Air Force following the Second World War.

The way he got his "second chance" to become a U.S. Army aviator, was typical of McDonnell's determination, sound thinking and do-it-don't-dream philosophy, an inherent nature. After serving seven months as a buck private in the Army, he finished college, graduating from Princeton with a Bachelor of Science degree in 1921. Furthering his desire and goal to get into aviation, he was one of four accepted in the school of aeronautical engineering in the fall of 1921 at the Massachusetts Institute of Technology. He was working on his Master's thesis when his appointment came through as a flying cadet.

One can almost sense what was going on in his mind: it would be pretty difficult, downright poor judgement on the part of the Army's Flight Training Qualifications Board to turn down a graduate aeronautical engineer who wanted to become a pilot. There were very few engineer-pilots in the Air Service, and rarer still was the military aviator who knew anything about what made an airplane fly and how to design one of the winged machines. A 'joystick' and a 'slide-rule' were about as far apart as the cloth-and-baling-wire "Jennies" he learned to fly in and the sleek jet-powered *Phantoms* that one day his firm would design and build, and in turn would be acclaimed in the 1970s as the best fighter planes in the world.

IT WAS NOT UNTIL 1925 that he was awarded his Master's Degree in Aeronautical Engineering from M.I.T.—the same school, remember, from which Don Douglas was graduated 11 years before. Times were different, however, in the post-war years so far as the job market in aviation circles was concerned. It was tough going to latch onto any position in the aircraft industry, struggling to stay alive in the absence of military orders. It was so tough, in fact, that even the Air Service had to fight tooth and nail to get Congress to give it enough money to buy gasoline for its planes. The private sector of avia-

30

tion was comprised mostly of wartime fliers in their war surplus planes "barnstorming" around the country trying to generate public interest in the future of aviation. The Air Mail under Post Office management, was just beginning to catch on, and passenger carrying airlines, except for a very few, very shaky fly-by-night operations, were non-existent.

pany of Buffalo, New York. He stayed with Consolidated several months, then joined the Stout Metal Airplane Company of Detroit, Michigan, as an assistant Chief Engineer. There, he worked on the design and development of the Stout all-metal trimotor which so interested Henry Ford, the automotive genius, that he bought out Stout and formed

Mr. Mac, at Huff-Dalland, worked on planes like this one, the *Petrel*, which was a forerunner of special planes designed for crop dusting.

Consequently, McDonnell even though he was a qualified pilot and a qualified aeronautical engineer, didn't have much luck trying to get a position in the aircraft industry. Indeed, the whole airplane industry in the U.S. at that time had only about 2800 employees. There were less than 200 professional engineers. "Mac" wrote to every aircraft manufacturer, job seeking. No one was interested. Ironically, he was turned down by Douglas, whose company he would one day lead out of the doldrums.

Persistence paid off, finally, and he went to work as a draftsman for the Huff Daland Airplane Co., Ogdensburg, New York. His salary was $108 a month. The job didn't last long, neither did Huff Daland, but he found himself a position as a Stress Analyst and Draftsman for Consolidated Aircraft Com-

the Aviation Division of the Ford Motor Car Company. McDonnell and his talent went along with the deal.

One result was the famous Ford all-metal, 10-passenger high-wing trimotor (affectionately called the "Tin Goose") which for a time in the late twenties and early thirties would become the most popular airliner in the small family of scheduled airlines then just coming into existence. Although William Bushnell Stout, grandson of William Bushnell credited with the invention of the first American submarine, is oftentimes called the designer of the fabulous "Tin Goose," that claim to fame is doubtful. The trimotor Stout built was a monstrosity. (See photo). The trimotor Ford put on the market was almost a chinese copy of Tony Fokker's plywood and fabric trimotor which Com-

31

William Bushnell "Jackknife" Stout, who got Henry Ford interested in the manufacture of airplanes. Stout is generally credited with the design of the famous Ford Trimotor, although he had really little to do with its final configuration. Here he is shown beside one of his early experimental designs, the *Air Sedan.* He did pioneer all-metal construction for aircraft.

When he joined Stout Metal Airplane Company, Mr. Mac may have worked on several different airplanes as an engineer-designer. This one, called *The Bat* because of its enormous wing, was a twin-engine Navy Torpedo bomber. Mr. Mac says he can't really remember, but he "thinks" he had a piece of the action in design of *Air Pullman* and first Ford trimotors.

Another Stout airplane was this single-engine, all-metal *Air Pullman*. It was this transport that got Henry Ford to buy out the Stout Metal Airplane Company, which became a division of Ford Motor Company. The *Air Pullman* became the backbone of a fleet of "airliners" and "air freighters" which Ford operated on a scheduled airline between plants in Detroit, Chicago, Cleveland as the Ford Air Transport Service. It was first plane to bear the name FORD.

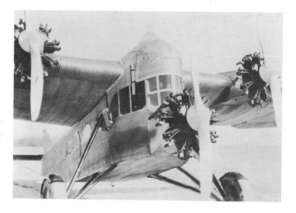

This was Bill Stout's first effort at a trimotor design. Ford called it a "monstrosity," didn't want anything to do with it, and sent Stout on nationwide tour while Ford engineers set to work designing first Ford trimotor, daddy of the famous *Tin Goose* series of air transports.

Gander of the *Tin Goose* was this 4-AT trimotor, first of Ford-engineered designs. Mr. Mac definitely had a part, when working in the engineering and design section of the Ford Motor Company.

mander Richard E. Byrd, in 1926, flew over the North Pole and into history. Its configuration was far different from Bill Stout's trimotor. Indeed, Old Henry had sent Stout on a nation-wide speaking tour, while Ford Motor Company Airplane Division's engineers—among them McDonnell—came up with the basic design of the "Gander of the Tin Goose family," one of the safest airplanes ever built. About the same time, they were also working on a small, single-place, single engine "flying flivver" which Henry Ford had dreams of turning into the Model-T of the Air Age. The dream died when the plane crashed during tests in Florida, killing one of Henry Ford's close friends, Harry Brooks, test pilot. Distraught over Brooks' death, Henry Ford lost all interest in aviation, and closed down his operation.

The "flying flivver" may, however, have had an influence on the career of James S. McDonnell, Jr. after he left Ford, by request.

The story goes that he got fired by Henry Ford, himself, because McDonnell showed up one day at the plant wearing knickers. In recalling the incident, McDonnell has said— "I didn't know the old man had an aversion to knickers." Maybe not, but Henry Ford had an aversion to eccentricities, one of them being *no one else around the plant except Ol' Henry would appear in knickers.* When young McDonnell asked for an explanation of his firing he was told the knickers were only part of the reason. Whatever else it was, he never learned about it.

No matter, anyway. After his dismissal, McDonnell was hired as Chief Engineer for the Hamilton Aero Manufacturing Co., Milwaukee, Wisconsin, and in two years, he would form his own company.

THE TIMING WAS PROPITIOUS. Harry F. Guggenheim, a World War I flier and his father, Daniel Guggenheim, who had made millions with their mining operations, gold, silver and other precious metals, had just announced the Guggenheim Safe Aircraft worldwide competition. The Daniel Guggenheim Fund for the promotion of aeronautics founded with more than $2,500,000 in 1926, was offering $100,000 as first prize to the winner in the safe plane contest. With his eye on the $100,000 plum, McDonnell quit his job with Hamilton and started James S. McDonnell & Associates. The partners were James C. Cowling, Jr., of Milwaukee, a Harvard graduate

The Ford *Flying Flivver,* which Old Henry had in mind to make the Model-T of aviation. The dream died when the plane crashed, killing one of Ford's closest friends. It may have lived, however, in the mind of Mr. Mac, who left Ford about the same time. Several years later, he designed and built his own *flying flivver.* (insert) Lindberg in *Flying Flivver.*

Mr. Mac's "flying flivver" vintage 1928-29. It was his first design, and a good one for its day. They called it the *Doodlebug*. He doesn't like to talk about it, probably because it was one of the few "dreams" he had —to give everybody wings—that he didn't make come true. The flivver idea died out when the depression of the early '30s clipped everybody's wings.

who worked for the Hamilton Company, and Constantine Levoyavich Zakhartchenko, of New York, a classmate of McDonnell's in graduate school at M.I.T. Early in 1928, the trio set out to design and build what McDonnell called "the flivver plane of the future." It would be the McDonnell entry in the Guggenheim competition. The design would compete with 25 other entrants. To be an official entry the machine had to be on the ground at Mitchell Field, Long Island, by midnight, Thursday, October 31, 1929, the contest deadline. Qualifying tests could be made thereafter.

On paper, the "flivver" began to define itself. It was to be a two-place front and rear open cockpit in tandem low-wing monoplane. The wings and fuselage would be of wooden frame covered with fabric. It would have a conventional tractor-type undercarriage, two main wheels and a tail wheel. The plane would incorporate special wing slots and wing flaps, which McDonnell had designed to enhance stability and increase the lift at slow speeds. It would have a theoretical speed of 110 mph, but it could slow down to permit landing on the proverbial dime.

After months of tests with models in the wind tunnel at New York University, with excellent results, actual construction was started in the Hamilton factory in Milwaukee. From then on, it became a race against time. And time ran out. But the contest committee granted J. S. McDonnell & Associates an extension until mid-November to fly their plane to New York. Other entries could make their qualifying trials first.

It was not until Friday, November 15, that the plane made its initial flight over the Milwaukee County Airport. There was drama. McDonnell climbed into the ship's rear cockpit, and took off just as darkness was setting in. He flew the plane for about 50 minutes, swallowed up in the black of night. Although once in a while the moon ducked out from behind a cloud. The handful of observers said he landed on a moonbeam, and with the aid of a couple of flashlights tied to the undercarriage. The plane's designer proudly announced his creation had performed beautifully, and that next day he would hop off for Mitchell Field, New York.

Saturday, November 16, at 4:35 p.m., J.S. McDonnell took off alone on the 900 mile cross country flight. The flight was not uneventful: a leaky gas tank forced him down at Racine, Wisconsin. The tank repaired, he flew to Chicago for an overnight stop. On Sunday morning he was off again with scheduled refueling stops at Toledo, Ohio, and Bellafonte, Pennsylvania. He was following the route of the Air Mail. He was forced down after the Toledo stop about 12 miles west of Cleveland. Thick fog blotted out everything, and he landed the plane in a small field.

It was a good test for the plane's wing slots and flaps, he reported to his associates. Any plane not thus equipped could not possibly have landed in a field the size of the one he had picked. Equally remarkable was the fact that he could take off again in the short distance available, and fly on to Cleveland where he landed in almost zero-zero visability. There he was grounded by fog and storms until Tuesday noon, when he was in the air again, heading for New York. He landed at Mitchell Field late Tuesday afternoon. At times, he said, he had let the plane fly itself. Over-zealously pleased with the ship's stability, upon arrival at Mitchell he wired his associates—"We will win the Guggenheim contest, yet."

Things looked pretty bright that he would do just that after the plane's first demonstration flight on Saturday, November 23. McDonnell took off after a very short run, put the plane through some stalls, flew past observers upside-down, did tailspins, loop-the-loops and whip stalls, after which he brought the plane down to an almost vertical landing. It rolled only about 15 feet after touch down. Observers declared that it had made the best showing so far compared with other entrants.

Then it happened. On his second flight, coming out of a steep dive, the stabilizer on the tail broke, and the plane was plunging earthward at a terrific speed. Spectators on the ground expected any instant to see the pilot pop out of the diving plane and use his parachute. Not McDonnell. About to "bail out," he made one last effort to get the ship under control. Because of the flaps and slots permitting him to brake the speed, he managed to stop the dive, level off and bring the plane down in an adjacent field to a rough landing. Everything would have been fine, except it hit a concrete block or stone knocking off the right wheel, causing a ground loop and damaging the right wing. It would take two or

"Barnstorming" aviator James Smith McDonnell, about age 30, with *Doodlebug*, which he flew around the country. The suit and chute weighed almost as much as the propeller.

Winner of the Guggenheim Safe Aircraft award was this Curtiss *Tanager* biplane. The *Tanager* used slots and flaps and floating ailerons on its wing tips.

three weeks to repair the plane. Hopes dimmed for chances of winning the big prize, even though officials gave J. S. McDonnell & Associates until December 23rd to get their plane in the air again, when it would be flown for evaluation tests by Guggenheim pilots.

The day the deadline arrived, McDonnell and his mechanic, C. L. Zakh, were in the air racing against time, once more making the flight from Milwaukee to New York. They didn't make it. Near Waukegon, Illinois, a connecting rod broke, the motor stalled and they had to land. A broken landing gear strut was the only damage, but repairs would require several days. There was no extension of time, and McDonnell's hopes for winning the Guggenheim competition went out like a faulty light on the Christmas tree. Ironically, it was Christmas Eve when he got the discouraging news. No more time.

On January 6, 1930, presentation of the coveted first prize of $100,000 was made to the Curtiss Aeroplane and Motor Company at appropriate ceremonies in New York City. The winning entry was a Curtiss "Tanager" biplane. Although it successfully performed almost all of the contest requirements, the *Tanager* was never heard much about after its winning of the Safe Airplane Competition. Certainly, it never became "everybody's airplane."

ALTHOUGH DISHEARTENED BY the twists of fate that knocked him out in the final rounds, McDonnell was far from discouraged with his "flying flivver" design. He again repaired the airplane and set out on a nation-wide tour to demonstrate its remarkable performance and airworthiness. J. S. McDonnell & Associates was dissolved, but he took a position as Vice President of the Air Transport Engineering Corporation of Chicago, a consulting firm, to help finance an intensive year of "barnstorming" and other flying exhibitions. Before the year was over he had flown his little monoplane 26,000 miles—over the Rockies, across Canada, East, West, North and South in America's skies.

The last week in August 1930, we find him at the National Air Races held at Curtiss-Reynolds Airport in Chicago. His plane, which he had named the *Doodlebug,* was an entry in the civilian free-for-all race. After that, he flew the plane in the 6,000 mile National Air Tour, sponsored, incidentally, by the Ford Motor Car Company, Aviation Division, for whom he had once worked. In January, the *Doodlebug* took part in the All-American Air Races held in Miami, Florida. Everywhere he went, the plane performed splendidly and attracted a lot of attention.

Despite a fine showing and a remarkable performance after thousands of miles of flying, over all types of terrain, in all kinds of weather, he couldn't raise the necessary funds to put the plane into production. It was not, however, any fault of the design or its creator. These were trying times, at the height of the Great Depression, and people—especially investors—were preoccupied with other things. Searching for risk capital to start an aircraft manufacturing company wasn't easy, when there were those on street corners

Martin B-12 bomber, one of the contenders in the 1935 bomber competition at Wright Field.
(Army Air Corps Photo)

begging—*"Brother, can you spare a dime!"*

In the spring of 1931 McDonnell abandoned the *Doodlebug* project. Fortunately, in Washington he sold the plane to the National Advisory Committee for Aeronautics (NACA) which would use it for experiments, testing for strains and stresses in the new big-mouthed wind tunnel at its Langley Field, Virginia, laboratory. The *Doodlebug* gained some glory by being one of the first planes to be tested in the huge wind tunnel, itself an experimental tool in aeronautical research.

There was a position open with the Great Lakes Aircraft Corporation in Cleveland, Ohio, builders of a popular trainer type biplane. McDonnell became engineer and test pilot for Great Lakes and remained there until 1933 when he joined the Glenn L. Martin Company, Baltimore, Maryland.

It is interesting to point out, perhaps, in the light of events in the distant future that both Donald W. Douglas and James Smith McDonnell, Jr. should both, early in their careers, work for Glenn Martin. Was there, perhaps, a common ground of thought and purpose between the two Scotsmen, both of whom would contribute so much to the advancement of aircraft design, and who one day would join forces?

At Martin, McDonnell rose rapidly to become Chief Engineer for land planes. There, he was project engineer on a twin-engined bomber design called the *Maryland*. He also worked on the Martin B-10 and B-12 bombers, successors of the *Maryland*—planes that would become famous because in the mid-thirties they were faster than the pursuit plane that was supposed to protect them!

In Baltimore, McDonnell seemed happy and satisfied. In 1934, he married Mary Elizabeth Finney, the daughter of a prominent surgeon. His two sons, James and John, were born in Baltimore. He seemed settled down.

But was he? "All my life," he confessed to one interviewer, "I had been deliberately studying and planning so that one day I would be qualified to head my own company."

In December 1938, he made the decision. "I was going to be 40 years old the next April," he said, "and I decided the time had come."

He resigned from Martin and set out to raise money to form his own company. An aircraft company, naturally. By this time, aviation was in his blood. The site he chose was Saint Louis, Missouri. There were a lot of reasons for this selection.

THE FIRST TIME McDonnell had been to St. Louis was when he was five years old, and his mother brought him and his brother, Bill, age ten, to the "big city" for a summer vacation in 1904. The city was alive with a World's Fair in progress, commemorating the 100th anniversary of the Louisiana Purchase. There were many sights, but one which attracted the five-year-old's attention the most was an airship floating above the fairgrounds.

Showing amazing recall, McDonnell, during an interview with the author Christmas time, 1976, described it—"a long sausage-like balloon with a framework platform suspended below on which the operator ran back and forth changing the weight fore and aft to make the balloon point its nose up or down." What he saw was Captain Tom Baldwin's airship, the *California Arrow*, powered with a motorcycle engine, and piloted by Lincoln Beachey, who would become one of the most famous names in the Earlybird days of American aviation. Beachey created a sensation at the St. Louis Exposition with his daring flying exhibitions. Certainly, the airship flights left an impression on the wee Scotch laddie, James Smith McDonnell, and it may well have planted the seed for his future interest in the science of aerostatics. Perhaps, when he came back to St. Louis to set up his own aircraft manufacturing business 35 years later and create his own sensation as one of aviation's most successful entrepreneurs, he was thinking that it was nice to come back and begin at the beginning.

Memories and sentimentality, however, had nothing to do with his picking St. Louis as home base for his own company, which one day would become the city's biggest employer, and industrial giant. Before he ever left Martin, McDonnell hired a team of specialists to survey the St. Louis area, and report back to him the geographical, sociological, political, financial, physical (facilities) and philosophical environment

and its potential growth factors. The report was encouraging.

St. Louis, McDonnell learned, had a lot going for it. The climate was moderate; there would be lots of good flying weather. The city's airport, Lambert Field, about 17 miles from the heart of town, could handle the largest aircraft then flying, and there was room for expansion. Curtiss-Wright, a big name in aviation was located there. American Airlines was well entrenched, and three other airlines, TWA, Chicago-Southern, Braniff, used the terminus. Moreover, St. Louis was aviation oriented. Far-sighted businessmen and civic leaders had backed an unknown airmail pilot named Charles A. Lindbergh in his 1927 non-stop New York-to-Paris venture. Lindbergh had named his plane, *Spirit of St. Louis*. His epoch flight made St. Louis world renowned.

St. Louis had a good skilled labor market: automobile assemblies were manufactured there, and small airplanes (the once popular high-wing Monocoupe for flying sportsmen) and shoes. The big International Shoe Company made its home there, plus many other smaller manufacturing plants. And there was the biggest brewery in the U.S., Anheuser-Busch, makers of Budweiser, the "King of Beers."

The city had culture, flower gardens, good schools, libraries, museums, and it was the

First office building and engineering department of the McDonnell Aircraft Corporation at Lambert Field in St. Louis. It was a modest beginning, compared with the towering new McDonnell Douglas Corporation headquarters building in St. Louis today, forty years later.

home of the St. Louis Cardinals, the "Gas House Gang" of the National Baseball League. The St. Louis *Post-Dispatch* was one of the world's greatest newspapers, established by Joseph Pulitzer, founder of the Pulitzer Prize awards for distinguished achievement in journalism, literature, drama and music. All in all, St. Louis was a good place to live. And most important, it had that Missouri "show me" attitude, and the spirit to never stop growing.

Back in Baltimore, McDonnell weighed all of these things over and over in his mind. Indeed, there were a lot of PLUSES. But in the final analysis he had some ideas of his own for deciding to head west.

The increasing tensions abroad, Hitler's massive build-up of the Nazi military machine, the takeover of the Saar region, the Czechoslovakian crisis, were ominous signs. And McDonnell saw the effect right here at home. It touched him personally. At Martin, he saw more and more orders coming in from the Army Air Corps for more and more bombers, indicating there was "serious concern" in Washington. In his "Fireside Chats" President Roosevelt was left-handedly warning the American people to prepare for

preparedness. FDR had talked Congress into a 5,000 plane program for the build-up of American airpower. It would be a good time, McDonnell thought, to get into the aircraft manufacturing business. His country, if there were a war in Europe—and his "sixth sense" felt it was coming—would need all the aeronautical know-how it could muster. He wanted a piece of the action, to help make America strong.

He had his own philosophy about National Security—in a troubled world on the brink of war, a nation could maintain its security and freedom only through a position of strength. He believed, as did "Teddy" Roosevelt— "talk softly and carry a BIG STICK."

Quietly, he made his move—to St. Louis. The deciding factor for establishing his company there: "I had studied the concentration of the aircraft industry on the West Coast and the East Coast, and I believed, in case of any potential enemy attack on this country, both coastal regions were the most vulnerable spots. I felt it would be a good thing to have something going for us in reserve, just in case. And I believed the Government might favor dispersion." As it turned out, he proved to be right.

Mr. Mac minus flying togs. The young executive, President of McDonnell Aircraft Corporation, punches in—just the same as all the other teammates—at first factory in St. Louis.

WHEN he came to St. Louis in early 1939, Mr. McDonnell had $30,000 in savings, as well as a solid background in aeronautical engineering and aircraft design. Furthermore he had an uncanny knack for business, lots of ideas, high hopes and the determination to turn his dreams into realities. He also had a lot of guts. Some skeptics were betting he wouldn't make it.

On paper, he had written down in broad terms his objectives: "The company intends to engage in the business of designing, developing, manufacturing, testing, selling and the repair of aircraft and parts thereof."

This was in essence the prospectus to show to potential investors. He needed a lot more money than his own $30,000. He figured at least $150,000. In six months time he raised $165,000. The money came from friends, relatives, acquaintances, and non-acquaintances. It came the hard way. "I guess," he recalled, "I walked ten miles in the St. Louis business district alone, going from one office to another."

Finally, when he put it all together, he organized the McDonnell Aircraft Corporation duly incorporated and ready for business on July 6, 1939.

He had rented a small room in an American Airlines building at Lambert—St. Louis Municipal Airport. There was a typewriter, some secondhand furniture, and the total staff of two—himself and a secretary named Lou Ritter. The secretary's first job was to type a letter to the Chief of the Contract Section, Materiel Division of the Army Air Corps at Wright Field, Dayton, Ohio. Wright Field held the purse strings on all Air Corps procurement programs, and McDonnell wanted to untie them.

In making his pitch, McDonnell wrote, "Our objective is to be of maximum service possible to the United States Government in the design and manufacture of airplanes. With this end in view, we are building an organization which will be exceptionally strong in creative airplane research and design and in economical factory production. We are going to operate as a constructive influence in this industry."

To the best of his memory McDonnell can't recall ever receiving any direct reply from the chief procurement officer. But he does remember—"A few weeks later we got a copy of an Air Corps' bid invitation to enter a fighter plane design competition. At least, we were on the mailing list; they knew who we were and where."

In the beginning, business was scarce as a fly in a spider's web. McDonnell, himself, has described it as "excruciatingly slow."

Three months after incorporation, however, the duo staff had increased to fifteen, and McDonnell had surrounded himself with a group of young aeronautical engineers, the nucleus of a "team" that one day would number in the thousands, turning out the best fighter designs ever built, as we shall see. Back then,

Factory scene, 1941, McDonnell Aircraft Corporation, St. Louis, about 400 employees. "Teammates" shown here are working on ribs for elevators on Douglas DC-3s and Army C-47s.

however, the "team" was put to work on a preliminary design study for the fighter plane competition, the result of a $3,000 contract. Nothing ever came of it.

"At the end of the first year," McDonnell would report, "our backlog was zero, sales zero, earnings zero!"

When he started his own company McDonnell also started a tradition which lives to this day. The small force of employees who began with him, he never has referred to by any other name than "teammates." The number of teammates has grown to tens of thousands. Among them there is loyalty, trust, and a great pride in their close knit relationship as a family of pioneers and producers of some of the finest aircraft, missiles, spacecraft and other multi-service activities. It is most evident in the quality and quantity of work they turn out.

The teammates have much respect and strong feelings for their management people. There is a camaraderie here that exists in very few giant corporations.

They in turn have a name for the man who founded the company where they are employed.

They call him affectionately—"Mr. Mac."

THE SITUATION in Europe, as McDonnell had sensed it would, changed from better to worse when Hitler invaded Poland in September 1939, and France declared war on Germany.

President Roosevelt almost immediately upped his 5,000 plane program ten-fold. FDR, like the Roosevelt before him, wanted a big stick. He told the nation that the aircraft industry might be expected to hit a "production rate of 50,000 units a year!"

The impact was felt in St. Louis. Early in 1940, McDonnell Aircraft got an Air Corps research contract for $20,000, and in August the same year there was an order for $7,672 for small parts for Stinson observation planes,

another larger order for gun mounts for bombers. The trouble was, there was no space to do the work.

St. Louisians proved their mettle. Hobbyists, who had machine shops in their homes became small-time "subcontractors", and some of the work was done in abandoned garages and buildings. But McDonnell got the job done.

Then came a crucial turning point in his company's history. Three months before Pearl Harbor, McDonnell Aircraft got a contract to build a bomber-destroyer fighter for the Air Corps, the first contract for an experimental aircraft of its own design. The die was cast. McDonnell was ready.

Mid-summer, 1941, the company, completing its second year, had $2,500,000 in orders for airplane parts on its books. The staff had grown to nearly 400. And McDonnell Aircraft had moved into its first factory, 36,000 square feet of space, the old plant once occupied by the Monocoupe Corporation at the St. Louis airport. McDonnell could see it from the second story window of his one-room office in the American Airlines' building, and he had been eyeing it for a long time. After the purchase, he acquired $150,000 worth of machinery, including a big hydraulic press, one of the first of its kind to be used in stamping out aircraft parts, a new technique in aircraft fabrication.

There followed another contract for $7,000,000 for turning out tail surfaces and engine cowlings for Douglas DC-3s, their military counterpart, C-47 cargo planes, Douglas and Boeing bombers. The work was significant because it marked the beginning of the McDonnell/Douglas relationship.

No one ever dreamed—not even McDonnell, himself, that one day his struggling, fledgling McDonnell Aircraft Corporation would "take over" Douglas Aircraft Company, 2,000 miles away, an established giant in the aircraft manufacturing industry.

In St. Louis, the fledgling McDonnell Aircraft Corporation, only two years old, was turning out tail surfaces for the Army Air Corps' C-47s (top), the Douglas B-18 bombers (center), and Boeing's fabulous B-17 Flying Fortresses (lower).

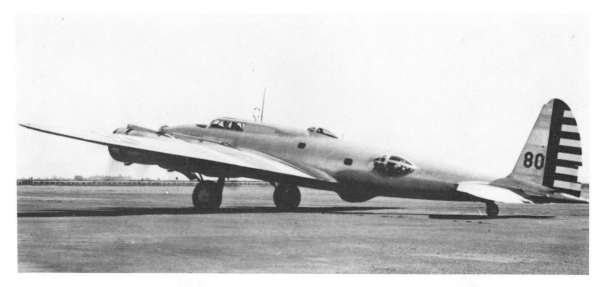

TWA Fokker trimotor. It was in such a plane that Knute Rockne, famed Notre Dame Football coach, was killed in Kansas crash. Tragedy led TWA to "look around" for a more modern transport, prompting Jack Frye to write Don Douglas letter which, it has been said, was the birth certificate of the DC-family.

Chapter Three

Birth Of The DC Family

WHEN DON DOUGLAS went down to his office in Santa Monica on Monday, August 5, 1932, in his mail he found a letter from Jack Frye, then vice-president of operations for Transcontinental & Western Air, Inc., forerunner of today's international flag carrier (TWA) Trans World Airlines. Frye's letter wanted to know if Douglas would be interested in submitting a bid for the design and development of a new air transport plane which would give TWA a competitive edge over United Airlines which was then flying its fast, twin-engine Boeing 247s coast-to-coast in 19½ hours. TWA was shackled with a fleet of cloth-and-veneer Fokker trimotors and all-metal Ford Trimotors whose best time was about 27 hours from New York to Los Angeles, with too many stops, up and down, to make it a pleasant journey. United was simply running away with the market. TWA was desperate.

Attached to the Frye letter were more detailed specifications as to the type of plane TWA desired: a monoplane, three engines, all metal construction, a cruising speed of 146 mph, service ceiling of 21,000 feet, a range of 1,080 miles to permit fewer stops, gross weight of 14,200 pounds, capable of carrying at least 12 passengers, a crew of two, pilot and co-pilot, a roomy cabin equipped with miscellaneous fixtures and conveniences generally expected in a commercial airliner,

plus radio, the latest flight instruments and navigational aids for night flying. Indeed, if TWA could come up with such an airliner, it would make the popular Boeing 247s virtually obsolete.

That night Don Douglas took the Frye letter and the specs home with him, read and re-read them until the wee hours. Before he went to sleep he had made up his mind. The Douglas Aircraft Company would submit a proposal to the TWA crowd. For a long time Douglas had wanted to get into the commercial airliner field, military orders for Army and Navy aircraft were getting slimmer and slimmer with the armed forces on a peacetime basis, Congressional appropriations harder and harder to come by, and the whole nation in the throes of a belt-tightening depression.

Early next morning Douglas called a meeting of his engineering design and production people. He outlined the TWA requirements, and all agreed the company should go after the TWA business. That night Douglas answered Frye's letter saying his company was interested, and requested a date when "Some of our people can get together with your people and present our views." He also gave the order for his own people to get to work, the new transport design getting top priority.

The men involved included James H. "Dutch" Kindelberger, Chief Engineer;

Arthur E. Raymond, Kindelberger's assistant; Fred Stineman, Ed Burton, Fred Herman, all senior design engineers; and Douglas, himself. Harry Wetzel, Vice President & General Mgr., and George Strompl, production chief, were also part of the "team." John K. Northrop, at that time head of a Douglas subsidiary, also influenced the structural design. Most of them had worked with Douglas at Martin, and had cast their lot with him when he started his own company on the West Coast. This background may have had some influence on their decision to build a twin-engined transport rather than a trimotor.

Douglas, himself, recalled a bit of prophetic writing he had done under his byline for *Aviation* magazine as far back as 1919. "The Martin twin," he had written, "is easily adaptable to commercial uses. As a mail or express machine, a ton may be carried (payload) or twelve passengers in addition to the pilot and mechanic, and can be carried non-stop up to 600 miles . . . Requirements for safety, so important in air transportation, are especially well fulfilled by this machine because it can fly on one engine only!"

Such performance was right in line with TWA's needs.

By the last week in August, the rough draft of the proposal, sketches and drawings were ready and Art Raymond and Harry Wetzel were enroute to New York to meet with the TWA people. There was a lot of enthusiasm over the proposal on the part of all concerned. But there were also a lot of disagreements over general approaches to specific problems. In general, Wetzel reported to Douglas, he thought the customer was interested. There would be a lot more meetings with the technical people before things would get down to brass tacks. For more than three weeks the discussions continued. One by one, the differences were ironed out. There were some positive signs Douglas would get the contract.

When Douglas got the good word from Wetzel in New York, he signed the work order to start work on the TWA plane. By now they even had a name for it— the Douglas DC-1—*Douglas Commercial Model No. 1*. She would be the first of a long line of DC skyships which would write the name Douglas across a thousand skies.

On September 20, 1932, the contract was signed in TWA's New York office. The price agreed upon for the service test airplane was $125,000 to be paid in gold bullion. If the costs of the service test model went over that figure, Douglas would have to stand the difference. An option clause in the contract gave TWA the right (and there was the intent) to buy all, or part, of sixty additional airplanes in lots of ten, fifteen or twenty at $58,000 apiece.

THE LAST WEEK IN JUNE 1933, little more than ten months after Don Douglas received Jack Frye's letter and bid invitation, the DC-1 was rolled out of the factory hangar and onto the ramp at adjacent Clover Field. She was a thing of precision and promise.

According to Douglas, the prototype had cost more than $307,000 to build which included design and engineering hours. She would have to pass every test, and there would have to be orders for many more in order to make any money on the risk venture. The Scotsman, at that point, may have been a little concerned. He was in for the surprise of his life.

She was a thing of beauty, this Douglas Commercial Model No. 1, four tons (empty weight) of metallic machine glistening in the sunlight; sleek and trim with lines that made her look born to the sky. The fuselage was sixty feet from nose to tail, half again as long as a Greyhound bus. There were six square windows along each side and a large door aft of the trailing edge of the wing. The cockpit was in the nose, with side by side seating for two.

AUTHOR'S NOTE: *Perhaps, there never was and never will be an aircraft with which so many persons associate themselves as the Douglas DC-3 airliner, some of which are still flying more than 40 years after the original model took wing on December 17, 1935. It was, too, the DC-3 and its predecessors, the DC-1 and DC-2s, which more than any single aircraft design "made" the Douglas Aircraft Company, and in a small way started the McDonnell Aircraft Corporation of St. Louis in the airframe manufacturing business. For a more detailed account of the history of the DC-3, the story is told in another Aero book—"THE PLANE THAT CHANGED THE WORLD."*

DC-1, the first of a long line of Douglas DC-skyships, on the line at Clover Field near Douglas Santa Monica plant.

The ship rested on the conventional undercarriage, two main wheels and a tail wheel. The nose was high in the air. The wing measured 85 feet, tip to tip, 789 square feet in area designed to lift a payload of over 6,000 pounds—fuel, crew, passengers, baggage and mail.

The DC-1's engines were the latest Wright *Cyclone* 710-horsepower, nine-cylinder, air-cooled radials. Propellers were three-bladed, nine-foot diameter Hamilton Standards incorporating a new changeable pitch mechanism.

The plane at the time of the roll-out was far from complete. Inside, the cabin was still raw frame and skin with no insulation or sound-proofing. No comfortable seats had been installed, only some bucket-type seats for test observers. The interior was filled with various kinds of test recorders. The "plushing up" would come later. She was, however, just about ready to try her wings.

Even those who had designed and built her were a little uptight. Before the engines were installed, she was already half a ton overweight!

Maiden flight DC-1, July 1, 1933. They called her "Old 300." Note number on tail.

There were also some die-hard skeptics. One TWA pilot who had stopped in for a look at the ship commented, "She's too damn big. It will never get off the ground."

A little after noon on July 1, 1933, a Saturday, with Carl A. Cover, Douglas Chief Test Pilot and Vice-President of Sales, in the left hand seat and Fred Herman, DC-1 Project Engineer, beside him in the co-pilot's seat, the silvery ship was parked at the end of the runway at Clover Field. Everything was set for her maiden flight.

Cover gunned the engines for a moment. Then he released the brakes and DC-1 came roaring down the runway. She lifted off gracefully, and started to climb.

She was still climbing when, suddenly, the port engine sputtered and quit. She dropped, but Cover poured the coal to the starboard engine, and she was climbing again. The next instant, the remaining engine sputtered, barked, coughed and died out. Although they had gained a couple thousand feet altitude, when the engines quit, the DC-1's nose dropped at a precariously sharp angle. She was in a death dive.

Observers on the ground were awestruck. "She's going to crash!" someone yelled. "My God, she's going to crash!"

As mysteriously as they had quit, the engines suddenly came to life again, and the ship began to gain altitude. There was that eerie silence again. Both engines had quit once more, and down came the ship's nose. She was losing altitude rapidly. Seconds later the engines caught on again, and once

more Cover averted a crash.

The whole sequence was repeated several times. Up and down, up and down, in a sawtooth pattern. Power on, power off, but somehow, Cover managed to gain altitude, foot by foot by foot. Finally, he got enough height to make a graceful bank, and virtually without any power at all coaxed the DC-1 down to a rough but *safe* landing.

"It was uncanny," Cover told Douglas, "we couldn't figure out what was going on. But we knew something was radically wrong."

The something wrong turned out to be in the carburetors. Ivar Shogran, Chief of Powerplants for Douglas, explained it this way: "They (the carburetors) had been designed with the floats hinged in the rear, with the fuel lines feeding gas from the same direction. Every time the plane would climb, the gasoline couldn't flow uphill, so the fuel was shut off, and the engines gasped for life. When the ship would nose down, fuel flow was normal, so the engines caught on. We didn't have pressure fuel systems, then. All we did was reverse the floats and feed lines. There was never any more trouble."

When she was ready to fly again, the DC-1 was subjected to one of the most rugged and extensive flight test programs ever required of any previous aircraft. One time they loaded the ship to about 18,000 pounds gross weight using sandbags and lead ingots to simulate a load of fuel, passengers, crew and mail. Without any difficulty, she climbed to 22,000 feet—far above the TWA specification requirement. There followed a series of takeoffs

Methods of testing were crude. To test strength of DC-1 wing, this was one way of doing it. Nothing happened.

and landings to see how quick she could get airborne, how short a distance she could land in, how slow a landing speed. With a full load she got off one time in less than 1,000 feet of runway. Using full flaps, she slowed down easily to below the 65 mph prescribed landing speed, rolled to a stop in a surprisingly short distance. In speed runs, back and forth over a measured course, on one fly-by the DC-1 hit 227 mph, almost racing plane performance. Whatever they asked her to do, she did with superb results.

On the strength of the performance reports of the manufacturer's tests, TWA placed an order for 25 of the planes. The Douglas Aircraft Company's beachhead into the commercial transport field was secure.

The production models were designated DC-2s—a stretched version of the DC-1. In the "Two" they had added two feet to the fuselage length, permitting a 14-passenger seating arrangement. In the new model there were other improvements that increased the payload, lifted the ceiling, increased the speed, to make the DC-2 the most luxurious airliner yet to be introduced by the airlines. There were even in flight movies!

By August 1, 1934, TWA, which got the

The Douglas *Dolphin*, an early flying boat.

first 25 of the DC-2s off the assembly line, proudly announced in its advertising—"Coast-to-Coast in 18 hours via 200-mile-an-hour luxury airliners. Called *The Sky Chief*, the through plane left New York (Newark) at 4:00 P.M. daily. Landing in Chicago shortly after the dinner hour, the plane was in the air again, Kansas City-bound. The next leg was a non-stop jump to Albuquerque, New Mexico. On the ground briefly for refueling, it took off again at 3:20 a.m., arriving in Los Angeles at 7:00 a.m."

For the first time, the air traveler could fly from New York to Los Angeles, without losing

The DC-1 ("Old 300") made history in 1934 when she carried last load of civilian Air Mail before FDR's famous cancellation order. Here with Jack Frye at controls DC-1 approaches Kansas City, TWA's home base.

any part of the normal business day. The TWA-Douglas team had taken the lead in air transport development.

Orders for the new transport piled up. Before long she was the prime mover in the fleets of Eastern Airlines, American Airlines, Pan American Grace Airways, Western Airlines, Braniff Airways, Northwest Orient Airlines, and she had been sold to foreign carriers such as K.L.M. *(Koninklyke Luchtvaart Maatschappy)* and Czechoslovakia's *Ceskoslovenska Letacka Spolecnost,* altogether flying the colors of the airlines of 12 nations.

At home, there were also orders from the Army Air Corps, and she became both personnel transport and cargo plane for the newly organized air transport squadrons. In one role, at Fort Benning, Georgia, as the C-39, she carried aloft the first U.S. paratroopers.

Altogether, in one version or another, there were 138 of the DC-2s built in Santa Monica.

Douglas, himself, was pleasantly surprised, "I remember early in the program," he reminisces, "I told Frye that I felt we might build fifty of the planes, but that would just about saturate the market. Then, when we passed that mark, I remember telling Raymond, one day, that it looked like we might make 100 of the ships. But, honestly, I couldn't see going beyond that figure.

"Now, looking back, it was never nicer to have been wrong."

Development of the DC-2 brought many honors to designer and plane builder Donald W. Douglas. More important, in monetary return, sales of the DC-2s took the Douglas Aircraft Company out of the red and gave it strong financial position in an industry that many said would never get off the ground.

Indeed, it was a happy Scotsman (Douglas) who stood before President Franklin D. Roosevelt in the White House on July 1, 1936 (three years to the day after the first flight of the DC-1) and received aviation's most coveted award, The Robert J. Collier Trophy. "This airplane," FDR read from the citation, "by reason of its high speed, economy, and quiet passenger comfort, has been generally adopted by transport lines throughout the United States. Its merits have been further recognized by its adoption abroad and its influence on foreign design is already apparent."

THE FIRST DC-2 AIRLINER had been in service less than a month when Congress passed a law that was to have far-reaching effects on the aircraft manufacturing industry and the future of America's scheduled airline system. Known as the Black-McKellar Bill (The Air Mail Act of 1934), the measure put all civil aviation under three branches of the federal government.

Under the new law, the Post Office Department was made responsible for awarding all

Douglas DC-2, which has been called "first of the modern luxury airliners."

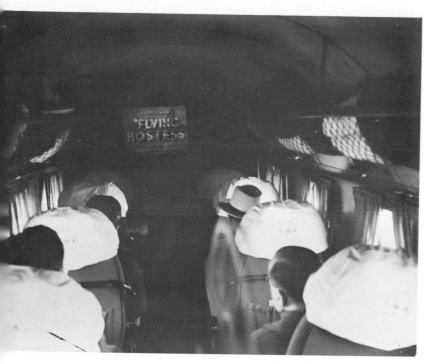

Aboard DC-2, which had seven seats along each side of a narrow aisle, passengers enjoy first in-flight movies.

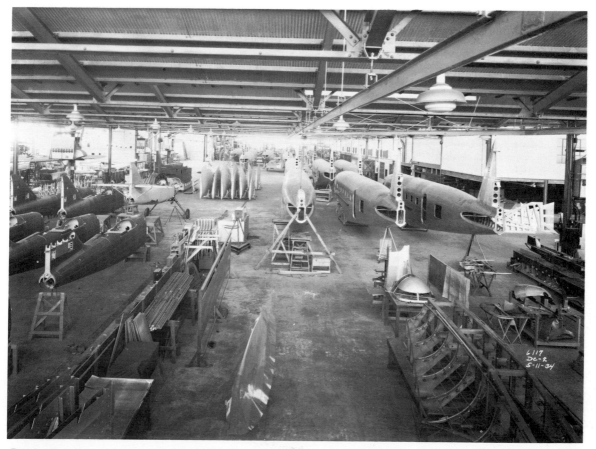

Production line of DC-2s at Douglas Santa Monica plant, 1934-35. Trainers and *Dolphin* amphibian were also in production.

air mail contracts and determining routes and schedules. The Interstate Commerce Commission fixed the mail rates and payments. The Bureau of Air Commerce had the authority to regulate the airways and license all pilots and machines. At the same time, the Act separated the aircraft manufacturing concerns and big holding company combines from their air transport operations because of the trend toward monopolistic empires. In short, it was illegal for an aircraft builder to own any part of an airline operation.

Some of the smaller operators were knocked out of the picture when the Post Office took away their mail routes. Others merged to produce a whole new pattern of airline networks criss-crossing the nation.

Of all the aircraft manufacturers, Douglas stood to benefit the most. The Douglas Aircraft Company never had had any affiliation with an air transport operation. Moreover, in the new DC-2, the company had an airliner that was far ahead of any other. Naturally, the new, financially stronger and larger airline companies rushed to buy the DC-2 in order to stay abreast of the competition.

One of the first of the new and stronger airline companies to come into being was American Airlines, Inc., an outgrowth of the old American Airways. Newly elected president of American was Texas-born Cyrus Rowlett ("CR") Smith, who had made a reputation for himself as a leader in the development of air passenger service with Texas Air Transport and Southern Air Transport, doing well as interstate airline operators. Smith, a student of law, economics and business administration, brought a new sense of business acumen to the air transport industry. Certainly, it was true of his American Airlines leadership.

His first act was to fight for a new mail contract and he won. The Post Office Department awarded American Airlines a third airway, coast-to-coast across America, the southern route. He was in the ring with the heavyweights—United and TWA. To stay in competition he ordered 15 Douglas DC-2 airliners, and the famous American Airlines' "Flagship Fleet" was born.

Smith knew, however, that offering the same type of equipment as his competitors over a longer, less populated route, wasn't exactly the key to success. Something new was needed.

It WAS THE SUMMER OF 1934 and Smith, with his Chief Engineer William (Bill) Littlewood, were on the ramp at Love Field, Dallas, Texas. They were going aboard an American Airlines plane to fly westward to Los Angeles. It was a different kind of plane than the DC-2, a big red and blue Curtiss *Condor* biplane, a twin-engined cloth-covered, 12-passenger airliner. The *Condor* had something the DC-2 didn't have. It was a "sleeper" plane. Passengers could climb aboard and get into a pullman-sized bunk and sleep all the way to the West Coast. American had pioneered "sleeper plane" service on May 5, 1934, between Los Angeles and Dallas.

When they climbed aboard the *Condor*, a pretty stewardess was already making up the bunks.

Smith, almost subconciously, remarked to Littlewood, "Bill, what we need is a DC-2 sleeper plane!"

Neither slept that night, though the flight was smooth.

They were both thinking the same thing—*Why not make the DC-2 a sleeper transport? It was big enough. It had the power.*

Littlewood, the engineer, was thinking it could be done. He was roughing it out in his own mind, how it might be done. He had some strong ideas on the subject. He knew the story of the DC-2, how they had stretched it from a 12-passenger into a 14-passenger airliner. With a little more wing and a fatter fuselage, the "rubber airplane" could be stretched again.

Smith was thinking, too. If he could put a DC-2 sleeper on the line, he could throw a hot curve at United and TWA. It would be a strong point for his sales people. The "hard sell" was on. In the next round in the battle of the giants for the transcontinental business, he was determined to come out slugging.

When they disembarked at Glendale Terminal, "CR" told Littlewood about his thoughts. They were a good team. Littlewood already had caught the signal. He said he would work up some preliminary specifications.

Smith didn't waste any time. Back in Chicago, American's home base, again he called Don Douglas on the telephone.

Could Douglas make the DC-2 into a sleeper plane?

If so, American was interested.

Douglas was a little cold to the idea. His first reaction was, "We can't even keep up with the orders for the DC-2's!"

That was what he told "CR" on the telephone.

Smith, however, wouldn't take NO for an answer. The long distance bill mounted into hundreds of dollars. Finally, he broke through Douglas' obstinacy by virtually promising he would buy, sight unseen, twenty of the sleeper planes if Douglas would build them for American.

Douglas agreed to have his people work up a design study.

Smith said he would send Bill Littlewood out to Santa Monica to help.

When he hung up, "CR" was almost in a cold sweat.

He had virtually committed American Airlines to a multi-million dollar order for an airplane that wasn't even on paper yet, and he didn't have any idea where he would get that kind of money.

Littlewood headed west.

Smith went to Washington to see his old friend and fellow Texan, Jesse Jones, who was the head of the Reconstruction Finance Corporation, an agency Herbert Hoover had set up to help business stay in business. FDR called it an organization "to ward off financial disaster" and invoked it on many occasions. The publicity was superb, and RFC did the job.

Smith believed what he read. When he walked into Jones' office to present his case, he came right to the point.

"Jesse," he said, "American Airlines *is* a disaster if you don't make us a loan."

He got the money—*a $4,500,000 loan.* But he still didn't have the plane.

The project—DST—Douglas Sleeper Transport, however, was moving along at a rapid pace.

A Douglas Company historical record reveals that a staff of 400 engineers and draftsmen were assigned to the project. Some 3500 drawings later the finalized design began to take shape. Then, in December of the same year, after more than 300 wind tunnel tests, the "keel was laid."

The DST was rolled out and made its first flight on December 17, 1935—thirty-two years to the day after Orville Wright made the first heavier-than-air, man-carrying flight in a power-driven airplane at Kitty Hawk, North Carolina. The airplane had come a

American Airlines' first DST (Douglas Sleeper Transport), which as a dayplane would become the popular 21-passenger DC-3. Note the small windows for berths.

long way.

The wingspan of the DST was 95 feet—almost equal to the entire distance that Orville Wright had flown during those 12 seconds that changed man's concept of the flying machine. The big, silvery airliner weighed a hundred times as much as the first Wright machine. Its engines were fifty times as powerful.

FOR HER DAY, the DST was a colossus. The biggest all-metal airliner flying in 1935. Capable of near 200-mile-an-hour speeds, she was also faster than any other airliner of that period. Her ability to fly on only one engine, de-icers for propellers and wings, duplicate instrumentation in the cockpit, autopilots, automatic fire extinguishers in engine nacelles, and other features brought to the airlines new and badly needed standards of safety.

The DST, which had 14 berths as a Skysleeper, was one of three configurations. Another was the 21-passenger dayplane which became the popular DC-3. And there was also a 14-passenger (Skylounge) which had chair-car accommodations, wider, more plush seats, more leg room. Each model set a new high in sheer luxury and comfort aloft for the air traveler: cabin air conditioning, stand-up head room, improved soundproofing, individual radios (in the pillows), airborne movies, hot meals aloft!

It didn't matter which version (DST or DC-3), almost immediately she became the vehicle that converted landlubbers everywhere to almost casual acceptance of the airplane as a safe and practical means of travel. About her, it has been said, that she did for aviation what the Model-T did for the automobile.

Acceptance by the airlines was phenomenal. She was just what the doctor ordered. She slashed coast to coast flight times to 15 hours eastbound, 17 hours westbound. Her all-metal construction and design simplicity cut maintenance cost in half; mechanics could change an engine in a couple of hours. She was seldom on the ground very long for repairs and inspections. And her capability to lift half again the payloads of previous airliners was like money in the bank. She was everybody's airliner, and everybody loved her.

Shuttling back and forth across the continent in all kinds of weather with timetable reliability, she set unprecedented safety records. Even insurance companies took a different look at the safety aspects of flying. For the first time, air travelers could buy $5,000 worth of trip insurance for 25 cents—the same rate that applied to travel by bus or train or ship.

Significantly, within two years after the first of her kind went into scheduled service,

Aboard American Airlines' Douglas sleeper planes, passengers could climb into Pullman-sized berths and ride the wings of night across the continent.

The DC-3s and C-47s blazed new air routes around the world. Even the ends of the earth were theirs. Above, on May 3, 1952, she landed at the North Pole.

The fabulous DC-3 in khaki-colors, as the C-47 military version(the famous "Gooney Bird")by the thousands became the workhorse of the air in World War II. On D-Day she flew thousands of paratroopers (above) to attack Hitler's fortress Europe.

the DC-3 was hauling 98 per cent of the world's air commerce. About her, "CR" Smith would declare, "She freed the airlines from the shackles of dependency on government mail pay. She was the first airliner that could make money just hauling passengers. Economically, the DC-3 let us expand and develop new routes and improve our services."

The DC-3 blazed new trails across a thousand skies. She flew in blinding snow storms and sub-zero temperatures where cold and salt water atmosphere played strange tricks. Then, with utter disregard for climatical change, she flew in the teeth of desert sandstorms that tried to grind her to a halt. She was equally indestructible on the ground at tropical bases in jungles where corrosive fungi threatened to eat her alive. Monsoons tried to drown her. Waterspouts slapped her a thousand feet into the sky. Jagged mountain peaks reached up to spear her to death.

Still she flew on, establishing air routes across the top of the world, the North Atlantic "aerial lifeline" that helped build up Allied forces in England for the ultimate invasion of Hitler's Fortress Europe; pioneering another supply route over the South Atlantic to feed the armies that drove Rommel out of Africa; elevating the historic Burma Road, when the Japanese closed it; two miles high in the sky— flying "over the Hump" of the treacherous Himalayas—maintaining the vital link between India and China; tying together the widespread island bases in the vast Pacific which were to become the jumping off places for the ultimate destruction of Japan's armies.

On D-Day, 1944, she kept a date with destiny. More than 1,000 DC-3s and C-47s flew in the first waves of paratroopers for the big invasion, and carried jeeps, small cannon, ammunition and planeload after planeload of heroes to secure the Fields of Flanders.

The DC-3 (khaki-clad as the C-47 and varied versions) had her sides ripped open by flak and riddled with machine-gun fire. She had engines blown out by direct hits, parts of her wings sheared off in mid-air collisions, her rudder shot to pieces, but still she lumbered home. She was bellied-in, ground-looped and somersaulted in crash landings and her crews survived. She lived through loop-the-loops,

In Vietnam, C-47 was modified as "Puff The Magic Dragon" gunship, mounting three rapid-firing guns. At last she had become an actual "combat aircraft."

terrifying dives, snap-rolls and tailspins. She was mauled and insulted by pilots who didn't understand her. She was overloaded, underfed, overworked, and maintained by Arabs and aborigines. But she never shirked a job and she never complained.

Before Douglas would shut down the production line on the DC-3 and the various model designations, more than 10,000 airframes of the basic configuration would be built.

FIRST FLIGHT—The Tri Turbo-3, a DC-3 twin-engine aircraft modified to a three-engine turboprop design with Pratt & Whitney PT-6 engines, met or exceeded its expected performance on its first flight (November 2, 1978). Outboard wing fuel tanks provide a range in excess of 3,000 miles, making it possible for the Tri Turbo-3 to take off and climb to 10,000 ft. cruising altitude, and with the center engine feathered (pictured here), fly a 3,000-mile mission with one hour of reserve fuel remaining. The aircraft is capable of carrying up to 12,000 lbs., cruises at 230 mph, and STOL characteristics enable it to operate from short, or high elevation airstrips. Developed by Specialized Aircraft Co., the Tri Turbo-3 is latest version of 45 year-old DC-3 family.

Consolidated B-24 "Liberators" were built by Douglas during the war at Tulsa, Oklahoma,facility. Today, Tulsa location is a beehive of activity, modifying DC-8s and F-4 Phantoms.

Designed by Boeing, the famous B-17 "Flying Fortress" was built by the thousands by Douglas Aircraft Company at its plant on the outskirts of Chicago, Illinois. After the war, plant was shut down, laying off thousands of workers.

Chapter Four

Planes By The Thousands

"FIFTY THOUSAND planes a year," the President had predicted. When Don Douglas, plane manufacturer and designer who was listening to FDR's speech over the radio that night, heard these words, he turned to some guests and said, "We can do it." He was, of course, speaking of the whole U.S. aircraft industry, not just Douglas Aircraft Company alone. There were those inside the industry, big names, who didn't agree with Douglas; they thought the President had picked an unrealistic number. As it turned out Douglas was right. When production reached its wartime peak, big four-engined bombers like the Consolidated B-24 *Liberator* and the Boeing B-17 *Flying Fortress* were being built at the rate of better than *one an hour*!

"Big Bill" Knudsen, President of General Motors who had donned the uniform of a Lieutenant General in the Air Corps to head up the aircraft production program, summed it up, "We won because we smothered the enemy in an avalanche of production, the like of which he had never seen nor dreamed possible."

It was "teamwork" on a gigantic scale that started the avalanche. The automobile industry and the airframe industry got together, and it was a good marriage, even if a martial one. A command performance. As a result the assembly line techniques that put America on wheels, turning out millions of cars, were applied to aircraft fabrication. Fuselage sections and wing sections were put on a moving assembly line in cavernous factories designed especially for airframe mass production. Day and night, the lines never stopped moving.

By the time the war ended, there were 26 different types of military aircraft—trainers, observation planes, fighters, bombers, helicopters, gliders, jet planes—in production at huge plants around the nation. Equally as many new experimental designs were in flight test stage, in prototype or on the drawing boards. Altogether, the U.S. had produced 2,483,304,900 pounds of airframes. The cost was astronomical; the Air Corps alone, in 1944, had an operating budget of $30 BILLION, most of which was earmarked for aircraft production. During one month, at the height of the war, the Procurement people at Wright Field were spending $1,000,000,000 a day!

The Douglas Aircraft Company got its share. At wartime peak, in 1944, Douglas net sales reached $1,061,407,485. In all, from 1942 to 1945, Douglas turned out a grand total of 29,385 aircraft—432,000,000 pounds of airframes. The Douglas Aircraft Company, which had started in a Santa Monica barbershop a quarter of a century before, had, besides its Santa Monica factory complex, plants in El Segundo and Long Beach, California, in Tulsa and Oklahoma City,

Oklahoma, and Chicago, Illinois. From 68 employees in 1922 in its first factory, the Wilshire plant, it had mushroomed to a work force of more than 157,000 in 1943.

As Douglas' public relations writer Crosby Maynard described it in his book, *Flight Plan For Tomorrow,* a company publication, "The loft operation on the second floor of a planing mill had zoomed to become the fourth largest business in the United States."

McDonnell Aircraft Corporation, just getting off the ground at the outbreak of World War II, by the end of hostilities had manufactured 7,000,000 pounds of airframe for which Uncle Sam had footed the bill to the tune of $60,000,000. By comparison with Douglas' billions, the sum was "peanuts." But it put the young company in the business for keeps. It never stopped growing, viable and sturdy as a Redwood, an unprecedented achievement in such a volatile industry. Example: the day would come when it would land a $775,000,000 contract—with no war going on—for production of a revolutionary fighter of its own design, the F-15 *Eagle.*

THE PLANES produced by Douglas during World War II were these: military versions of the DC-3 commercial transports, C-47s for the Army and R4Ds for the Navy, as personnel transports and cargo planes; medium bombers, the B-18s and B-23s, adaptations of the DC-3 design; the DB-7s and A-20s, and a more advanced A-26, attack bombers; the SBD dive bombers for the Navy, and A-24s, the Army version of the same design; C-54, four-engined cargo planes that became the backbone of the military airlift, and R5Ds, the Navy version; Boeing-designed B-17s and Consolidated-designed B-24s, four-engined heavy bombers; an experimental design, the XB-19, the biggest aircraft ever built up to that time; a limited number of experimental gliders.

Douglas, in 1944, had also built the XB-42, an experimental design with engines in the fuselage driving counter-rotating propellers.

The Douglas planes had names as well as numbers. The C-47 was called the *Skytrain;* the C-54, the *Skymaster. Bolo* and *Dragon* were the B-18 and the B-23. The A-20 was the *Havoc,* the A-26 the *Invader. Dauntless* was the Navy's SBD dive bomber. The XB-19 didn't have a name, but it should have had "Mr. BIG" for, indeed, that it was—a wingspan of 212 feet, fuselage length 132 feet, a gross weight of 160,000 pounds!

To build it, Douglas constructed a gigantic hangar at Santa Monica. The XB-19 was unique: it never fired a shot at an enemy, or dropped a single bomb. But in its role as a "flying laboratory" it contributed much to the advancement of aircraft design in war and in peace: The first bomber to have revolving

In Santa Monica, the DC-3, modified as the military C-47 cargo version, was turned out in such numbers that before the line was shut down more than 10,000 had been produced. The C-47s were being built here before Pearl Harbor.

An "off shoot" of the DC-3, the B-18 bomber was one of our front line aircraft in 1939-40. Many were destroyed in Pearl Harbor attack. "Bolo" was the nickname for the B-18s.

This B-23 bomber also used DC-wing, but with radically different tail. The B-23 was better liked as a personnel transport, because of its speed, than it was as a bombardment aircraft.

A-20 *Havoc* attack bomber was outgrowth of DB-7 bombers, which Douglas sold to French and British before U.S. entry into the War. With U.S. Forces, it flew missions in all theaters.

gun turrets, a virtual "flying battleship." A flying test-bed for the Wright R-2200 horsepower radial air-cooled engines (almost twice the power of the engines in the B-17s and B-24s) and the wartime developed Allison V-2600-horsepower, liquid-cooled in-line engines installed in the XB-19A, a modified version. And, probably most important of all, because of its size, it pioneered new fabrication techniques and production ideas for building large aircraft, revolutionizing the state of the art.

These new methods were used in building the Douglas C-74 cargo plane (124-foot wingspan, four 3,000-horsepower engines, 125,000-pounds gross weight), the biggest cargo plane flying before the war ended. The C-74 was the forerunner of the still bigger C-124 (*Globemaster*), which would come along in the early 1950's.

When it came time for the DC-10, the "know-how" was like money in the bank.

The best known of the Douglas combat types to see action in World War II were the A-20 *Havoc* and the SBD *Dauntless*, which also led in production numbers. Altogether, there were 7,478 of the A-20s built at Santa Monica, Long Beach, El Segundo, and 240 by the Boeing Airplane Company in Seattle, Washington. It saw action at Dieppe, one of the first Allied raids of the war before the U.S. entry. After that, the *Havocs* were in every theater, Africa, Europe, the Pacific. Likewise, the *Dauntless*, carrier-based, was in the thick of things in the Marshall and

The A-26 (later changed to B-26) was called the *Invader*. It proved to be a good all-purpose bomber, but came along late in the war.

Gilbert Islands, in the skies over Bougainville, Wake, Marcus, Tulagi, the Battle of the Coral Sea, at Midway, Santa Cruz, the Solomons, and on the other side of the world in the North African campaign. One Admiral in praise and gratitude said, "It has sunk more enemy combatant tonnage than all the other branches of the service!" A *Dauntless* record for the history books.

The A-20s had another distinction. They were among the most versatile combat aircraft: attack bomber, photo-recon airplane, and as the P-70, a night fighter!

Out of the Douglas plants in Oklahoma City and Chicago came another plane, a non-combatant, which would write its own name

Revolutionary design, the XB-42, had two Allison in-line engines buried inside the fuselage driving two counter-rotating pusher propellers in the extreme tail. Unique feature was the plane could fly on one engine, one propeller.

"Mr. Big," the XB-19, which flew first in 1939, was largest landplane ever built up to that time. Only one was ever built, but it proved invaluable as "flying laboratory." Wing was so thick a mechanic could crawl out to outboard engines.

As possible replacement for the C-54, Douglas offered this bigger cargo plane, the C-74. Pilots sat in side-by-side canopied cockpits in the extreme nose. They called it "old bug eyes" because of this arrangement.

The *Globemaster* (C-124) introduced in the early '50s was capable of carrying tanks and other heavy army equipment. The C-124s were workhorses during Korean police action. Many are still flying.

Navy SBD-4s on the line at Douglas El Segundo plant.

in the annals of aviation—the C-54 *Skymaster.*

Don Douglas likes to recall that back in 1940 he had a "secret project" of his own going on behind a curtained off area in the big hangar where the XB-19 was built. It was a four-engined commercial airliner to replace the DC-3. Douglas Aircraft even had orders from United Airlines and American Airlines for the king size luxury airliner. Construction of the prototype was kind of a surreptitious operation, because the word had come from Washington that the aircraft manufacturers should concentrate on bomber and fighter production, not transports.

Chief of the Air Corps, General Henry H. "Hap" Arnold, a close friend of Douglas, on a visit to the plant had peeked behind the curtain and saw the new commercial airliner under construction. He didn't make it an order, but he implied it, when he remarked, "Doug, we need bombers, not airliners."

Douglas reminded Arnold that he was already turning out the DB-7s and the A-20s in large numbers. He had a suggestion of his own, "Hap, we're going to need a bigger cargo plane than the C-47s before this thing is over." He kept on building the plane behind the curtains.

His suggestion proved prophetic. The Ger-

Douglas also produced a large number of the AD-1s.

mans, with a great aerial armada, invaded the Greek island of Crete. U.S. military observers returned with reports of giant gliders and huge four-engined Junkers transport planes that had made the invasion swift and successful.

The teletype from Washington was hot to Santa Monica—"Top priority on the big transport." As the C-54, it would be the prime mover of men, machines and supplies to ground forces everywhere, the plane that put the word "airlift" in the dictionary. In her war role, the C-54 *Skymaster* hauled VIPs— Roosevelt, General Marshall, Prime Minister Churchill, General Eisenhower, and other wartime leaders— all over the world. One specially equipped C-54 became *"The Sacred Cow,"* FDR's personal aircraft, the first of presidential planes, giving the White House wings, and bringing the capitals of the world and their leaders closer together.

In the post war years, poshed up with seats, soundproofing, and the best known conveniences for the air traveler, the C-54, as the DC-4 (Douglas Commercial No. 4), was the first landplane to inaugurate trans-ocean routes for the airlines.

The specially equipped C-54 for FDR, showing elevator to accommodate wheelchair.

ONE PASSENGER aboard a C-54 who crossed the Atlantic during the war was James Smith McDonnell, who wanted to

Airlift "on the shelf." A derivation of the DC-4E, the C-54 *Skymaster* became the heavy-duty workhorse of World War II. In the beginning, the C-54 was to be the airlines' next generation airliner, Pat Patterson's "dream plane." It had to fight a war first. First commercial versions did not appear until 1946-47.

In its first year (1939) McDonnell Aircraft Corporation began design studies for a fighter plane that would become the XP-67, a twin-engined aircraft. It represented "breakthrough" for McDonnell, because it was the corporation's first contract from Air Corps for a fighter design. Called the "Bomber Destroyer," only one was flight tested.

McDonnell's XP-67 had two Continental XI-1430 engines with superchargers, housed in large torpedo-shaped nacelles flared into the wings. Here, the XP-67 rests in front of McDonnell Aircraft Corporation's original headquarters building in St. Louis. Picture was taken in 1943.

observe the British aircraft industry first hand. There he met Air Commodore Frank Whittle, credited with the invention of the first successful gas turbine engine for aircraft, for which he would later be knighted by King George. McDonnell was fascinated by the "potential of jet propulsion for aircraft." He predicted the day"when all military bombers and fighters would be jet-propelled . . . within ten years, and there is a great future also for the commercial jetliner." His small company back in St. Louis, 4,000 miles from war-torn Britain, was already involved, jet oriented. That early $20,000 Air Corps contract was for research studies in the field of jet propulsion.

In January 1943, McDonnell Aircraft got a Navy contract for the design of a jet-propelled fighter, and was set to become the producer of a long line of jet fighters for the Navy, Air Force, Marines and many free world nations. Its twin-engine jet-powered fighter designs would be acclaimed as the "best fighter planes ever built." The company also spent a large sum of its own monies in the design and development of a jet transport. The Jet Age for McDonnell really began in 1945 when the first prototype gas turbine engine fighter was completed for the Navy.

During the war years, McDonnell Aircraft's design efforts were concentrated mainly on the development of its first all-McDonnell-designed, twin-engined, piston-powered, propeller-driven fighter for the Air Force, designated the XP-67, and named the *Bomber Destroyer.*

What the Air Corps people wanted was a single-place fighter with a range of 2,000 miles, 350 mph plus speed and a service ceiling above 35,000 feet. The XP-67 was designed around that concept. In the final months of 1943, the plane emerged with a rather unusual configuration. It had a bat-like wing (55 foot span) with two Continental 1060 hp in-line, liquid-cooled engines mounted in streamline nacelles that looked more like external fuel tanks, one on each side of the fuselage, which was 44 ft. 9 inches from nose to tail. In the nose was a cluster of six 37mm cannons, more concentrated fire-power of a heavier caliber (37mm) than any other fighter. It had a gross weight of 20,000 pounds.

"Although only one experimental airplane was built," explained Kendall Perkins, project engineer on the XP-67, "this difficult pioneering project proved a worthwhile engineering exercise for designing the McDonnell jet propelled fighters of the future."

A native of St. Louis, Ken Perkins, a lifetime "teammate," joined McDonnell in 1941 and in 10 years climbed the ladder to become Engineering Vice President, responsible for engineering work on aircraft, missiles and spacecraft. Plus his engineering degree from Washington University, Ken brought to the company a gold mine of experience. Starting in 1928, as a shop mechanic for the Curtiss-Robertson Airplane Manufacturing Company of St. Louis, he became project engineer handling engineering changes on such famous name planes as the *Curtiss Robin, Thrush, Kingbird* and *Travelair.* In 1939, he was project engineer on design and engineering development of the Curtiss-Wright twin-engine transport, the commercial prototype of the Air Force C-46 (*Commando*) which in the China-Burma-India Theater opened up the aerial supply line over the towering Himalayian peaks, the "worst flying weather in the world," when the Japanese closed the historic Burma Road. The following year (1940) he joined American

Kendall Perkins

Airlines as an engineering consultant to the vice-president engineering, "in on" the decision to give Douglas the green light to go ahead with the DC-4 transport. In Washington (1941, before Pearl Harbor), he was head of the Aircraft Scheduling Unit of the Office of Production Management, predecessor of the War Production Board, resigning to go with McDonnell.

In April 1967, Perkins was made Corporate Vice President, Engineering and Research, a guiding hand in the development of the DC-10, F-15 USAF fighter, and NASA space projects.

Another "teammate" who, like Perkins, would begin as an aerodynamicist on the XP-67 project and work up to become President of McDonnell Aircraft Company (1971) and a member of the McDonnell Douglas Corporation Board of Directors (1973), is George S. Graff. One of the youngest of MAC's original talent team, Graff, only 25 when he joined the company in 1942, would play a leading role as McDonnell moved into the jet propulsion field and the Space Age.

In other areas than design and engineering—management and production—McDonnell acquired the services of men like C. Warren Drake, Dolor P. Murray, William R. Orthwein, Jr. Each brought with him special talents. Each rose to high-level corporate executive positions. They did it the hard way, from the bottom up.

Drake, for example, came to McDonnell in 1940 as Factory Manager. Before that, from 1928 to 1935, he had worked in all of the factory departments at Waco Aircraft Company in Troy, Ohio, builders of the popular Waco biplanes of the thirties. When he left Waco he joined Beech Aircraft Corporation, Wichita, Kansas, where the famous Beechcraft, "reverse stagger wing" biplane was born, and wartime producers of a light, twin-engined utility cargo and transport plane. In five years, at McDonnell, he would become Director of all Manufacturing, and in 1972, a Corporate Vice President, Manufacturing, Quality Assurance and Facilities.

Coming to McDonnell in 1942 from the Ralston Purina Company, with a sales merchandising and industrial engineering background, Dolor Murray started out as an estimator, became Manager of Customer Contracts, was elected Vice President of Fiscal in 1961, a member of the Board of

George S. Graff

Directors in 1962, and in 1971 Chairman of the Board of the McDonnell Douglas Finance Corporation, a subsidiary. Likewise, Bill Orthwein, who started in 1942 with the company as a Personnel Clerk, would become a Vice President, Personnel and General Services 15 years later, and in 1966 President of the McDonnell Automation Company.

Such is the calibre of the personnel and personal friends whom McDonnell surrounded himself with from the early days of his organization. There were many more. The number would grow into tens of thousands. Among all, there is an *esprit de corps* that probably more than anything else has been responsible for the steady growth of the company from an obscure, unknown, small factory operation in 1940 to become one of the world's largest and best run corporations engaged in a wide and diversified sphere of activities.

Working together, the teammates, from the beginning have pulled a lot of chestnuts out of the fire. But no one has worked harder, with more dedicated purpose and mission than the boss himself. Always, he has tried to stay in the background, although it is well known

William R. Orthwein, Jr.

Dolar P. Murray

that his drive and enthusiasm and strong leadership qualities have been the keys to the company's success.

In an industry well known for its tons of press releases, self-praise hoopla and fanfare every time a new plane made its debut, McDonnell Aircraft for a long while was virtually unknown, until its *Mercury* spacecraft put the first American in space. Even today, its public relations policy is to keep a low key profile.

One "teammate" likes to tell the story of what happened recently when he was flying to the West Coast aboard a McDonnell Douglas DC-10. In the seat next to him was a well dressed executive-type who introduced himself, and over a couple of drinks proudly boasted that he had been flying for more than 40 years, a two-million miler or more.

"I've flown in 'em all," he enumerated, "the noisy old Ford trimotors, the DC-3s, Boeings, Lockheeds, even the *Concorde*, but I like the DC-10 best."

Pridefully, the teammate who had worked on the Ten interjected, 'I work for McDonnell . . ."

A puzzled look crossed the face of his traveling companion. Then, very politely, he remarked, "I love your hamburgers, too."

BACK IN ST. LOUIS in 1940, when his company showed zero profits, McDonnell may have wished he'd started in the hamburger business instead of the airplane business. Even though McDonnell Aircraft was building assemblies and accessories for Boeing, Douglas and Lockheed planes, and managing to stay alive, this wasn't by any means what he had hoped for. Even the XP-67 contract didn't make him jump up and down and click his heels; after all, it was just for one experimental aircraft. He had come here to produce airplanes, lots of airplanes, McDonnell-designed airplanes.

In the spring of 1942, things started looking up when the Army Air Corps Materiel Command at Wright Field placed a contract with McDonnell for the production of an AT-15 advanced trainer design. The order called for a considerable number of the trainers to be produced, and in order to handle the program, additional manufacturing area was necessary.

Following a study by a firm of consulting engineers covering the area from the Appalachians to the Rockies, from Detroit, south to the Gulf of Mexico, Mr. Mac decided on a site in Memphis, Tennessee, about 300 miles down river from St. Louis. When the new factory was ready, by the end of 1942, the Air Corps changed its mind about the AT-15 and in its place asked McDonnell to produce a new type, all-plywood, twin-engine trainer designed by the Fairchild Aircraft Division of Hagerstown, Maryland. Originally, the new plane designed as a bomber trainer was designated the AT-13, but later became the AT-21 by the time the Memphis plant was geared up for production. McDonnell Aircraft Corporation, the Bellanca Aircraft Corporation, and a Fairchild plant in Burlington, N.C., were to concurrently produce this airplane.

"It put us in the airframe manufacturing business on a mass production scale, and that was fine," McDonnell laments, "but we were still in the same rut, building someone else's airplane." He didn't complain. The Govern-ment had constructed the new facility.

Upon receipt of a preliminary bill of material and preliminary drawings from Fairchild in March of 1943, procurement activities were started in St. Louis, and in May operations were started in the Memphis plant. Less than 20 teammates were originally transferred from St. Louis to Memphis to form a nucleus for more than 1,100 additional personnel, who joined the Memphis operation in the year that followed.

Before the AT-21 production line at Memphis would be shut down, McDonnell would produce 30 bomber trainers, and the contract would amount to 15.2 million dollars.

By that time, too, the company was well along on the contract for the carrier based jet-propelled fighter for the Navy, 100 percent a McDonnell Aircraft Corporation concept.

There were also other turbine-powered designs on the boards and McDonnell had his foot in that door that opened up into the Jet Age.

McDonnell Aircraft Corporation's first production contract for the Army Air Corps was for building this AT-21 Advanced Trainer, a twin-engine, all-plywood, bomber trainer. Plane was not McDonnell design. It was designed by Fairchild Aircraft Division, Fairchild Engine and Airplane Company, Hagerstown, Maryland. Contract gave McDonnell mass production experience.

Production line at McDonnell plant in Memphis, Tennessee, turning out AT-21 bomber trainers.

With Bell Aircraft Company test pilot Bob Stanley at the controls, America's first jet plane the XP-59 makes its first flight at a secret test base in the California desert. (It is now Edwards Air Force Base.) Plane was given popular name of *Aircomet*. It and twelve others (YP-59As) never did become combat fighters.

Chapter Five

On Wings Of Fire

WHEN GENERAL OF THE AIR FORCES "Hap" Arnold heard about Air Commodore Whittle's gas turbine engine, and that it had been successfully flown in a specially designed aircraft in 1941, he didn't waste any time flying over to Britain to see first hand what some people called "the breakthrough that can win a war." Our British allies were most cooperative, and when Arnold returned stateside, in his briefcase were documents that would literally "set fire" to the whole U.S. aircraft manufacturing industry. Like the "shot heard round the world," what the general had to say to a group of the nation's best aeronautical engineers, powerplant people and production people—military and civilian—whom he summoned to his office in Washington for a secret meeting, started a revolution in aircraft design and propulsion methods.

Present were some of Arnold's "first-team"—Major General Oliver P. "Red" Echols, Assistant Chief of Air Staff Material Maintenance and Distribution, the policy-dictating agency for Wright Field; Brigadier Generals B.W. "Benny" Chidlaw and Frank O. Carroll, of the Engineering Division, Wright Field; Colonel Donald J. Keirn and Colonel Ralph P. Swofford, Chiefs of the Powerplant Laboratory and the Aircraft Laboratory at Wright Field, respectively; some engineers and officers of the General

Electric Company and the Bell Aircraft Company. The meeting lasted for hours, and the group remet several times in the course of a week.

At the opening session Arnold announced, "Gentlemen, what we're going to talk about here is a project that has top priority from the White House."

He took from his briefcase some papers and said, "These, gentlemen, are preliminary drawings of the Whittle jet engine that you've heard rumors about. Your job is to build one like it and better. Then, design an aircraft around it. Both FDR and Prime Minister Churchill want it done, yesterday!"

Before the meetings ended, Arnold had handed out the assignments: Ben Chidlaw was to be liaison officer, in charge of coordinating the activities with G.E., which would build the engine, and Bell Aircraft, whose job was to design and build the airframe for the new powerplant. Col. Swofford was to be project officer, and Frank Carroll, overseer at Wright Field. Don Keirn had a very special secret assignment.

A few days later at his desk at Wright Field, Keirn received an envelope by special courier. In it were his orders stamped SECRET. There was really little need for the classification, because nobody could have made much out of the mumbo jumbo language anyway. In part, the orders read: *"You will proceed . . to*

USAF's General Henry H. "Hap" Arnold is credited with pushing for the development of XP-59 and "an all-jet air force."

determine the desirability of adopting package power plants and to investigate late developments of sleeve valves."

Keirn hopped a plane to England. Not until he arrived there did he learn that "sleeve valves" was the code word for the RAF's new jet plane, and "package power plants" were Frank Whittle's gas turbine engines. Not too long after that Keirn was winging his way

across the Atlantic aboard a B-24 *Liberator* bomber that carried a precious cargo in its bomb bay—one complete working model of the Whittle gas turbine engine and a complete, detailed set of blueprints for building it.

The engine and plans were delivered to General Electric in Lynn, Massachusetts, where engineers studied the British engine part by part, incorporating its better points in an engine of their own, which would emerge finally as the I-40 turbo-jet engine, whose thrust was about equal to 2,000 horsepower. By the middle of March 1942, the engine was on the test stands.

Meanwhile, at Bell Aircraft in Buffalo, Larry Bell—designer of the revolutionary P-39 *Airacobra*, with its in-line piston engine inside the fuselage driving the propeller in the nose by a long geared shaft arrangement, and the first U.S. fighter to mount a 37mm cannon—had accepted the challenge to build the first U.S. jet fighter. The plane was designated the XP-59 *Aircomet* and by the end of the summer of '42 it was for real, and it was shipped in sections to a secret Air Force Base at Muroc Dry Lake, now Edwards AFB, California, for final assembly.

At Muroc there was a restricted area fenced off where they put it all together. Security was so tight that on one occasion an Air Force general tried to pull his rank on an M.P. to get the enlisted man to tell him what was going on inside the secret hangar. When the guard refused, cocking his rifle to bar the way, the

British-designed and American-made, this 1300-pound thrust turbojet engine is one of two that provided thrust for the XP-59. It has been said that British used U.S. metallurgical secrets of General Electric turbo-superchargers to make their first Whittle turbo-jet engine a success.

general threatened to have him court-martialed. The general walked away to report the incident to the base commanding officer.

The response he got was, "General, nobody gets in, "Hap" Arnold's orders. But I can tell you this—behind those closed doors is the hope of tomorrow. We are coming out with a gadget that will revolutionize the sewing machine."

The gadget referred to was Lawrence Bell's XP-59. On October 2, in 1942, Bell Aircraft's chief test pilot Robert M. Stanley took the XP-59 up for its maiden flight, and the day of the jet Air Force had its beginning.

Before the war was over, the U.S. had a combat jet fighter, the Lockheed P-80 *Shooting Star,* ready to join the propeller-driven fighter fleets of Republic P-47 *Thunderbolts,* Lockheed P-38 *Lightnings,* North American P-51 *Mustangs,* Grumman F-6F *Hellcats,* and Chance Vought F-4U *Corsairs,* which had gained Allied superiority in the skies over Europe and the Pacific. There was a backup jet fighter being built by Republic, the XP-84 *Thunderjet.* The P-80 and the P-84 production models saw very little action in World War II. Other U.S. plane builders also had new jet fighter and bomber designs in the experimental stages.

THE PRINCIPLE of jet propulsion wasn't new, far from it. An Egyptian named Hero invented the first jet engine more than 2,000 years ago. Hero's engine, called an *aeolipile* was a steam turbine, although its principle was the same as that in today's gas turbines. The principle was based on Sir Isaac Newton's third law of motion—*to every action there is an equal and opposite reaction.*

Hero put a kettle filled with water over a hot fire. When the water boiled inside the closed kettle, steam escaped through pipes into a ball, where extreme pressures were built up. Released through small jets in the ball, the steam caused the ball to spin rapidly. Even its inventor didn't know *why* it worked, but Hero had an engine that made things go round and round. He had discovered a new mysterious source of power. Newton's law wasn't published until 1687 to unscramble the mystery. Hero had invented the first *reaction-type* engine.

How a jet engine works is described in simple terms by Professor H. Sheldon Stillwell, Head, Aeronautical and Astronautical Engineering Department, the University of Illinois.*

The Professor writes, "You can understand the *force* or *reaction* which moves a jet engine if you watch a small floating log when a frog jumps off it. The action of the legs of the frog sends him through the air in *one direction.* His legs apply a reaction to the log, causing it to move through the water in the *opposite direction.*

"A jet engine drives forward by using a similar *reaction.* The engine takes the place of the frog. When the jet exhaust shoots backward into space, the *reaction* to it drives the engine forward. For this reason jet engines are sometimes called *reaction-type* engines."

Today, there are four types of jet engines—the *ramjet, turbojet, turbofan* and *turboprop.* The latter three types are used in most jet aircraft, military, commercial and private.

Turbojet engines were used to power the first jet-propelled winged aircraft designed and built by the Douglas Aircraft Company and the McDonnell Aircraft Corporation.

Both got into the jet-propelled field about the same time, Douglas with a twin-engined medium bomber design for the Air Force, the XB-43, and McDonnell with its twin-engined XFD-1 Navy fighter.

The two experimental jet aircraft were flying in 1945, before World War II ended. For both companies, which one day would join forces, it was the beginning of a new era, the so-called Jet Age.

The jet engine, which had been delayed for almost 2,000 years until the discovery and development of high heat resistant metals necessary for the tiny buckets on the gas turbine wheels, came along at just the right time to give a needed shot in the arm for the aircraft manufacturing industry. As the war drew to a close, billions of dollars in contracts for aircraft and engines were cancelled.

Don Douglas summed it up when he said, "The future is as black as the inside of a boot."

At the time he made the remark, he had just laid off 90,000 workers in one week's time. Having produced an average of about 10,000 planes a year from 1942-45, Douglas production in 1946 totaled 127 aircraft, mostly transports. He had three big government-owned plants shut down. He was think-

*Writing in the WORLD BOOK Encyclopedia.

ing seriously of going into the aluminum boat business.

There was one glimmer of hope in a contract that hadn't been cancelled, development of the AD-1 attack bomber named the *Skyraider*. A single-place low-wing attack bomber, the *Skyraider* was first delivered to the Navy in 1945, primarily for use on anti-submarine surveillance missions. As it turned out, the plane was very versatile, and served as a cargo carrier, ambulance plane and personnel transport.

Powered with one Wright R-3350 engine, the most powerful piston engine available, the *Skyraider* was a big, heavy airplane and in one version (as a transport) carried ten passengers and pilot. Altogether there were 27

basic configurations of the AD series produced between 1945 and 1957. Mainly because of the Korean situation, orders piled up, and before the line was shut down, 3,180 had been produced.

One *Skyraider*, in 1953, set a world's record carrying a 10,500 pound bombload, and the *Skyraider* served with distinction in the Vietnam war. The plane made history of a sort, as the last piston-engine, propeller-driven combat aircraft to be produced by Douglas. The 1950s were to be the decade of the jet.

Douglas got off to a slow start in the Jet Age. Although there had been a lot of preliminary design studies incorporating jet powerplants, the first Douglas jet aircraft to take wing was the XB-43 twin-engine

Douglas A5D *Skyraider,* one of the most popular planes in WWII. Navy pilots swore by them.

bomber. Only two were built. Another early effort was a modified version of the *Skyraider,* the XA2D-1 *Skyshark,* powered with an Allison *turboprop* engine driving two counter-rotating propellers. There were seven built and the project was cancelled.

The company did get a contract, in 1945, to build several experimental jet-propelled and rocket-propelled planes in conjunction with a collaborative effort of the Navy and the NACA, the National Advisory Committee for Aeronautics. The result made major contributions to high-speed flight research.

It was not until the mid fifties when the A3D and the A4D appeared— the *Skyknight* and the *Skyhawk,* respectively—that Douglas got any sizeable production orders for jet aircraft. The *Skyhawk,* for more than a quarter of a century, would set many production and performance records.

About the same time (1954-55), Douglas produced for the Air Force, a twin-engined jet bomber, the B-66 *Destroyer,* a derivative of the Navy A3D attack bomber. In speed, range and capacity, the B-66, with a three man crew, met all tactical requirements for

The XB-43, a twin-engined jet bomber with similar configuration to the A-20s and B-26s, was first Douglas venture into the Jet Age.

Early Douglas jet fighter for Navy was F-3D *Skynight.*

Douglas A4D *Skyhawk* No.1 takes to its wings June 22, 1954. In various versions, *Skyhawks* would still be in production almost 25 years later. Total of 2960 were built.

delivering the most potent weapons. As the RB-66, it was modified for night photo reconnaissance.

DURING the same ten year period (1945-55) McDonnell Aircraft Corporation was getting a head start as designer and builder of several jet-propelled aircraft. Paradoxically, at the end of World War II, the St. Louis company was expanding, mainly because of the Navy contract for its first jet-propelled carrier-based fighter, which resulted in a healthy production order. McDonnell also had taken a different approach to the coming era of the jet.

Setting up a Helicopter and Propulsion Division, as far back as 1943, McDonnell engineers came up with a lightweight *ramjet*

In early sixties, Douglas offered this F6D, the *Missileer*, as a flying launch pad for air-to-air missiles. It was a large aircraft, wing span of 70 feet with a fuselage length of 53 feet, carried no armament. No prototype was built.

Douglas twin-engine RB-66 bomber *Destroyer*.

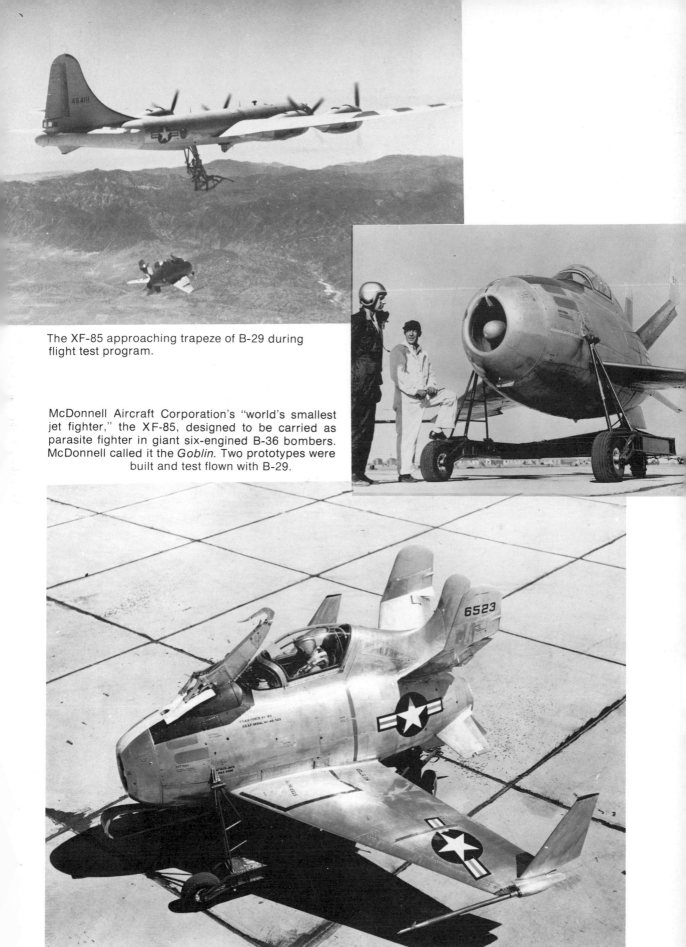

The XF-85 approaching trapeze of B-29 during flight test program.

McDonnell Aircraft Corporation's "world's smallest jet fighter," the XF-85, designed to be carried as parasite fighter in giant six-engined B-36 bombers. McDonnell called it the *Goblin.* Two prototypes were built and test flown with B-29.

McDonnell XF-88 was designed as a new class of penetration fighters. It was single-seater, but one of largest ever built in order to carry large amounts of fuel for long-range escort duties.

engine nicknamed the "Tom Thumb powerplant," which was later applied to a small helicopter design. More important, perhaps, it established McDonnell's reputation in jet propulsion research, and led to other contracts to build more conventional jet-propelled aircraft.

One of these contracts was to design and build a parasite fighter for the big six-engined B-36 bombers of the Strategic Air Command, the "striking force," just in case we had to fly great distances from homeland bases to a potential enemy target. The idea wasn't new. In the early thirties the Navy had small fighter planes that were carried by its giant dirigibles, the *Akron* and *Macon*. The small planes were launched from the dirigible in flight. After completing their mission against any "enemy" fighters to protect the mother ship, they returned to hook onto a trapeze-like arrangement and were pulled up inside the big gas bags. The *Akron* and *Macon* were the world's first airborne aircraft carriers.

The size of the Consolidated-built B-36 permitted a similar system of launching and retrieving a small fighter. Thus, the A-bomb carrier bomber (B-36) would have its own fighter protection if attacked by "enemy" fighters over the target area.

On August 23, 1948, McDonnell's parasite fighter made its first flight. It was the world's smallest jet-propelled aircraft—wingspan 21 feet 1¼ inches; length 14 feet 10¼ inches; height 8 feet 3 inches; weight 5,600 pounds. It looked more like "an engine pod with wings" than it did an airplane. But it could carry a crew of one and was fitted with four forward firing guns. The little fighter had a top speed of 600 mph and a service ceiling of 40,000 feet. For its size, it was a heavyweight.

The Air Force had a number for it, the XF-85. McDonnell called it the *Goblin*. After two prototypes were built, the concept was abandoned. By that time the B-36 was an obsolete aircraft soon to be replaced by the B-47 and the B-52 jet bombers which had developed faster than many had believed possible.

Within two months of the *Goblin*'s first flight, another McDonnell experimental jet made its debut in the sky, the XF-88, originally designed for the Air Force as a long range penetration fighter. After two prototypes were built, however, the Air Force lost interest because of restricted budgets. McDonnell, however, continued with the basic design, making a lot of modifications and improvements with the company's own research and development funds.

Original XF-88 also became testbed for Allison XT-38A turbo-prop engine, redesignated XF-88B. The configuration gave McDonnell the distinction of having world's first turbojet-propjet trimotor. Some wag called it the "Whodoo" not *Voodoo*.

It was money well spent. With the outbreak of hostilities in Korea in 1950, the Air Force revived its interest in the long range penetration fighter concept and announced a competition, the winner virtually assured of a big production order. McDonnell, with its second generation XF-88, got into the competition. Its persistence in staying with the basic XF-88 concept, step by step upgrading the performance with new design features, gave it an edge, and the McDonnell entry, which would become the vaunted F-101 *Voodoo,* won the blue ribbon.

Meanwhile, McDonnell Aircraft had been turning out a whole family of jet fighters for the Navy.

The plane that really put McDonnell Aircraft Corporation of St. Louis into the spotlight, the XFD-1, progenitor of the later fabulous and ageless *Phantom II*, flew maiden flight in January 1945, before end of World War II, and succeeding models would become Navy's first jet carrier force.

Chapter Six

Phantoms, Banshees And Demons

IT WAS NEW YEAR'S EVE, 1942, and Mr. Mac was getting in some twilight hours of overtime in his office when he received a telephone call that would greatly influence the future of McDonnell Aircraft Corporation."The phone rang," he recalls, "and I was surprised that it was Washington calling. The Navy Department, an Admiral, was on the other end of the line. The gist of our conversation was that he wanted me to be in Washington the next morning to talk about a hush-hush project, the design of a new carrier-based fighter aircraft powered by jet propulsion."

Would McDonnell Aircraft be interested in undertaking such an assignment? The Admiral wanted to know.

"We had been doing a lot of research studies in the area of jet propulsion, a lot of our own monies," McDonnell points out, "and I saw the opportunity to accept a tremendous challenge in a new concept of aircraft engineering.

"I told the Admiral I'd be there. And I was. As it turned out, within a week's time, we had roughed out a design proposal. The Navy people bought it, and we had a contract to build the experimental prototype."

The project had a name. The Navy designation was the XFD-1—a defensive experimental fighter. McDonnell also had a name for it. He called it—the *Phantom*.

THE GREATER SAINT LOUIS Magazine tells an interesting story about why McDonnell chose the name *Phantom*.

According to the magazine, "There are some general requirements for airplane names. They should have only one or two syllables, standard spelling and be recognizable and comprehendable. They should be easy to pronounce and remember, and, if possible, should help to identify the products with the company that produced them. Aerospace firms stake out an area from which to draw such names."

In discussing this subject in 1947, McDonnell explained, "There are few fields from which such names have not been frequently drawn. One of these rare fields is the world of animism. Such a field is appropriate because even inanimate objects possess a conscious life or vitality. It is good and nourishing to treat all things as alive."

Officially, the Air Force assigned the spirit world to McDonnell. McDonnell was right at home. When he was a student at Princeton, young Mac had read a book, *Human Survival After Bodily Death,* by English essayist Frederick W. H. Myers. The book aroused an interest in the young student in matters psychical. McDonnell attended seances, became deeply immersed in the study of the science of psychology.

The XFD-1 Phantom, progenitor of a long line of Navy aircraft, displayed in front of the American Airlines building (now demolished) in which McDonnell Aircraft Corporation began operations.

It may or may not, but it probably did, influence McDonnell in the selection of names for McDonnell-designed aircraft. Names such as—*Phantom, Banshee, Goblin, Demon* and *Voodoo*. It may also have influenced him to take a deep interest in all things ethereal including the design and development of spacecraft which would put man in outer space and let him live among the stars.

Project *Mercury* and Project *Gemini* would put the first U.S. astronauts in space and put the McDonnell Corporation in the public limelight as designer and builder of the astronauts' spacecraft of the same names.

Mercury and *Gemini* were far in the future when the *Phantom* was born. The Navy contract to build the XFD-1, however, put McDonnell Aircraft Corporation on the launch pad. That contract according to company records amounted to $4.4 million, and it launched the McDonnell Aircraft Corporation into a long and illustrious career of producing jet-propelled fighters for the military services whose sales dollar value would run into the billions.

In Washington the first day of the new year 1943, McDonnell was joined by teammates,

Kendall Perkins and Bob Baldwin, whom he had alerted before departing St. Louis.

"The Navy chaps really meant business," Ken Perkins remembers. "They put us up in a small office in the old Navy building, supplied pencil and paper and a drafting board, and told us to go to work. We were surprised at things moving so fast."

What the Navy Bureau of Aeronautics top brass wanted was a single-place tactical fighter that could take off from the deck of carrier, fly out a couple of hundred miles or so, be able to fight the enemy out there for about an hour, fly back to the carrier and land there. The Navy wanted a plane that was faster than its propeller aircraft, in the 500-mph range, but still capable of a slow landing speed essential for the limited sea-borne airstrip. It must have a service ceiling of at least 15,000 feet. And it had to have folding wings so as not to take up too much space on the carrier's deck.

THE NAVY already had committed itself to a powerplant source, Westinghouse Electric Corporation. It would be a team effort—the

Bureau of Aeronautics (USN), Westinghouse and McDonnell Aircraft. Westinghouse had several experimental engines, axial flow, multi-stage compressors and single-stage turbines in the design and development stages, but the state of the art was so new that it would be months before they were available. These engines were of different sizes, shapes and with a wide range of thrust.

The builder of the airframe (McDonnell) had to work within this framework. In their cubbyhole office in the Navy building, McDonnell's teammates faced a major decision *before* the first lines were drawn on paper for the new fighter. Should they go all out with a completely new and revolutionary design concept, an airframe built around the best engine which would meet performance requirements? Or should they apply previous know-how gleaned from their experience with the XP-67 and wait for the right engine to come along, then fit it into the fighter? Wisely, they chose the latter course, and as things turned out, it proved to be the right move.

In the early conceptual stages of the new fighter, Ken Perkins points out that several different engine configurations were tested before the final decision that the design would be a two-engined aircraft. Initially, they thought of using six engines of 9.5-inch diameter each, the "cluster" providing a total of about 2200 horsepower. They also tried different size diameter engines in different "clusters" ranging from six 11-inch diameter engines to four 13.5-inch diameter engines. But in the last analysis they settled for two 19-inch diameter engines which emerged on time from Westinghouse as the 19-XB turbojets, each producing 1600 pounds of thrust. This duo combination would give the plane an equivalent horsepower rating greater than that of any then in-use piston-powered Navy fighter.

The airframe configuration also took many twists and turns. At one time, they considered making it a tail-first design to "keep the tail out of the jet blast."

Another design consideration was a unique cockpit arrangement. Some studies were made that had the pilot in a prone position, which would permit a smaller diameter fuselage, reducing drag of frontal area air resistance. It was also believed that this would give the pilot better protection against G-forces (gravity) during high speed pull-outs.

The prone position idea never got farther than the drawing boards.

Where to put the engines was another design dilemma. In a paper about the evolution and design of the XFD-1, Ken Perkins writes, "The most obvious course was to put the engines side by side within the fuselage. A number of layouts of this configuration were made trying by every conceivable means to avoid the necessity for long tail pipe extensions and either long or curved inlet ducts, but no neat solution was found.

"Furthermore, it was found that with the engines in the fuselage there was insufficient fuel space without putting tanks in the wings or making the fuselage abnormally large. In view of the amount of fuel required for a jet airplane, which at that time seemed abnormally large, and since unobstructed space was required for bullet sealing tanks, it was felt that the fuselage could be put to better use to enclose fuel than to enclose engines."

In the end, it was decided to locate the engines in the wings, one on each side of the fuselage, employing a similar arrangement as that on the McDonnell XP-67 *Bomber Destroyer*. The engines were located as close to the fuselage as was thought to be safe without permitting the jet to contact the fuselage skin.

According to Perkins, "A tricycle landing gear was clearly indicated in spite of the fact that there was little experience with this type for carrier operations and that the weight was generally greater . . . It was not known how much the hot jet ("kick-back") might damage wooden carrier decks if allowed to impinge directly on the deck for warmup. It seemed better from this standpoint and from that of the deck crew to have the engines parallel with the deck when the airplane was at rest. . . It was felt that the characteristics of a tricycle gear, whereby the nose tends to drop instead of the tail upon first contact with the deck would be particularly beneficial in carrier operation."

With the engines filleted into the wing and near the center of gravity it was possible to put the cockpit forward of the leading edge, giving the pilot an excellent forward visibility. Another advantage, Ken Perkins pointed out, "was that it provided a place to put guns where the barrels were close to the pilot's line of sight. The combination of such a cockpit and gun installation made possible with this engine arrangement was thus very nearly ideal from the standpoint of the pilot in combat."

There were other problems which arose that challenged the design team. But one by one they were overcome, and the Navy's first carrier-based jet fighter emerged from its cacoon, a sleek, trim, efficient design, pleasing to the eye, and a good performer as subsequent tests were to prove.

The plane had a wingspan of 40 feet 9.3 inches, about the same as that of the Republic P-47 *Thunderbolt*. The fuselage was 37 feet 2.5 inches nose to tail, about a foot longer than the P-47's, but in profile it was long and slim, almost half the cross-section of the *Thunderbolt* fighter with its big radial engine in the nose, hanging there like a horse collar around the neck of a thoroughbred. In the nose were mounted four .50-caliber machine guns. With its crew of one, armament and fuel aboard the XFD-1 grossed out at 10,000 pounds, more than 4,000 pounds under the biggest of the P-47s. And it had half again as much horsepower. Its top speed was faster than any piston-powered World War II combat land-based fighter.

The plane first flew in January 1945. After meeting all the requirements of the original contract with the prototype model, McDonnell Aircraft Corporation was awarded a contract to build sixty FD-1 production models and within a month, the Navy, so pleased with its first jet fighter, gave McDonnell another contract to design an improved experimental version. In the years ahead, McDonnell and the Navy would become teammates in many technological triumphs in the design and production of a whole family of jet-powered aircraft.

A key milestone which greatly enhanced the partnership occurred in the summer of 1946, when the XFD-1 prototype flew into history. Naval Aviation from that day to this has never been the same.

On Sunday, July 21, 1946, the McDonnell XFD-1 *Phantom* became the first jet propelled aircraft to take off and land aboard an American carrier at sea.

On the 2-½ acre flight deck of the U.S.S. *Franklin D. Roosevelt*, steaming into an early morning wind off the Virginia Capes, a select audience of more than 2700 high ranking naval officers, aeronautical experts, representatives of newspapers, newsreels, and aviation magazines watched as the *Phantom* lowered its wings and started its engines.

Navy pilot Ltd. Cdr. James T. Davidson then pushed the throttles forward, released the brakes, and just seconds later, after a 400 foot run, pulled the *Phantom* up and away into a beautiful, climbing turn. Then, without retracting the wheels, Commander Davidson banked his aircraft around for an approach and came in for a perfect landing.

Again and again the *Phantom* took off and landed. Commander Davidson demonstrated the practicality of a jet fighter's taking a wave off successfully when he was waved off on his fourth approach. At an approach speed of 95 mph, the *Phantom* pulled up and climbed away rapidly and safely, to circle the ship and complete the landing.

After completing five takeoffs and landings, Commander Davidson lifted the *Phantom* from the deck of the carrier for the sixth time, and following a brief demonstration, flew the airplane to Patuxent River, Maryland, where a McDonnell pilot took over the cockpit once more.

A McDonnell Vice President, John Sutherland, who was an observer aboard the FDR, later told McDonnell, "The *Phantom* demonstrated all the ease and grace of conventional aircraft during her takeoffs and landings. I'll never forget, after her sixth takeoff she buzzed the ship at extremely high speeds and then ascended slow rolling!"

McDonnell, although he contributed a lot of ideas, didn't have a lot to do with the actual design of the *Phantom*. Teammates, Ken Perkins, Bob Baldwin, Irv Sheppard and many others put the lines on paper. By his own admission, McDonnell, himself, says that he got too busy putting the company together and chasing around the country trying to drum up business to spend much time over the drawing board. The last time he played the role of designer was when he was at Martin, and worked on the *Maryland* bomber.

"There are times when I wish I were back in the role of a project engineer and closer to the design and development problems," he confesses. "I haven't flown, either, since back in the late thirties; . . . Sometimes, when I see one of our creations take off and climb up there, I say to myself, 'Ole' Mac, you're really missing something . . .''

In the role of "entrepreneur," as Ken Perkins calls him, McDonnell, with superior

Navy Lt. Commander James J. Davidson flew into history when he made takeoffs and landings with XFD-1 from flight deck of USS *Franklin D. Roosevelt.* New era in naval aviation had its beginning that day.

McDonnell XFD-1 *Phantom* takes off from deck of carrier *Franklin D. Roosevelt* in July 1946.

business acumen and good salesman's savvy made it possible for a lot of guys to fly in a wide variety of aircraft and spacecraft. Flying faster than twice the speed of sound in today's F-4 *(Phantom II)* or riding in comfort hundreds of miles above the earth in a McDonnell spacecraft, or dining aloft in the commodious comfortable cabin of a DC-10, is an *experience* one doesn't easily forget. A high heritage, indeed.

To see his company grow as it has, to recap its many, many accomplishments in so many diversified fields, must be an experience and satisfaction to McDonnell. For more than four decades he has been at the helm, a leader in ideas and ideals.

PHANTOM I, the XFD-1 prototype was just the beginning. Almost two years to the day after the first *Phantom* flew in 1945, on January 11, 1947 another McDonnell-designed fighter for the Navy, the XF2D-1, which was named the *Banshee,* made its first

flight. Re-designated the F2H-1, the first production model of the *Banshee* was delivered to the Navy in August 1948. Altogether, the company would produce a total of 895 *Banshees*. It has been said that the *Banshee* is the plane that "made" the fledgling McDonnell Aircraft Corporation. The statement is probably true. Certainly, the total sales amounting to $318.7 million for the different versions of the *Banshee*—day fighter, night fighter and a long-range photo-recon airplane—didn't hurt the young company's financial status. McDonnell Aircraft, like its airplanes, was off and zooming.

Essentially the *Banshee* was an improved version of the successful *Phantom I,* although there were significant design changes: (1). The engines (two Westinghouse J34 axial-flow turbines) were about twice the thrust equivalent in horsepower to the four engines on a B-29 bomber. (2). The airframe was larger; the wings and tail surfaces were thinner with a much smoother skin. (3). The

F2H *Banshee* production line in St. Louis. When *Banshee* finally got into mass production it resulted in vast expansion program for McDonnell Aircraft Corporation.

McDonnell F2H-2 *Banshee*, capable of carrying up to 3,000 pounds of offensive weapons, gave us new muscle during the Korean conflict.

Banshee could carry twice as much fuel, and four .20mm cannon replaced the .50-caliber machine guns in the nose.

The *Banshee* was also a larger aircraft than the *Phantom I,* a wingspan greater by about four feet, another three feet added to its fuselage length. It grossed out at 16,000 pounds weight, more than half again the gross weight of the *Phantom I.* Most of that weight was translated into payload, which permitted carrying enough fuel to double the effective maximum range. While the *Phantom I* was considered to be in the 500-mph class, the *Banshee* had a top speed of 600-mph plus. Launched off the deck of a carrier by catapult augmenting its own thrust, it could climb at the rate of 9,000 feet per minute up to operational altitudes 35,000 feet and above.

As rapidly as the *Banshees* rolled off the production lines in Saint Louis, they were delivered to carrier forces with both the Atlantic and Pacific Fleets. "The *Banshee,*" said Rear Admiral Selden B. Spangler, Maintenance and Material officer of the Atlantic Fleet, "is the backbone of carrier jet aircraft . ."

During the Korean War, *Banshees* first went into action aboard the carrier *Essex.* Their combat record was remarkable.

They flew strafing missions using the forward firing cannon with armor-piercing shells. They flew strike after strike at bridges and other installations with two 500-pound bombs slung under the wings. Time and time again, they limped home with one engine out, and sometimes, badly shot up. But sturdy, rugged construction held them together.

With such performance, the *Banshee* for all time changed the concept of naval aviation tactical warfare. Carrier-based, the *Banshees* proved they could hold their own against the best ground-based fighters. And they were soon to be joined by a third member of the family of McDonnell jets, the F3H *Demon.*

Before the Korean fracas began, as early as September 1948, McDonnell had entered a Navy competition for a single-engine fighter interceptor. The single-engine concept was not McDonnell's idea. It was, however, what the ground rules called for, and McDonnell Aircraft accepted the challenge.

With McDonnell the *Demon,* like the *Doodlebug* was, in the beginning, a loser of sorts, and he doesn't like to talk too much about it. The trouble was with the early models. They were grossly underpowered. The Westinghouse J-40 turbojet engine which the Navy insisted on didn't come along as well as was expected. And when the Navy raised its original spec from a 22,000 pound aircraft designed as a short-range interceptor, to a 29,000 pound medium-range, all-weather fighter, all Hell broke loose.

In a letter to Washington, McDonnell had warned that the design would be "alarmingly underpowered." The Navy said to go ahead, anyway. McDonnell did, and sixty *Demons* were built around the J-40 engines. Eleven crashed, killing four pilots. Several times the aircraft were grounded until an engine switch was made.

The design itself was basically sound. It simply didn't have enough thrust to perform its required mission. When the new Allison J71-A-2 turbojet came along, the re-designed *Demon* turned out to be a breadwinner. A total of 519 *Demons* were sold to the Navy.

In its new configuration, bigger and heavier, and with the more powerful engine, the *Demon,* with greatly increased performance, joined the Fleet as a fully qualified, first-line, all-weather defense fighter. It was the first operational aircraft to be equipped with *Sparrow III* air-to-air guided missiles.

With armament consisting of four 20mm rapid firing cannon, missiles, rockets and bombs, the *Demon* was deployed in the Mediterranean, Caribbean, and Far East. Flying day and night, *Demons* were the primary fleet defense fighters during the critical operations in the Lebanese and Quemoy crises.

Capable of operating above 46,000 feet, the *Demon* also had great speed, approaching Mach I, the supersonic range.

Breaking the so-called sound barrier would be the next challenge.

It would be another McDonnell design, a refinement of the XF-88 prototype, which would become the F-101 Air Force attack fighter and interceptor that would thrust McDonnell Aircraft Corporation into the Supersonic Age. A long line of famous faster-than-sound fighters would follow.

McDonnell concept of "two engine reliability" gave way reluctantly when company produced single-engine *Demon* to meet hard set rules of Navy competition. Early models proved to be underpowered, suffered a series of tragic crashes. New more powerful engines in re-designed *Demon* (F3H-2N interceptors) having more wing, large fuselage, proved to be good defensive fighters, capable of operating above 40.000 feet at near supersonic speed, carrying four *Sparrow* missiles.

Douglas Model D-558-2 *Skyrocket,* which smashed the brick wall to pieces when it took off under its own power (unlike XS-1), climbed to altitude, exceeded Mach 1 in straight and level flight, landed under its own power the same as any subsonic jet fighter.

Chapter Seven

Brick Wall In The Sky

HIGH ABOVE the San Fernando Valley, not far from the Lockheed factory at Burbank, California, where his plane was built, Air Corps test pilot Lieutenant Benjamin S. Kelsey pushed the nose downward, and the fork-tailed, twin-engine YP-38 went into a steep dive. "The plane reached a vertical dive screaming down at better than 500 miles per hour," Kelsey later wrote in his official report. "Investigating recovery technique, I forced the plane into an attitude where the loads caused it to start disintegrating.

"The plane went into a series of violent maneuvers, so confusing and so rapid, that I had difficulty recalling in detail the sequence of events, never quite sure until floating down in the parachute and looking up at a stairway of parts in the sky, that the machine had broken up in flight . . ."

Studies of what happened revealed that the plane had run into a series of shock waves built up by its own terrific speed—a phenomenon that aero-engineer-scientists diagnose as "compressibility." It was no mystery that these problems occurred as the aircraft neared the speed of sound, or Mach One—about 760 mph at sea level.*

*Ernst Mach, an Austrian-born physicist and psychologist, is credited with having developed an accurate method for measuring the action of bodies moving at high speeds, relating their speeds in terms of the speed of sound. Until aircraft began approaching these high velocities, Mach was virtually unknown. But today the Machmeter is important relative to supersonic flight.

Indeed, strange things happened in the unknown sonic regions. Shock waves—exploding shells of compressed air—hammered at a plane's skin and frame like trip hammers trying to tear it apart. The rudder, ailerons and elevators developed severe buffeting, violent vibrations and flutter, all symptoms of that new disease, "compressibility." Sometimes, the controls froze. A pilot was helpless. There was a new danger in the sky.

Eventually, engineers would design around the problem, but for a period of time there was the school of thought that when aircraft reached certain high speed ranges linked to the speed of sound there was an impenetrable barrier. Pilots and scientists alike often called it "the brick wall in the sky." When planes hit the barrier: Blewee! They disintegrated.

What happened in the skies over England on September 27, 1946, more than six years after Ben Kelsey's experience, only made the alarmists scream louder that their theory was sound. Geoffrey R. DeHavilland, the eldest son of the famed British plane designer, was testing a new experimental jet-propelled, tailless monoplane (the DeHavilland DH-108) when it suddenly disintegrated in flight. Unfortunately, DeHavilland didn't get out and was killed. He had been flying at or near the speed of sound, according to recording instruments. The so-called experts were more certain than ever that there was a "sound barrier."

Larry Bell's XS-1, with then Captain Charles "Chuck" Yeager at its controls, streaks through the sound barrier. Nothing happened, and from that moment on supersonic flight no longer was the big "bugaboo" holding back progress in aircraft design for high speeds.

The theorists declared that aircraft could only fly so fast. That was that.

Their theory itself "blew up" little more than a year after DeHavilland's death when a young Air Force Captain, Charles E. (Chuck) Yeager (now a retired Brigadier General), made history when he flew his Bell XS-1 through the so-called "sound barrier." The date was October 14, 1947.

Built by the Bell Aircraft Corporation of Buffalo, N.Y., the XS-1 was an odd-looking aircraft. No propeller, no jet intakes, only a cluster of rockets in the tail. Her fuselage with short stubby wings and a long needle-nosed probe gave her a profile like a swordfish. She was built of special metal alloys to withstand high ambient temperatures, friction heat of the rushing air over her sleek skin surface. It was said she could withstand aerodynamic forces up to eighteen times her own weight. The idea was she would ram her way through "that damned brick wall."

For the big test, they carried her up to 21,000 feet above California's Mojave Desert (Muroc Dry Lake, today's Edwards Air Force Base) snuggled beneath a modified B-29 like a baby whale suckling its mother. Then, they dropped her like she was a king-sized bomb. Only she had a man aboard!

According to Yeager: "We dropped several hundred feet to be sure of clearing the mother ship. Then, I hit the switch igniting the rockets. BOOM! It sounded like I had fired a big cannon. The XS-1 shot forward. There was

some vibration and a lot of strange noises, but I had control, positive control and we were climbing at a normal angle. . . . Up, up, up to above 40,000 feet. I had a comet by the tail and couldn't let go . . . And the real sensation was that flight was smooth and virtually silent, only the hissing sound of rushing air over the plane's skin. Airplane control and stability were completely normal as 1.0 Mach was attained and passed . . ."

Later on the ground, after a long glide back to the lake bed and a safe landing, Yeager would insist—"If the Machmeter hadn't been in the cockpit, I would never have noticed the smashing of the barrier that wasn't there . . ."

Planes have been flying faster than sound ever since.

THE DOUGLAS AIRCRAFT COMPANY got into the supersonic sky early in the game. Its first entry was an experimental design, Model D-558-1, the *Skystreak*, built at the El Segundo, California Division with the cooperation of the National Advisory Committee for Aeronautics (NACA), the predecessor of today's National Aeronautics and Space Administration (NASA), and the United States Navy. Its mission: to "nibble" at the so-called sound barrier exploring the unknowns of the transonic regions.

Skystreak, a straight-winged aircraft powered with a General Electric J-35 turbojet engine, never did fly faster than sound, but it flew into history. During high speed trials in

August 1947, the plane twice shattered the world's speed record for subsonic aircraft. The plane hit speeds in excess of 600 mph! During the speed runs one observer remarked—"It didn't just nibble at the speed of sound, it took big bites!"

An advanced sequel to the *Skystreak*, Model D-558-2, the *Skyrocket*, shattered for all time the myth of the sonic wall to become the first manned aircraft to fly twice the speed of sound.

Skyrocket, although similar in profile to *Skystreak*, had a swept back wing and was unique in that it was powered by both a turbo-

Douglas Model D-558-1 *Skystreak* was design "tool" which shattered subsonic speed records (faster than 600 mph) and resulted in improved version D-558-2 *Skyrocket* that would be first aircraft to fly twice the speed of sound.

Douglas *Skyrocket* Model D-558-2 takes off using rocket motors. *Skyrocket* also set new altitude record, climbing to 83,000 feet!

jet engine and rocket motors. One engineer described it as a "helluva problem in design arrangement, because it meant two powerplants and two types of fuel systems to feed them." The rocket motor alone, built by Reaction Motors, Inc., required several different chemicals to motivate it.

Original specifications for the *Skyrocket* called for an airplane to fly at the speed of sound at sea level and designed to investigate transonic flight phenomena. Design studies began in the summer of 1946, almost 15 months before Yeager and the XS-1 first flew faster than sound. On November 14, 1947, the *Skyrocket* was taken out of the shop at Douglas El Segundo for its first public appearance.

She had a wingspan of 25 feet, and an overall length of 45 feet, and fully loaded she weighed about eight tons. She had another unusual feature, a long needle-like spear protruding forward of her slim nose to register air speeds ahead of the turbulent air currents set up around the fuselage. The probe earned her a nickname—"Old Needle Nose." She stuck her nose into regions above the earth where no other manned aircraft had ever dared venture before. And she served her purpose well, bringing back urgently needed knowledge to help in the design of safer and more efficient airplanes of the future.

Skyrocket made her first flight on February 4, 1948, with Douglas Chief Test Pilot John Martin at the controls. On the initial flight only the plane's turbojet engine was installed. Meanwhile, Douglas engineers were trying out its rocket motor on test stands.

It was not until February 25, 1949, more than a year later, that the *Skyrocket* zoomed aloft for its first trial under simultaneous rocket engine and turbojet power. Climbing almost vertically, the *Skyrocket* reached an altitude of 11,000 feet using her rocket power alone. Fuel exhausted, her pilot switched on the Westinghouse J-34 turbojet engine, and the plane continued on a routine research flight for almost half an hour, landing under turbojet power on the desert floor. She had not yet challenged the brick wall. But now she was ready.

Again and again, through a series of 41 flights, the *Skyrocket* was flown repeatedly through the speed of sound to demonstrate the routine practicability of supersonic flying. Each time it was different than the flight of

the XS-1. The *Skyrocket* took off under its own power and then, with rocket motor turned on, streaked in level flight at speeds exceeding Mach 1. And each time she landed under her own power the same as any jet fighter.

"Passage of the exploratory craft into the supersonic regions has become routine," declared Scott Crossfield, a NACA research test pilot who made many of the supersonic flights. The sound barrier was no longer a deterring factor. Airplanes designed properly and with sufficient power could fly as fast as man wanted them to fly.

Crossfield proved it when on November 20, 1953 he flew the *Skyrocket* at a speed of 1327 mph (Mach 2.01), better than twice the speed of sound. It was a modified *Skyrocket* that did the trick.

Douglas engineers had concluded that their research plane was capable of far greater speeds than were possible by taking off from the ground and climbing to moderate altitude using both jet and rocket engines. If they could carry the plane as high as possible in the belly of a B-29—the air launch principle employed in the XS-1 flight—they were certain the *Skyrocket* could accelerate into much advanced high-speed regions. The Navy, whose monies were being spent for the project, said "go ahead, try it."

Result was that the *Skyrocket* was refitted for aerial launchings from the underside of a specially modified B-29 "mother" ship. For these tests the *Skyrocket's* turbojet engine was removed and three tons of additional rocket fuel put aboard in its place. The D-558-2 became for the first time a purely rocket-powered aircraft. Hence, the name *Skyrocket*.

Altogether, eleven flights were made with the rocket-powered craft, and virtually each time she set a new record of some kind. On August 21, 1953, with Marine Lt. Colonel Marion E. Carl at its controls, *Skyrocket* was dropped from the bomb bay of a B-29 at an altitude of about 37,000 feet. Seconds later Carl fired the rocket engines, and the plane headed upward in a steep climb. By the time he reached 75,000 feet, all the rocket fuel had been expended, but his speed carried him up over 83,000 feet, a new world's altitude record.

Then, almost three months to the day, Crossfield made his historic speed breakthrough. Levelling off at a predetermined altitude after being launched from the B-29, Crossfield, with a second shot of rocket

Launched from belly of B-29, *Skyrocket* was first aircraft to fly twice the speed of sound. In modified version, Model D-558-2 used only rocket power, the turbojet engine being eliminated.

power remaining, sent the *Skyrocket* in level flight at double the speed of sound. His rocket fuel gone, he glided the plane to a safe landing, much the same as today's Space Shuttle *Enterprise* has done before the eyes of millions of viewers on the TV screen.

Skyrocket showed them the way.

In all there were three *Skyrockets* built and designed by Douglas El Segundo, California Division. The planes more than doubled their specification requirements.

WHILE *SKYROCKET* was showing its stuff, another faster-than-sound aircraft, the X-3, designed and built by Douglas at its Santa Monica plant, made its appearance in the supersonic sky. Sponsored by the Air Force, NACA and the Navy, the X-3 was specifically designed for sustained flights at extremely high speeds. Equally important, the X-3 was a test vehicle for new materials and new fabrication techniques that would effect aircraft design and construction far into the future.

Striking in appearance, the X-3 had a slender fuselage and short wings that were located well back toward the tail. The fuselage

(66 feet 9 inches) was nearly three times the wingspan (22 feet 8 inches) and it was so long and narrow that some observers said the plane resembled a stiletto. In like fashion she stabbed away at the sonic wall, providing valuable data which would become the basis for eventual development of operational supersonic aircraft.

Unlike *Skystreak* or *Skyrocket*, the X-3 had no rocket power. Her powerplant consisted of two Westinghouse J34-WE-17 turbojet engines. She was the first jet-powered (not rocket) to fly faster than sound. And for a whole year, from October 1952 until November 1952, in numerous flights she demonstrated the feasability of sustained manned flight at extremely high speeds.

Although the X-3 never did exceed the supersonic speeds set by the *Skyrocket*, what Douglas engineers learned from her design and construction led to a whole new family of supersonic fighters, the famed F4D *Skyray* and the F5D *Skylancer*. Both would give the U.S. Navy a super, supersonic Sunday punch.

THE F4D *SKYRAY* would also give Douglas Aircraft Company a share of the

Needle-like X-3, a joint Air Force-NACA-Douglas design was first turbojet to fly faster than sound. She had no rocket power assist. X-3 provided "know-how" that led to design and production of new family of supersonic fighters.

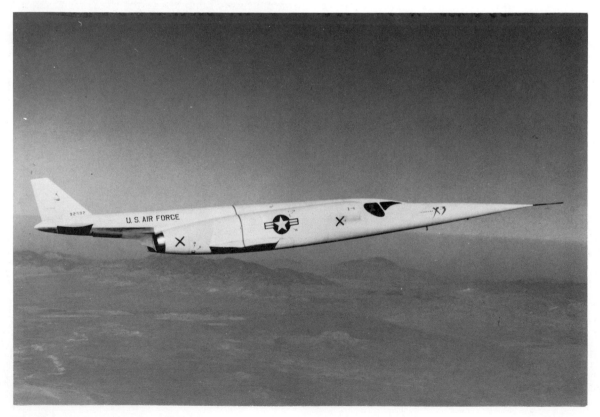

Douglas F-4D *Skyray* takes off from carrier deck.

The XF4D-1 Skyray, which set a world absolute speed record in October 1953.

President Eisenhower presents Collier award to Ed Heinemann for design of *Skyray*. Heinemann shared award with J. S. "Dutch" Kindelberger, for design of North American F-100 *Sabre* series. Both worked for Douglas during design of the famous DC-1 which launched DC family.

coveted Collier Trophy, aviation's highest award. The other recipient was the North American built F-100 *Super Sabre*. Both were production aircraft going into service with Navy and Air Force operational squadrons. Paradoxically, both were the creations of two Douglas-oriented design engineers, J. H. (Dutch) Kindelberger, whom we met earlier in the first chapter, one of the first engineers Don Douglas hired when he founded his company in the early twenties, and E. H. (Ed) Heinemann, whom Kindelberger himself later hired to work for him at Douglas. Together, the two shared the Collier Trophy award, Kindelberger credited with the design of the *Super Sabre* and Heinemann credited as the designer of the *Skyray*.

At the time, December 1954 when the award was presented at the White House by President Eisenhower, Kindelberger was Chairman of the Board and Chief Executive Officer of North American Aviation, Inc., and Heinemann was Chief Engineer of Douglas Aircraft Company's El Segundo Division.

About Heinemann, incidentally, "Dutch" Kindelberger once told the author—"Ed is one

of the most brilliant and creative aeronautical engineers in the country." He added with a twinkle in his blue eyes, "that's why I hired him for $18 a week back in the late 1930's. Don't laugh, it was good money in those days. The average Douglas worker was getting only about ten bucks a week!"

Ironically, Heinemann came to Douglas with only a high school education, which included a course in mechanical drawing, plus a recommendation from a Los Angeles firm that said he was a good designer—*of fire truck bodies.* As it turned out, he was a damned good designer of airplanes, too, playing a major role in the design of such famous Douglas planes as the SBD *Dauntless*, the AD *Skywarrior*, the A-4 *Skyhawk*, and, of course, the *Skystreak*, *Skyrocket* and the X-3 supersonic pioneers. The *Skyray* and its successor, the *Skylancer*, however, were his crowning achievements.

For Ed Heinemann, the F4D *Skyray* has a special significance, as well it should. Not only did it bring him a share of the Collier Trophy but in a competition for the world's speed record in October 1953 under Federation Aeronautique Internationale rules (F.A.I. being the world's monitoring organization for official aircraft performance records), his *Skyray* brought the world's speed record back to the United States. On October 3, 1953, *Skyray* flew at an average of 752.943 miles per hour over the official three kilometer course to beat the previous record held by Great Britain. *Skyray's* record, incidentally, was bettered a few weeks later on October 30 when Dutch Kindelberger's F-100 *Super Sabre* flew at an average speed of 755.149 miles per hour over a sanctioned 15-kilometer course. Both feats undoubtedly helped in the winning of the Collier.

Both speed runs were made at sea level and, admittedly, the *Super Sabre* and the *Skyray* were both capable of much greater speeds at higher altitudes. What made the record flights most impressive to the world was that both these aircraft were already in service with their respective defense service organizations, the Air Force and the Navy. Both services regarded them as the "hottest things in the sky."

For this book Ed Heinemann's *Skyray* warrants a more detailed description. Designed as a supersonic interceptor, it was one of the first American-built planes to have a delta wing—a triangular shape with rounded tips. With a very short span, there was no need for wing tips to be folded upwards to make room for more planes on a carrier's flight deck. Some called the *Skyray*—the "mighty little midget." Indeed, it was the smallest of any carrier-based fighter of that period.

Interestingly, in its first configuration, *Skyray*, designated the XF4D-1, never attained supersonic speeds. Not until later, when it was fitted with the newer, more powerful Pratt & Whitney J-57 jet engine, did it become a supersonic performer. The P&W jet engine, capable of developing in excess of 10,000 pounds of thrust, coincidentally in 1953 also had won the Collier Trophy for its designer, Leonard S. Hobbs. *Skyray* was also equipped with an afterburner, a device that reburns the main engine's exhaust to give an extra boost in power. With this combined thrust the single-place, single-engine *Skyray* could be shot off a carrier's deck (catapult-launched) and climb to 10,000 feet in less than a minute.

With such sterling performance the Navy ordered and was delivered more than 400 *Skyrays*, contracts worth hundreds of millions to Douglas. There followed a vastly improved version, although similar in configuration, the F5D *Skylancer,* the Navy's first 1000-mile-an-hour fighter.

Only 56 of the *Skylancers* were delivered to the Navy because of heavy budget reductions. But the F5D, which made its first flight on April 21, 1956, proved to be a versatile design, a multi-purpose aircraft capable of performance as an all-weather day fighter or interceptor.

Skylancer was also capable of carrying the most modern weapons systems, including bombs, rockets and missiles. Still, it was designed for catapult takeoff from all types of aircraft carriers and capable of slow enough speeds for landing on the floating airfields or extremely short runways.

The Navy also proudly proclaimed that it was (for its period) faster than any American jets in squadron service!

It would not remain in this front position for very long.

In St. Louis, at the McDonnell Aircraft Corporation's facility, a radically new design adapted from the original XF-88 was taking shape. Later to be designated the F-101 and named *Voodoo*, it was to have a far-reaching impact on the whole complexion of Mr. Mac's position in the aircraft manufacturing industry and his role in the conquest of space.

Douglas F-5D *Skylancer.*

Real "teammates" in name and in the sky, an F-4 *Phantom* is refuelled by an A-4 *Skyhawk*.

Chapter Eight

Phantom II And The Skyhawk

IT WAS THE *Banshee* (F2H series) that "rang the multi-hundred million dollar gong," according to McDonnell. And according to a company press release these versatile twin-engined carrier-based fighters were "immortalized" in James Michener's great book, *The Bridges at Toko-ri*. There was only one thing wrong—to date McDonnell Aircraft Corporation was fast becoming very much Navy oriented. It was getting the reputation of building good airplanes for the Navy *only*, a healthy partnership to be sure, but McDonnell wanted to branch out and get some Air Force business also. His initial attempt after the XP-67 effort was a single-place, twin-engine design, the XF-88 which he called the *Voodoo*. Unfortunately, it lost out in a competition with the North American entry, the F-86 *Sabre*. Perhaps it was a good "loss" because McDonnell never gave up the basic concept of the XF-88, which evolved into the F-101 *Voodoo*, a long-range, supersonic, penetration fighter. Before the *Voodoo* line would shut down, it would almost equal the *Banshee* in number of planes produced. More important, perhaps, the F-101 put McDonnell into the supersonic sky.

The original *Voodoo* (XF-88) was transonic and by the time it made its first flight in October 1948—more than a year after Chuck Yeager's historic first supersonic penetration—there was every indication that the next generation of fighters, to keep pace with

progress, would have to fly at supersonic speeds. With its own monies, McDonnell Aircraft Corporation accepted the challenge and continued to improve the original XF-88 design, incorporating new powerplants, a more efficient sweptback wing and other innovations to come up with one of the most beautiful airplanes ever built.

First flown on September 29, 1954, the prototype F-101 *Voodoo* won a production contract from the Air Force, and in various versions (807 were produced in all) it served with three different Air Force commands. The original F-101 *Voodoos,* which were designed as single-place fighter-bomber versions, were used with the USAF Strategic and Tactical Air Commands. A modified version, the F-101B with more powerful engines and designed for a crew of two (the radar observer was added) went into service as an all-weather interceptor with the Air Defense Command. Yet another version, the RF-101 *Voodoo*, joined the USAF Tactical Command as a long-range photo-reconnaissance aircraft. In all configurations the *Voodoo* family established many remarkable performance records. With USAF Commands, the planes were in service all over the world.

The *Voodoo* was the first operational aircraft to fly at twice the speed of sound. In November 1957, the *Voodoo* established a new transcontinental speed record, flying west to east at 781.74 mph, east to west at 677.73

McDonnell designed F-101 *Voodoos* were first in-service fighters to fly twice the speed of sound. When McDonnell Aircraft landed contract to produce F-101, it marked first time company had large production order from the Air Force.

mph and averaging 721.85 mph over the 4891.8 mile round-trip distance. Too late for the Korean conflict, *Voodoos* were an on-the-shelf aircraft for the Vietnam fighting. There, the RF-101s distinguished themselves carrying out key reconnaissance missions.

The *Voodoo* (RF-101 versions) extended the art of aerial photography into the supersonic field. Carrying three different camera systems, these planes can take photographs from 45,000 feet and higher, covering an area 217 miles long by 8 miles wide. Flying at low levels at supersonic speeds they brought back evidence of the Soviet missile build-up in Cuba. As "spies in the skies" they gave the U.S. a decisive edge in photo reconnaissance.

Early in its conceptual stages the F-101 design was powered with two Westinghouse J-46 engines. But the design which won the Air Force production contract was built around the Pratt & Whitney J-57 engines, the advanced powerplants which had made the Douglas *Skyray* the Collier Trophy winner. Quoted in *Fortune* magazine, McDonnell himself said—"We could see that engine would be a winner. That was a good marriage, a good union of airframe and engine."

"Including spare parts and so on," he added, "the *Voodoo* produced over a billion dollars worth of business."

For McDonnell Aircraft Corporation, the *Voodoo* was a splendid exemplification of a basic company design philosophy.

Sanford N. McDonnell, who today is President, Chief Executive Officer and Director of McDonnell Douglas Corporation, emphasizes—"Early in our company history, we took into consideration the combat requirements of not just one service but all services. We designed not just for one mission, but many missions. We call it *multiple mission engineering*. The *Voodoo* was a shining example."

"Sandy," who is McDonnell's nephew, joined the company in 1948, at age 26, with degrees in economics, mechanical engineering and applied mechanics from Princeton University, the University of Colorado and Washington University, and under uncle's demanding and watchful eyes climbed up the ladder, rung by rung. As stress engineer, aerodynamicist, design engineer, he cut his teeth to become group leader, assistant project engineer and company-wide project engineer on the successful *Voodoo* program. Few, if any, top executives in the aerospace industry are better qualified to hold the reins.

THERE WAS FOR "SANDY," perhaps, a moment of great personal satisfaction when in 1961, he became Vice President and General Manager of the F-4 program which saw McDonnell Aircraft Corporation producing the fabulous *Phantom II* that was then, and is still, one of the world's most versatile and best performing fighter aircraft, a legend in the annals of military aviation. There probably never was and never will be again a plane born in peacetime that so met the needs of the rapidly changing concept of aerial warfare. Indeed, the *Phantom II* itself changed the concept.

What happened?

"The (F-4) Phantom had its beginning not by winning an aircraft competition, but rather by losing one," says Herman D. Barkey, who was Engineering Manager of all F-4 programs. "In 1953, McDonnell Aircraft Corporation lost a competition for a carrier-based fighter which was won by Chance Vought with the F8U. McDonnell previously had been the designer and producer of . . . more than 1,000 carrier-based jet aircraft prior to 1953, in the form of *Phantom I, Banshee* 1-2-3-4 and 5, and F3H *Demons.* With this background it was determined to continue design and production of carrier-based aircraft . . . McDonnell engineers canvassed numerous Navy operations personnel . . . willing to listen and return questionnaires to determine their desires for the next version of carrier-based aircraft."

"Numerous studies and layouts were made during the next year, and a full-scale mock-up of the aircraft which was believed to most nearly represent the desires of the majority of Navy operations personnel was constructed," Barkey continues his recollection. Invita-

tions were sent to numerous Navy operating commands, overhaul and repair facilities, Bureau of Aeronautics and Chief of Naval Operations (personnel) requesting they visit McDonnell (in St. Louis) and "offer their criticism or recommendations on our mock-

Sanford N. McDonnell

Herman D. Barkey

Air Force F-4C (*Phantom II*) was originally designated F-110. Originally, *Phantom IIs* were built for Navy, continuation of a long-time association with that service arm that started with *Phantom I* airplanes. Navy versions outclassed Air Force F-106 fighters in competition and Air Force turned to *Phantom* version designated F-4C air superiority fighter. F-4E version in Vietnam War was equipped with rapid-firing 20mm cannon as well as missiles. In F-4E version, up to 16,000 pounds of conventional or nuclear bombs can be carried externally.

up. Finally, in November 1954, the Bureau of Aeronautics gave McDonnell a letter of intent to design and build two aircraft similar to the mock-up display. Many of us considered this a consolation prize for having lost the F8U production contract."

It was a beginning, but not the kind of a start that McDonnell envisioned to make his company No. 1 in the production of the world's best fighter plane, an accolade that in its many versions the fabulous Phantom II (F-4) one day would enjoy. Perhaps, one big obstacle in the early stages was that no military requirement existed for the aircraft. In view of this, perhaps, McDonnell Aircraft was lucky to get any government monies to go ahead with the building of two prototypes. One was a single-place configuration, the other a two-place version.

Design performance specifications called for *Mach 2-plus* speeds in level flight, a slow

speed range of about *140-knots* for carrier operations, a service ceiling of over 60,000 feet. The aircraft was to be equipped with guns, radar and necessary fire control systems. Its designed-for mission was fleet air defense. That is, the aircraft was to be deployed from a carrier, cruise out to a radius of 250 nautical miles, stay on CAP and attack any intruder when required, and return to the carrier with a total deck cycle time—takeoff to landing—of three hours.

Later F-4 and RF-4 specifications: wingspan 38 feet five inches; fuselage length 58 feet 3 inches and 62 feet 11 inches; weight, about 44,000 pounds gross; powerplants, two J79 General Electric turbojet engines, one on each side of the fuselage, and each developing about 18,000 horsepower.

Essentially some of these design and mission objectives were spelled out in the proposal that McDonnell took to Washington in the summer of 1954. "I remember," he says, "I talked to the Attack Desk about it. No dice. Then, I talked with the Fighter Desk about it, and they wouldn't buy it, either. The runaround was deliberate. I think they (the Navy) wanted to bracket both fields. We set our sights in that direction, and what we finally came up with was an all-purpose aircraft, designed for growth and versatility."

McDonnell stresses the fact that the *Phantom II* didn't just come into being overnight. It was no airplane designed on the back of an envelope. "No siree," he declared emphatically, "we had one of the greatest fighter teams ever assembled, more than ten years experience in the jet fighter field and they pulled out all the stops. One might say, *Phantom II* took the best ideas from the *Phantom I*, the *Banshee*, the XF-88 and the F-101 *Voodoos* plus a lot of improved innovative features and put them all together."

A close look reveals definite clues to the *Phantom II's* ancestral lineage. The twin powerplant arrangement, for example, comes from *Phantom I* which we already know was one of the first fighter designs to get away from the conventional single-engine concept. From the *Banshees* came such things as a more compact and comfortable cockpit, a new longitudinal control system and a big radar nose. The *Voodoos* contributed to a longer, fatter fuselage to accommodate the bigger

engines and the sweptback wing. In these respects, *Phantom II* evolved as a kind of composite design. But it contributed many unique design features of its own.

From concept to its first flight on May 27, 1958, the *Phantom II* was five years in design, development and fabrication. That period represented hundreds of thousands of man hours and millions of dollars in expenditures, most of it McDonnell Aircraft Corporation's own money. The first limited production contract did not come until December of 1958. The initial order, a Navy contract, was for a carrier-based attack fighter version.

What the Navy got was a rugged, heavy, complex piece of hardware that was *Phantom II*, with a long bullet-shaped nose, a hump-backed fuselage because of the large canopy enclosure for a crew of two in front and back cockpits, wide-rooted sweptback wings having flip-up tips, and a bent down horizontal tailplane, probably its most distinctive feature. Technically called an anhedral tail—an inverted shallow V-shaped horizontal stabilizer—the design was necessary to keep the elevator control surfaces away from the jet exhausts. With its droop-snout and unconventional tail, *Phantom II* never was hailed as one of the most beautiful aircraft in the skies. Far from it, there are those who say it is downright ugly looking. But from those who fly it, there is virtually a common concurrence—"the best

Cut-away drawing shows interior arrangement of popular F-4C Air Force version of the *Phantom II*.

Phantom production line at McDonnell Aircraft's St. Louis plant.

McDonnell Douglas A-4 *Skyhawks* and F-4 *Phantoms* parked aboard USS *Independence*.

damned fighter plane ever built."

THE PHANTOM II's phenomenal performance was clearly evident before it became operational with service squadrons. During pre-service development, the airplane established its place in aviation history by zoom-climbing to a record 98,557 feet. On December 5, 1961, it set a world's class record for horizontal flight at sustained altitude, maintaining 66,443.8 feet over a measured 25 kilometer course.

Another measure of the *Phantom II's* potential lay in its ability to maneuver at high speeds. On September 5, 1960, a *Phantom II* set a 500-kilometer closed-course record of 1216 mph, and 20 days later it established a 100-kilometer world closed-course record of 1390 mph. While flying a circular path less than 20 miles in diameter, the airplane sustained a continuous centrifugal load of more than 3 Gs throughout the Mach 2 turn.

In August 1961, a *Phantom II* flew four times through a low altitude 3 kilometer course (at times less than 50 feet above the ground) at an average speed of 902.77 mph to capture the world record for that distance and establish its low altitude attack and re-attack capability.

In May 1961, a *Phantom II* crossed the North American continent at the rate of a mile every four seconds to set a new transcontinental speed record for the 2421.42 statute miles from Los Angeles to New York.

The *Phantom II's* intercept capability was exhibited in setting the world's absolute speed record of 1606.3 mph. During this record flight on November 22, 1961, the *Phantom II* reached peak speeds in excess of 1650 mph (Mach 2.5+).

During the months of February-April 1962, the *Phantom II* set eight official world time-to-climb records.

These records emphasized the *Phantom II's* capability for reaching any altitude from a standing start in record time. In establishing the 30,000 meter time-to-climb record, the airplane eclipsed its previous peak altitude mark by zooming to an altitude of over 100,000 feet.

The global range capability of the *Phantom II* was demonstrated in an 18-hour, 10,000 mile, non-stop flight of four Tactical Air Command *Phantoms* from MacDill AFB, Florida, on December 1-2, 1964.

THE BEST PERFORMANCE of the *Phantom II* was not in establishing so many world records but, rather, when prototypes won two competitions that resulted in McDonnell getting production contracts for thousands of planes. In the first instance, the *Phantom II* beat out the Chance Vought F8U-3 *Crusader*—an improved F8U design—in a "fly off" at Edwards Air Force Base, both aircraft being flown by Navy pilots under simulated combat conditions. Result: A Navy contract to go ahead with a production order for the *Phantom IIs*. In the second competition held in 1961, the *Phantom II* was pitted against the Air Force Republic F-105 and Convair F-106 land-based fighters with USAF pilots flying the planes. Again, the tests were held at

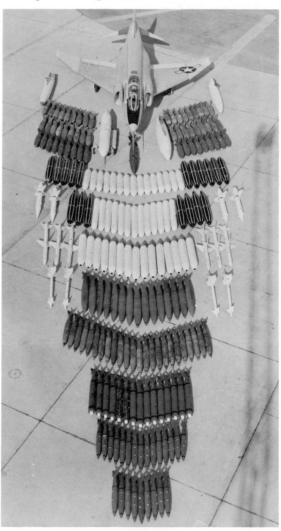

An early model *Phantom II* with the variety of bombs and missiles which it was capable of carrying. In addition, later F-4Es were armed with cannon. Note fold-up wing tips, space savers for carrier-based operations.

Edwards. Again, the *Phantom II* emerged victorious. Result: an Air Force contract for 1,000 *Phantom IIs*!

By the end of 1961 *Phantom IIs* (redesignated F-4s) were flying with all three branches of the U.S. military establishment— Navy, Marines and Air Force. At peak production McDonnell was turning out 70 planes a month. Today, more than twenty years after the first flight of the F-4 prototype, twelve versions later, the *Phantom IIs* (F-4s) also are flying in air forces of nine other nations— England, West Germany, Spain, Iran, South Korea, Turkey, Japan, Greece and Israel.

The reason for such a phenomenal success can be attributed to the fact that the *Phantom II* right from the start was designed for versatility and for potential growth. Certainly, it has been a "Jack of All Trades"—all-weather fighter, interceptor, attack fighter, reconnaissance aircraft. In various roles, it is capable of carrying a multi-ton load of conventional bombs, rockets, missiles, guns and napalm weapons, in addition to its own Sparrow III armament. It is both missile fighter and gunfighter armed with defensive rockets. As a gunfighter, it has a six-barrel 20-millimeter cannon mounted in the nose, which is capable of firing 6,000 rounds per minute for air-to-air

or air-to-ground operations. It can also be an A-bomb carrier!

When the U.S. got involved in the Vietnam war, the *Phantom IIs* were ready and got into action from carriers in the Tonkin Gulf, Marine airstrips at DaNang and from USAF bases as well. In fighter-versus-fighter "dogfights," *Phantom IIs* held their own against the vaunted Russian-built MiG-21. Their supersonic speed capability and sophisticated radar enabled them to do battle against the SAM missiles when other fighters fell victims. They flew ground attack missions, escort missions, recon flights. And in the end official credit was given to the "Phabulous Phantoms" for helping to maintain U.S. Air Superiority over North Vietnam.

Perhaps the greatest tribute of all is the fact that the 5,000th *Phantom II* was delivered on May 24, 1978, almost twenty years from the date of its first flight. The production line closed in August 1979.

Various versions of the *Phantom* are operating in Europe and Southeast Asia, and from aircraft carriers in the Atlantic, Pacific and the Mediterranean. It is still regarded as one of our nation's first-line interceptor, fighter-bomber and escort aircraft.

Small wonder McDonnell should remark,

The A-4 *Skyhawk* for Navy and Marines, in seventeen different versions, including two-place trainers, in production longer even than the fabulous *Phantom*. Weighing only 10,000 pounds empty, the A-4 can take off fully loaded from a carrier at a gross weight of 24,500 pounds, including 8200 pounds of bombs, missiles, rockets and machine guns. Marine Corps operates *Skyhawk* as tactical aircraft, flying it out of forward landing strips on close support missions.

"The *Phantom II* rang the multi-billion dollar gong!"

PRODUCTION LONGEVITY for the *Phantom II* is exceeded only by the Douglas A-4 *Skyhawk* which made its first flight on June 22, 1954, almost four years before the first *Phantom* F-4 took wing. Because of the McDonnell and Douglas merger (Chapter Eleven) the "phabulous Phantom phathers" also can be proud of their role in the design and development of the equally "fabulous" *Skyhawk* series. So says the following news release from the McDonnell Douglas Corporation's western news bureau.

A formation of A-4 "Mighty Midgets, saluting Mt. Rushmore presidents, and being readied for launch from USS *Hornet.*

The A-4 *Skyhawk* Blue Angels flight demonstration team thrills millions worldwide with spectacular exhibitions of precision flying.

"LONG BEACH, CALIF. — Newest and most sophisticated international version of the rugged A-4 *Skyhawk* military aircraft series is the *Skyhawk II*, designed by the McDonnell Douglas Corporation for use in tactical and quick-response strike fighter missions.

"Equipped with the powerful Pratt & Whitney J52-P-408 jet engine, *Skyhawk II* possesses outstanding maneuverability and survivability. These attributes, plus the combat-proven features of earlier models, give this bantamweight aircraft impressive capability for close air support, interdiction or strike fighter assignments.

"Like earlier *Skyhawks,* this new model carries more than 9000 pounds (4082 kg) of multi-mission armament, including air-to-air and air-to-ground missiles, bombs, rockets and guns, for its combat air patrol and tactical missions from forward airfields or from carriers.

"Optional equipment in the *Skyhawk II* includes two 30-millimeter cannons and an advanced navigation and weapons delivery system equal to or better than any operational system today.

"Weighing only 10,400 pounds (4717.4 kg) empty, *Skyhawk II* can take off fully loaded at a gross weight of 25,500 pounds (11,475 kg), including 9195 pounds (4170 kg) of varied tactical armament. The aircraft is 41.3 feet (8.4m) long, 15 feet (4.57m) high and has a wingspan of only 27.5 feet (12.59m). As with other *Skyhawks*, this wingspan permits it to be housed comfortably in carriers without folding the wings.

"Authorized by the U. S. Government, *Skyhawks* have been exported overseas for operation by the Israel Air Force, Royal Australian Navy, Royal New Zealand Air Force, the Argentine Navy and Air Force, Singapore Air Force and the Kuwait Air Force.

"Two versions of the *Skyhawk II*—the A-4M and the A-4N—, plus the TA-4J trainer, were in production at Douglas Aircraft Company division of the McDonnell Douglas Corporation in Long Beach and Palmdale, California."

The *Skyhawk* production lines were not shut down until the spring of 1979. Aircraft number 2960 was the last *Skyhawk*.

Building military aircraft today, however, is far overshadowed by the McDonnell Douglas production of the DC-10 which has become the most popular of the wide-bodied jetliners, judging by the growing numbers in service by the airlines of the world. The DC-10, like the *Phantom II*, evolved from a long line of famous ancestors.

The trend toward bigger airliners began a long time ago.

F-4B escorted by a bevy of A-4s.

The DC–4 was first of Presidential flagships. This is crew of *Sacred Cow*.

Chapter Nine

The DC Family Grows Up

"We can reasonably expect to continue to improve the reliability of our engines, instruments, radio, plumbing and other vital gadgets. But at the moment, we can only visualize a general betterment in the airplane itself by such changes as a four-engined transport capable of flying on two engines . . . Comfort development certainly is an open field and includes the problem not only of comfort but sustentation of life at high altitudes at which we may soon wish to fly . . . Pressure cabins and/or free oxygen in the cabins are both being experimented with today. Our airlines are working diligently with our designers on these points and we look with confidence to some solution soon."

THIS WAS DON DOUGLAS talking back in 1935. Obviously, he was thinking then about airliners much larger than the DC-3, which had just made its debut as the Douglas Sleeper Transport. It may well, indeed, have triggered his thoughts on passenger comfort aloft. And, perhaps, he could see beyond its wing tips to the larger skyliners of the tomorrow.

Within a year he had "laid the keel" of a four-engined super airliner—the DC-4E prototype of the C-54 (*Skymaster*), the Navy version (R5D) and the postwar DC-4 airliner.

It has been said by some that World War II spawned the development of the four-engined airliner. The truth is that *before* war was declared, in September 1939, the U.S. airframe manufacturers and the air transport industry had four-engined luxury airliners in production, and programmed to go into service, introducing a whole new concept of comfort, speed, and safety to the traveling public.

The Boeing Airplane Company in Seattle, Washington, had its Model 307 (*Stratoliner*), a four-engined, pressurized cabin airliner capable of carrying 33 passengers plus crew, in production and on order from several airlines. By 1939, the *Stratoliner* was in scheduled airline service with Pan American World Airways and TWA, flying high over the Andean peaks of South America and the towering Rockies at altitudes (because of its pressurized cabin) where the air traveler never had been before, and at five-mile-a-minute speeds.

In fairness, it must be said that Boeing pioneered the high roads, permitting passengers to enjoy living room comfort in the substratosphere (20,000 feet and above) once the private domain of airmen alone, who had to bundle up in cumbersome teddy bear suits and wear grotesque oxygen masks and face protectors. But it must also be said that the *Stratoliner* was a direct outgrowth of famous four-engined Boeing-built *Flying Fortress* (B-17s), a design paid for by tax monies. It had the B-17's wings and tail, and the advantage

The DC-4E pioneered new luxury aloft. It had berths, onboard galley, even air-to-ground phone service. She had triple tail because she stood so high off the ground on tricycle gear. One vertical fin would have needed to be so large that plane could never be parked inside a hangar.

of a lot of production experience. Model 307 was not a wholly designed commercial development.

The DC-4E was. W. E. ("Pat") Patterson, then President of United Airlines, as far back as 1935 had talked with top executives at Pan American, TWA, Eastern Air Lines and American Airlines, and they had agreed to "pool" monies for the development of a four-engined airliner. It was an unprecedented example of "teamwork" within a highly volatile and vehemently competitive industry. But, somehow, "Pat" put it all together.

"It was evident that there was a need for a bigger transport. Everybody agreed on that," Patterson later explained. "With this in mind, I told them that if we tried to finance it individually we'd go broke, one by one."

The airlines involved agreed to come up with $300,000 to help defray the experimental design costs of the new super airliner. They not only "pooled" the seed money, but their engineering people worked closely together in roughing out the specifications for the plane. The specs went the rounds of the various airframe manufacturers. There was some interest, but nobody really wanted to take the gamble, even with the $300,000 dangling there for bait.

When Patterson talked with Don Douglas in early 1936 about his "dream plane," the latter remembered the gamble he had taken with Jack Frye and TWA when they tackled the DC-1 project. It had cost the Douglas Aircraft Company a bundle to get the DC-1 into the air. He also remembered that he had an order for the production models (DC-2s) before the prototype had flown.

"The $300,000 looks good," Douglas told Patterson, "but can you guarantee the airlines will follow up with orders?"

Patterson promised United Airlines would buy. He said he was "pretty sure" the others would follow suit. They had all certainly indicated this in their conversations.

Douglas accepted the challenge. The super transport—roughly three times the size of the DC-3—came to life behind huge curtains that screened off a section of the Santa Monica plant. Workmen called the place "The Holy of the Holies." There was a bit of irony in all the secrecy. This was no military development. The competitive airlines knew all about what was going on. They were footing part of the bill.

W. E. "Pat" Patterson talked several airlines into pooling monies for development of four-engined airliner. It turned out to be the DC-4, but a war made it wait before the carriers could put it into service.

By the time the plane was ready for its maiden flight on June 7, 1938, the total cost was astronomical—$992,808 for labor and engineering; $641,804 in materials and overhead. It had taken eighteen months to build: 1,300,000 rivets, some 20,000 different pieces of metal formed to different shapes. It represented 500,000 hours in engineering and design, another 100,000 hours of ground and laboratory tests.

The DC-4E was big, a wingspan of 138 feet three inches; fuselage length of 97 feet seven inches. She was powered by four Pratt & Whitney 14-cylinder engines (two seven cylinder radials back to back) producing horsepower the equivalent of two diesel locomotives. The engines drove 14-foot diameter, three-bladed propellers, and she rested on a tricycle landing gear to give the big fans plenty of clearance room. The DC-4E grossed out at 65,000 pounds, a third again the gross weight of Boeing's *Stratoliner*.

The DC-4E, incidentally, was the *first* of the big commercial transports to take wing. She was flying six months *before* the *Stratoliner,* which didn't make its first flight until December 31, 1938. This lead time didn't mean much, as it turned out. The big Douglas, with its revolutionary triple-tail, her 40-seat main cabin, on-board galley, "Ladies' Lounge" and "Men's Dressing Room," plus a separate compartment up front called the "Bridal Suite," proved to be too slow and too expensive to operate. Douglas had to make a lot of changes before the airlines signed on the dotted line for a production model.

For her day, the DC-4E was a plane to remember. "The Grand Hotel with wings," one reporter called her. She could accommodate 42 guests by day and 30 by night in Pullman-style berths. Cabin decor and passenger appeal offered lounge-type chairs, color blends, lighting, soundproofing, air conditioning and other modern conveniences, hot and cold running water. Those who stepped through the door to board her walked into a new world of comfort in the clouds.

The author remembers the day they brought her to Vandalia, Ohio—the airport serving Dayton—as part of a nationwide demonstration tour. Orville Wright, the co-inventor of the aeroplane, was there to welcome her one day in 1940.

The author flew in the DC-4E that day. What I remember most of all was that she had a telephone on board. I picked up the phone and called my managing editor.

There was one other moment I remember about that flight in the DC-4E. We flew a course that took us over a spot at Wright-Patterson Air Force Base which once was old Simm's Station, where the Wright Brothers made their flight in 1904, the year after Kitty Hawk. We could look out the windows of the DC-4E and see down there an old white shed where the 1904 Wright Aeroplane was once housed. It has long since been destroyed.

But then it was still there. And it was in this patch of sky that the aeroplane was truly born. It was in this little acre of sky that Orville made the first *complete circle* with the improved 1904 Model *Wright Flyer*.

"This was the truly great moment," Orville Wright once confided. "When we made the great circle. When we proved the machine could take off and go where we wanted it to go and come back again."

What the grand old gentleman was saying was quite simple. At Kitty Hawk they flew. At Simm's Station, when they made the circle, the aeroplane became a practical vehicle for the speedy transport of people and things

from here to there to anywhere; above the highest peaks, over the vastness of oceans, shrinking time and space to bring the peoples of the world, for better or worse, closer together.

There was only one DC-4E ever built. She died an ignominious death. Douglas sold her to the Japanese before Pearl Harbor for a reported $180,000. The story is that on her first flight they dumped her into a watery grave in Tokyo harbor.

Meanwhile, back in Santa Monica, they were already at work on an improved model. She emerged first as the C-54 (*Skymaster*) and made her first flight on Valentine's Day, 1942. This was the original DC-4 which General Arnold had seen in its secret niche. This was the plane Arnold suggested to Don Douglas he stop building, and get on with the business of building combat aircraft. She was, at the time, strictly a commercial venture. She would not assume that role again until after the war when the first of the DC-4 airliners was delivered to Western Airlines in January 1946. Then, she was a much different design configuration than the original DC-4E.

She had a single tail, vertical rudder, like the DC-3, only about five times its area. She had a shorter wingspan than the DC-4E (117 feet 5 inches) and her fuselage was 2 inches shorter, but the wing had a better airfoil, thinner and much more efficient. She had more powerful engines, a total of almost 6,000 horsepower, and she grossed out at about 75,000 pounds with a payload of 10,000 to 25,000 pounds, profitable for any airline operation.

She was fitted to carry from 44 to 80 passengers, depending upon the customers' desires. She could cruise at about 180 knots at an operating altitude of 10,000 feet. Her only fault was that she didn't have a pressurized cabin.

But she had the range, 3,700 miles maximum, and it was enough to make Don Douglas' "dream" of a transoceanic airliner come true. Which she did, with American Overseas Airways, the first to operate landplanes across the Atlantic.

As the C-54 (*Skymaster*), the basic model DC-4 sold more than 1,162 in various versions to the military. Don Douglas' gamble had paid high dividends. The postwar DC-4, however, sold only 74 to the commercial airlines. Too many C-54s, declared war surplus,

The DC-4, which really belonged to the airlines, was "drafted" to become the C-54 *Skymaster*, and during World War II she played a vital role flying just about everything, just about everywhere.

went on the market. In all, as pioneer of the four-engined airliner, Douglas records show that with its transport models the company showed a profit of about one-half of one per cent on its own investment.

It probably will be forever an argument among historians: Did the war build the air transport industry? Or did the air transport industry do more to help the war effort? The fact is: the strong arm of *airlift* which played such a vital role in the allied victory in World War II, Korea and Vietnam was in the beginning an "on-the-shelf" item.

By war's end, there was another competitor in the skies, the Lockheed *Constellation*, a four-engined, pressurized cabin airliner. The Douglas supremacy in the field of four-engined transports was facing a real challenge. To take up the challenge was another Douglas design, the DC-6 which, like the DC-3, would become the world's most popular airliner. Before it would come into being, Douglas had other ideas.

Who said the twin-engined concept was dead?

WORLD WAR II DID, as history tells us, prove once and for all that air transport was a vital adjunct to airpower. The role of the DC-3s, C-47s, C-54s in airlifting supplies as paratrooper carriers, personnel transports and for a variety of other missions ranked the transport plane with the combat aircraft on equal terms of contribution to winning the war. Air transportation had become a way of life.

In the aftermath of the great conflict there was a sudden surge in the use of air transport. Airlines saw and realized a tremendous upsurge in traffic. More and more persons were taking to the airliner as a preferred means of travel over the Greyhound Bus, the railroad and surface vessels. Only the motor car remained a serious threat to the ballooning growth of air transportation. Even so, it was a threat only in the short-haul operations. There was definite need for a new, improved, short-haul airliner to replace the DC-3. Some said it couldn't be done.

Douglas, the "father of the DC-3," tried twice and failed.

The first attempt was the so-called "Super DC-3." In principle, the idea was quite simple: Take the original DC-3 and puff it up a little bit, bigger fuselage, more wing, more horsepower. As it turned out, according to M.K. Oleson, chief engineer on the Super DC-3 project, "By the time we were through with all our improvements the airplane emerged sixty per cent all new airplane."

It was true, the "Grand Old Lady of the Skies" was all gussied up and ready to go to the ball. Fate, or, perhaps it was progress, destined her to be a wallflower. Despite the fact that she could carry ten more passengers than the 21-passenger DC-3, and was almost 50 mph faster at cruise speeds, the *Super Three* simply didn't sell to the airlines. Only three of the planes were sold to one carrier, Capital Airlines. Maybe the price tag was too high: $140,000 to $200,000 per article, depending upon the interior.

119

Father and son, Donald Douglas, Sr. and Donald Douglas, Jr. in rare photograph alone, together, beam pridefully from the cockpit of DC-3 "Super Three" which they took around the country trying to interest the airlines. Unfortunately, the newer, larger and faster Martin and Consolidated airliners had already captured the market.

After World War II, back in civilian colors again, the DC-3 was still the prime mover among the world's airlines until larger planes came along. Douglas even tried to revive the line with a Super DC-3 (above), but bigger DC-ships soon took over the airlanes. Still, as of 1979, more than 46 years after her debut, there were said to be more than 1200 DC-3s still flying.

More likely, it was because there were new-comers in the arena to challenge the once almost exclusive domain of the DC-3 skyliner. The Glenn L. Martin Company of Baltimore had a new, much faster, larger capacity airliner to offer, the twin-engine Model 202. Consolidated-Vultee of San Diego, California, had its Model 240, another twin, bigger than the *Super Three*, on the market. As one airline president quipped, "Why take a grandmother (DC-3) to the dance, when you can take a debutante?"

There was one bright spot. In Washington, Douglas, himself, talked with friends in the Navy Department. The Navy ordered 100 of the *Super Threes* to be modified as R4D-8s for special missions. But that was the end of it.

Back in Santa Monica, Don Douglas faced a hurtful decision. After two decades of turning out the DC-3 in numerous versions, he shut down the line.

The same fate befell another Douglas twin-engined airliner, the DC-5, a pre-war design, which Douglas had in mind as a possible

The DC-5 was one of few Douglas-designed planes to have high wing. Note round windows, which would appear later in the DC-4. Airlines expressed little interest.

replacement for the DC-3. Many people never heard of the DC-5, with its high-wing design. There were only twelve built, one of which was sold to W. E. Boeing as his personal aircraft. Four of the aircraft were sold to K.L.M., and the remainder to the U. S. Navy and Marine Corps.

There are those who say that the DC-5 was simply a DC-3 with the wing on top instead of on the bottom of the fuselage. To an extent this is true; many of the systems and structural developments of the DC-3 were adaptable to the DC-5, but it actually was pretty much a "new" airplane.

In profile, there was a great resemblance to the DB-7 medium bomber which Douglas sold to the French. Likely, this production order paid for most of the development costs of the DC-5, a commercial version. The high-wing placement created a greater empty weight, and operating costs ran too high to generate much interest from airline customers.

Although the DC-5 first flew in February 1939—ironically, three years before the DC-4—and was delivered to K.L.M. fourteen months later, Douglas already had decided to abandon the project. He never went back to the high-wing configuration. It was not until more than a quarter of a century later, when popular DC-9 jetliners appeared, that he turned to a twin-engine design.

In the postwar years, the emphasis was on the development of the four-engined airliner.

WHEN WORLD WAR II was over, the military immediately cancelled all orders for the C-54 *Skymaster*. What was even worse for Douglas Aircraft, the Government threw its surplus four-engined C-54s on the open market, up for sale to the highest bidder. In some cases, you could buy a C-54 for as low as $10,000. Some fly-by-night "airlines," started mostly by returning wartime pilots, bought the surplus planes, refurbished them, and started flying passengers and freight in non-scheduled operations.

The so-called *non-skeds* forced a whole lot of different thinking among the scheduled air transport people. If they did anything really constructive, it was that they brought about a reduction in fares, which put air travel within the reach of almost anyone's pocketbook.

A "rash" of crashes brought new and stricter rules and regulations for the non-sked carriers, but the regularly scheduled airlines

had to do something to keep the fares down, and still provide a new and better service. On February 15, 1946, a new Douglas skyliner made her maiden flight, and when she went into service about a year later, the air traveler made her his sweetheart. They called her the DC-6, and the *Six*, like the DC-3 before her had done, virtually dominated the world's skies as a common carrier.

"The DC-6 was to the DC-4 like the DC-3 was to the DC-2," explained one Douglas engineer. Indeed, there was a lot of similarity between the DC-4 and the *Six*, although the latter had many improved features and much improved performance.

The *Six* had almost the same wing as the DC-4, although it had been beefed up here and there to take the much more powerful and larger engines. The fuselage was longer by about seven feet, and the *Six* had a differently shaped vertical fin or rudder. Outwardly, if you put her on the ramp alongside her predecessor, the DC-4, a lot of people couldn't tell the difference. There was one sure way to do so: the *Six* had square windows. The DC-4 had portholes!

When Douglas introduced the DC-6, the advance publicity acclaimed her as the first "entirely new" postwar airliner. Certainly, she introduced new standards of safety, speed and comfort. She had a pressurized cabin and could zip along at altitudes up to 28,000 feet at near 300-mph speeds or better. Inside, she set new standards of luxury aloft. Depending upon the individual airline's request, the *Six* could be seated for as many as 100 passengers. She was one of the first airliners to introduce high-density seating, popularly called "air-coach service."

The *Six* had four Pratt & Whitney engines producing a total of 8400-plus horsepower, the first commercial airliner to be fitted with the engines originally built for the B-29 *Superfortresses*. With so much power, she could lift a payload varying from 19,000 to 23,000 pounds—passengers and cargo—which permitted the airlines to operate her profitably.

"For the first time," one airline president told his stockholders, "we've got a good nickel-a-mile airplane."

Most probably this factor, plus her growing popularity with passengers, resulted in sales to the airline operators around the world, keeping the Douglas tradition of building the

The DC-6 was first Douglas airliner to have pressurized cabin. There were improved versions (DC-6Bs) and also a cargo DC-6A, and before the "Six" production line ended Douglas had sold more than 600 to virtually every free-world airline.

best commercial transports very much alive. With more and more orders coming in, Douglas produced a cargo version, the DC-6A, and a more efficient passenger carrier, the DC-6B, which was to be acclaimed almost unanimously by airliner operators as "the most efficient airliner ever built."

By the time the *Six* was ten years old, Douglas had sold more than 600 to forty-four different airlines plus some military orders, and there were one hundred more on order. The airlines, alone, had a total investment of more than $700,000,000. It turned out to be a very rosy picture.

Things turned fiery red at an early stage in the plane's history. Over Bryce Canyon, Utah, a DC-6 suddenly burst into flames and crashed, killing all fifty-two persons aboard.

Pieces of the wreckage were shipped back to Douglas where they rebuilt the plane as best they could from the charred remains. It was one of the most thorough and most scientific post-mortem operations ever performed; but nothing really positive turned up. The examiners were almost certain, however, of one fact: fire had started somewhere in the bottom of the fuselage. Could it happen again? Everybody had his fingers crossed.

Many refinements over original DC-6 made the DC-6B (above) one of the most economical and efficient airliners ever built. In some parts of the world, even in the Jet Age, they are still in daily service.

It happened again. Or something similar happened. An American Airlines DC-6 made an emergency landing at Gallup, New Mexico. The pilot had reported in flight that there was fire in the belly. Luckily, he made a safe landing and the fire was extinguished. There were no casualties.

But all DC-6s were grounded!

Investigators swarmed over the American Airlines' plane. They took hundreds of photographs. An enlargement of one photograph provided a hint of a clue. A fuel transfer switch had been left on. Standard procedure to maintain proper weights-and-balance characteristics meant switching from one fuel tank to another. It was just possible . . .

There followed a succession of test flights with a specially fitted DC-6 simulating all possible contingencies. Results showed that during the fuel transfer, if the switch was not turned OFF, there was an overflow as the high-octane gasoline flowed from one tank to another. Worse, the overflow of fuel, caught in the slipstream of air was sprayed under the belly of the fuselage *right into the duct of a cabin heater.* Poof! There was fire! But there was the culprit.

Engineers redesigned the heater scoops, placing them ahead of the wing. Time and time again they tested the new arrangement. Nothing happened. It couldn't happen. The DC-6s were back in the air again. There never again was any incident involving the aircraft's structural integrity.

In the piston-era of air transportation there was no other four-engined plane quite like the fabulous *Six.* In 1953, she flew non-stop for 5,700 miles in 20 hours and 30 minutes—a world's record. The year before, she had become the first plane carrying passengers to fly over the North Pole, pioneering the famous Polar route for scheduled airline operations. In Pan American colors, she made the first scheduled round-the-world flight—83 hours and 4 minutes. The DC-6A cargoliner proved her mettle when she carried a 23,000-pound extrusion press, Philadelphia to Los Angeles.

Altogether, according to a Douglas estimate, in her first ten years of operation—including the six months she was grounded—the planes flew nearly 88,000,000,000 passenger miles. Breadwinner of the combined airline fleets, the *Sixes,* at one time, were flying an average of 500,000 miles every

twenty-four hours!

Before the advent of the jetliner, there were some who said the *Six* never would be "replaced" by a propeller-driven airliner. But there was yet another member of the DC family that would join her along the world's far-flung airlanes.

HISTORY WAS REPEATING ITSELF. It was American Airlines again, which had conversations with Douglas about "stretching" the DC-6 to make it a bigger airliner with improved performance that would permit non-stop scheduled operations coast-to-coast. "CR" Smith, who had talked Douglas into upgrading the DC-2 into a sleeper plane (DST) and the 21-passenger DC-3, was back at the helm as American's president after serving as an Air Force General during the war years, guiding the Air Transport Command. "CR's" airline was in a bind with its DC-6s, which couldn't keep up with the faster TWA Lockheed *Constellations* (Model 749s) on the non-stop New York-Chicago-Los Angeles run. Smith decided they would have to do something to beat the competition. "Non-stop coast-to-coast service," he told Douglas, "will do the trick. Can you give us such a plane with that kind of range?"

If Douglas could deliver, Smith guaranteed

Art Raymond. As with the DC-3, he played a big role in DC-7 design.

an order for a sufficient number to make the project worthwhile. As he had done in the case of the DST and DC-3, he committed American Airlines dollar-wise, and Douglas started work immediately on a design to fill the bill.

Don Douglas, himself, has admitted that it was a tough decision—"which way to go." Should he gamble on a completely new aircraft using turbojet powerplants? Intelligence reports inside the airframe industry told him that Boeing was almost ready to come out with a four-engined jetliner, and that Lockheed had a four-engine turbo-prop design called the "Electra" it was about to offer the airlines.

Some of the "old gang," who had worked on the DC-1 and all the other DC models—Art Raymond, Ivar Shogran, Ed Burton and some of the others—were still around, and Douglas tossed the problem into their laps.

"We kicked around a number of airframe-engine combinations," Art Raymond explained, "but all the while in the back of our minds was the big question of how reliable the new jet powerplants were for commercial operation. Could the engine people stifle the turbojet's fuel-guzzling appetite?"

American Airlines' "CR" Smith, who talked Don Douglas into building the DST (DC-3) and also talked him into going ahead with a stretched version of the DC-6 airliner.

Advent of DC-7 permitted first coast-to-coast nonstop service. Plane had range, with plenty of fuel to spare. It did pose a big problem: Flight took longer than pilots were allowed to fly by regulations and union orders. Until rules were changed, extra crews rode DC-7s "deadhead."

What finally tipped the scales in favor of sticking with a more conventional design—a bigger DC-6—was the advent of the Wright Aeronautical Company's new and test-proved, 27-cylinder (three 9-cyclinder radial, air-cooled engines in a "corn-cob" arrangement) R3350 turbo-compound engine. Douglas' powerplant man, Ivar Shogran, was convinced—"this is the most efficient large piston engine ever developed."

The Douglas crowd took a look in another direction: why not put the new engines in a DC-6 to increase the range and payload? That was the simplest way to give "CR" what he wanted.

"Finally, that was what we decided to do," Art Raymond has explained, "but when we got down to brass tacks the airframe that finally emerged to accept the engine, although it looked a lot like the DC-6, was a helluva lot more airplane. It became the DC-7—Douglas Commercial Model No. 7, the last of the propeller-driven, piston-powered airliners in the DC family."

The DC-7 flew for the first time on May 18, 1953, and six months later, American Airlines proudly announced *non-stop, coast-to-coast service.* United Airlines, Eastern and some foreign carriers also placed orders for the DC-7s. Two years later, April 21, 1955, an improved version, the DC-7B, was flying, and on December 20, 1955—twenty years plus three days after the first Douglas DC-3 (the sleeper plane version) made its maiden flight—the DC-7C made its first flight. They called it the *Seven Seas,* an appropriate name, because it was truly the first intercontinental airliner.

Pan American World Airways was first to take delivery of the *Seven Seas,* on April 18, 1956—the fourteenth anniversary of the famous Doolittle raid on Tokyo. A few months later, Pan Am introduced trans-Pacific service with the DC-7C, San Francisco to Honolulu to Guam to Tokyo.

In both passenger and cargo versions the DC-7C became, like the DC-3 before it, the "workhorse" of the airlines.

The *Seven Seas* had the same wingspan as the DC-4, thirteen years her predecessor. But she was eight feet longer; room for thirty more seats; capable of carrying half again as much payload twice as fast at altitudes well above 25,000 feet, with a maximum range of 5,000 miles. And there was little question, she was the most luxurious air transport for her day.

With inboard engines farther out on the

The DC *Seven Seas* (DC-7C) was—and still is—the largest piston-engine, propeller-driven airliner built in the U.S. Advent of jetliners caused Douglas to stop production. The big, long-range DC-7C simply could not compete with faster jetliners.

wing, she was the quietest propeller airliner. Her pressurized cabin was commodious, bright and colorful; wall-to-wall carpeting, air conditioning, an on-board galley.

Despite all this splendor and her splendid performance qualities, the DC-7C, which began service in 1956, was soon to have strong competition. Boeing's jetliner was no longer an "on paper" design. The prototype 707 had made its first flight on July 15, 1954, and she was to join the DC-7s and DC-6s in scheduled passenger service in the not too distant future. Although early models of the 707 didn't have near the range of the DC-7s, they were nearly a hundred miles per hour faster. The Lockheed turbo-prop *Electra* was

also flying. For the first time, a foreign built airliner, the British four-engine turbo-prop *Viscount* was also flying U.S. domestic routes in the colors of Capital Airlines. The jetliners were harbingers of wings to come.

There was no question they had one advantage. The jetliner, depending upon the thrust available and aerodynamic design, seemingly had unlimited speed potential. The propeller airplane, on the other hand, had limits when it got into high speed ranges.

Douglas turned his attention to the design and development of a jet-powered transport. It was either that or the DC family would have no heirs.

The DC-3 joins the Jet Age. British fitted some DC-3s with Rolls-Royce "Dart" turbo-prop engines. Arrangement lifted the ceiling and increased speed, but the "turbo threes" soon gave way to the coming generation of jetliners.

Chapter Ten

Day Of The Jetliner

ABOUT THE SAME TIME that the Super DC-3 made its debut, another modified DC-3 was flying in Europe's skies. The roar of her engines had a new sound. This DC-3 had been fitted with Rolls-Royce *Dart* turboprop engines. The roar of the piston-engine was replaced by the shrill, high-pitched whine of the turbines driving the propellers. Literally, she whistled while she worked, and she was promptly put to work by British European Airways in regular scheduled service between London, Copenhagen, Paris and Milan.

Pilots "loved" the jet-powered DC-3, but up at altitudes above 20,000 feet where the jet engines were most efficient, she had a major handicap. There was no pressurized cabin. Flight crews and passengers had to wear oxygen masks. Moreover, in freight operations for which she was primarily used, not being pressurized she couldn't carry livestock, wine in bottles (a principle cargo out of Paris and Milan) and certain other goods. The service was shortly abandoned. But for the record: it was a Douglas DC-3 that helped launch the day of the jetliner.

The first pure jet airliner, the *DeHavilland Comet I*, came along a little later. Its first public appearance was at the 1950 Air Show in Farnborough, England. The *Comet* was a machine of beauty. In the silver, white and blue colors of British Overseas Airways Corporation, she attracted the attention of thousands. She was the main attraction: a low-wing monoplane with four turbojet engines buried in the wing, tricycle landing gear, wide, comfortable fuselage with sleek lines, a cabin capable of carrying more than 90 passengers at 500-mile-an-hour speeds. There was little question that she had the look of the future.

The future was closer than many believed. On May 2, 1952, B.O.A.C. introduced jetliner service from London to Johannesburg, South Africa. Flying regular schedules, *Comets* made the 6,724 mile journey in less than 24 hours!

Less than a month after the *Comets* went into service, back in Santa Monica, Douglas set up a Special Project Office where a group of his key people headed by Ivar Shogran, started design studies for a jet-powered passenger transport. Only those in this inner sanctum talked about the project by name—the DC-8. It would be almost six years later that the "studies" would for a time become the world's largest jetliner.

Meanwhile, there were a lot of milestones and millstones along the path to progress, and a lot of decisions to be made.

Nobody really questioned that sooner or later Douglas would come out with a jetliner. It seemed the next logical step. But in the light of fast moving events and rapidly growing competition in this field, the timing had to be a delicate decision to make, and the cost factor was out of sight. This time there was no

DC-3 Turbo-prop Jetliner.

World's first commercial jetliner was this British DeHavilland *Comet I* which began service London to Johannesburg. *Comet* later had structural troubles and suffered several crashes that grounded planes. New, improved models joined fleets later.

"stretching" the DC-7C, installing jet engines, beefing up here and there, applying old fabricating techniques. The DC-8—if there was to be one—meant starting from scratch.

It would be a whole new ball game. Admittedly, the Douglas "team" was a latecomer in the league. It was no reflection on their ability or capability to design and develop a jetliner. The expertise was there.

Perhaps no other airframe manufacturer had had so much experience building large aircraft dating back to the B-19. The jet powerplants were no mystery. In the XB-43, Douglas had built the largest aircraft to use the earliest General Electric jet engines,

before World War II was over.

These early experiments had paid off handsomely. Big plane "know-how" produced the C-74, the C-124, and the C-133, a whole family of huge cargo planes that performed herculean tasks.

Example: manufactured in 1949, the C-124 *Globemaster* went into service during the Korean War. With its 10,000 cubic foot cargo compartment the C-124 could carry up to 70,000 pounds payload—small tanks, trucks, cannon, 200 fully equipped troops, 125 litter patients. Douglas records say between 1950-56 these planes flew more than a million hours, an aggregate distance equal to a round trip to the sun. Mostly they carried men,

supplies and military equipment across the Pacific for our Korean forces.

The C-124, three box cars long and half again as wide, was the last of the piston-powered big cargo planes. Over 450 were built. They were replaced by a larger, much faster turbo-prop cargo carrier, the C-133, a high-wing design capable of a 100,000-pound payload. Two 40,000 pound earth movers could fit inside, and it could carry a complete *Atlas* missile. A bigger version, the C-133B, had a range of 4,000 miles carrying a 50,000-pound payload.

On the strength of these experiences, Douglas engineers knew they could build a big airframe and that it would fly. There was a lot of thought about a passenger version of the C-133 which never got beyond paper studies. Boeing had virtually killed the idea—for Douglas at least—of the interim turbo-prop jetliner when the airlines went for its 707 turbojet four-engined airliner that came out of the KC-135 USAF tanker design. The Boeing 707 prototype was flying in 1955 *before* Douglas made the decision to go ahead with the DC-8.

Douglas had to go it alone without money from the military to help develop the company's first jetliner. It had lost to Boeing a $100,000,000 contract to build a jet tanker,

Douglas C-124 *Globemaster* gave engineers and production people a lot of big plane "know-how." Later, when thinking of the DC-10, designers looked at C-124 "double-decker" feature.

and another big jet bomber design which actually had won an Air Force design competition. But the Air Force had opted to buy the Boeing eight-engined B-52's which were farther along.

"There were probably three major factors that made Douglas decide to go ahead," one of his top executives told the author. "*One*: surveys indicated that the growth potential of air transportation, both passenger travel and freight, most likely, would continue its upward climb, and that the air traveler wanted the faster, quieter jets. The sooner the better. *Two*: every intelligence report showed the engine people were making good progress in developing the turbojet powerplants with piston-engine reliability and comparable fuel appetites. A jetliner could be operated economically, especially over long distances. *Three*: there was very little potential military business on the horizon, and if Douglas wanted to maintain its reputation in the commercial field, something had to be done. It was the DC-8, or back off and start planning ten years ahead, a supersonic transport, perhaps . . ."

What happened is history. Douglas, with private monies, poured more than a *billion dollars* into design, testing and development costs of the DC-8 jetliner, plus new facilities, tooling and labor to build it. The first DC-8 went on the assembly line in February of 1957. The line didn't shut down until May 17, 1972, and in between, Douglas Aircraft had produced 556 of the big *Eights* in eleven different model designations. These planes have been acclaimed by passengers and airline operators alike, as the best, quietest, most economical jetliner ever built.

The Eight, which originally sold for about $6,000,000, had many new and outstanding features: in various versions it could carry from 117 to 259 passengers plus crew. It had a cruising speed of from 490 knots to 512 knots, a range from 4,000 to 6,500 miles. The DC-8 grew from a standard version with a wingpan of 142 feet 6 inches, to the *Super* 63, with a span of 148 feet 5 inches. It was stretched from 150 feet 6 inches in length to 186 feet 5 inches, with maximum gross weights ranging from 273,000 pounds to 355,000 pounds. For its day, until the advent of the wide-bodied Lockheed L-1011, Boeing 747 and the McDonnell Douglas DC-10, she was the biggest jetliner flying.

The first DC-8 flew on Memorial Day, May 30, 1958, and 95,000 persons, mostly Douglas employees who had helped build her, and their friends, gave up their holiday to see the *Big Eight* take off on its maiden flight from Long Beach International Airport. She was built there in a $20,000,000 building, 1,150 feet long and 480 feet wide, erected on 26 acres adjacent to the airport. Inside the building were two assembly lines, one for individual structures, the other for final assembly. At production peak in 1968, they were turning out between 8 and 10 of the big planes a month.

Before the last DC *Super Sixty-Three* series rolled out of the plant, Douglas had sold more than $3,000,000,000 worth of the planes and spares to 37 airlines around the world. A decade later, there are nearly 500 DC-*Eights* flying world routes with 76 different operators.

Now more than eleven years old, the DC-8s are getting a new lease on life—as flying freighters.

At its Tulsa, Oklahoma, facility, McDonnell Douglas is providing air carriers with an economical way to meet growing freight demands. Using production DC-8 freighter engineering and materials, passenger versions of the DC-8 are being converted into high performance air freighters at relatively low cost.

For the military, Douglas produced the turbo-prop C-133 cargo plane, then decided to jump into the middle of the commercial jetliner market with DC-8 design, by-passing the turbo-prop era.

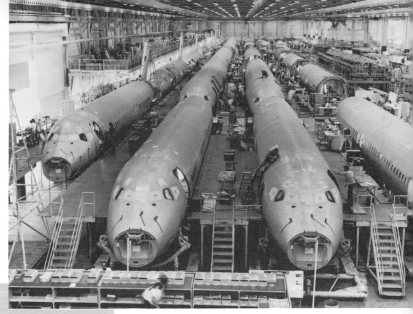

At Long Beach facility, DC-8 jetliners move along assembly lines.

First Douglas DC-8 takes off on its maiden flight.

DC-8 SUPER 61, giant transcontinental jetliner capable of carrying up to 251 passengers, was introduced into regular airline service early in 1967. Although designed for a normal operating range of 3500 miles, the Super 61 made the first nonstop flight by a commercial jet between Southern California and Tokyo, covering the 5630 miles in 11 hours 32 minutes and 49 seconds.

Super Sixty versions of DC-8 fill final assembly line at Douglas Aircraft Company division of McDonnell Douglas Corporation in Long Beach, California. McDonnell Douglas produced three models of the four-engine DC-8, the DC-8 Super 61 for transcontinental service, the DC-8 Super 62 for ultra-long range flights, and the DC-8 Super 63 for intercontinental routes. Super 61 and Super 63 versions, 187.4 feet long, will accommodate up to 259 passengers each. Super 62 will carry a maximum of 189 passengers in its 157.4-foot-long fuselage.

133

Donald W. Douglas riding in a DC-8.

Modifications include removal of passenger-oriented equipment and installation of a 7-track freighter floor and a (85-inch x 140-inch) cargo door. Plug windows, cargo liners, smoke detection equipment and barrier nets are installed, and the aircraft is certified at new maximum operational weights. Re-engine modifications are accomplished as desired.

The result is an efficient freighter, ready for years of profitable air freight service.

Beyond this, DC-8 operators, some, at least, are considering re-engining their DC-8-61s and DC-8-63s because of the big *Stretch Eights'* operating economy, already proven. The new powerplants probably will be either the General Electric/Snecma (CFM56) high

Family of DC-8s pose for their picture: Left to right, Super 61, Super 62 and Super 63. More than 20 years after first DC-8 flew, the big jetliners are flying with fleets around the world. In 1979, some operators announced re-engining program which should take planes well into the '80s along world airways.

The DC-8 is popular all-freighter. Some airlines are modifying Big Eight jetliners as all-freighters. Work is done at McDonnell Douglas facility in Tulsa, Oklahoma.

The DC-8F all-freighter version called the *Jet Trader*.

Line of cargo containers illustrates amount of freight that can be loaded into a McDonnell Douglas DC-8 Super 63F.

The DC-8 Super 62, designed for ultra-long-range operations, can carry up to 189 passengers at ranges over 6,000 miles. Seven feet longer than standard DC-8, it incorporated aerodynamic improvements and other modifications. Deliveries to airlines began in May 1967.

Biggest member of the DC-8 family is the Super 63 which flew for the first time April 10, 1967 and was introduced into commercial service on July 27 the same year. The Super 63 was designed for service on high-density, long-range routes. It was largest commercial jet flying until 747 came along.

bypass-ratio turbofan or Pratt & Whitney JT8D-209 refanned engine.

Both engines would make the Big Eights compatible with newly imposed FAA noise regulations.

Such a modification program amounts to giving the DC-8 "longies" a second lifetime.

With a target date of 1981 for first deliveries the "revitalized" DC-8 Stretch aircraft likely will still be flying in the 1990s.

SOLIDLY ENTRENCHED in the jet transport field with its domestic and international versions of the DC-8s, Douglas management had turned its attention in another direction. It was obvious that the big DC-8s could not be operated from smaller community airports or, economically, over shorter airline distances. Yet it was in this area that surveys of the air transport industry indicated there was a need for a replacement airliner to provide service to smaller communities and for short-haul operations. The DC-3 had given way to the more modern Martin and Convair twin-engine piston planes. But in 1963 these airliners were fast approaching "old age" and retirement. Moreover, the air traveler flying the shorter routes was tired of the noisy, slower, piston-propeller airliners. The so-called "Mainstreet Airlines"—those serving the smaller communities—were searching for a vehicle to bring the Jet Age to their patrons who represented a big segment of the passenger business.

To fill this vacuum, Douglas announced on April 8, 1963 that it was going to build a twin-engined jetliner. Douglas Commercial Model No. 9 was born. Named manager of the DC-9 program was John C. Brizendine, who ten years later on July 17, 1973 would become president of the Douglas Aircraft Company Division of the McDonnell Douglas Corporation.

Born in Harry Truman's hometown of Independence, Missouri, Brizendine was 25 when he joined Douglas as a test pilot after graduating with an aeronautical engineering master's degree from the University of Kansas. During World War II he had served as a Naval Aviator flying multi-engined land-based bombers. As engineer and test pilot he became test project engineer on the DC-8, and later DC-8 program manager, bringing a strong background of experience to the DC-9

John C. Brizendine

design, development and production activities.

According to Brizendine, looking back a few years, the DC-9 program was top priority at Douglas. More than 1,000 engineers were assigned to the design work on the new jetliner. Before they settled on a final configuration, wind tunnel tests involved six major design models, and during the plane's evolutionary period 40,000 man-hours a week were poured into the effort.

Douglas assigned a top management team to direct the DC-9 design, development and production. To focus its depth of experience most effectively on the DC-9, Douglas used a project-oriented concept known as "Program Management" which integrated the many functions involved in producing an aircraft and brought business management and technical management closer together. The DC-9 Program Management team, it was estimated, had a combined Douglas oriented background of 358 years dating back to the revolutionary and evolutionary period of the DC-1 in 1932.

"We had a four-pronged goal throughout the program," Brizendine recalls. "Throughout its inception and detailed design, the DC-9 evolved from the fundaments of *simplicity, reliability, main-*

Nose to nose. North Central's famed DC-3 No. 728, which amassed 84,875 hours time (left), and DC-9, first twinjet airliner to be produced by McDonnell Douglas. Old "728" was retired in 1975 and now rests among other great aircraft, Byrd's Fokker *Josephine Ford,* first to fly over the North Pole, and replica of Lindbergh's *Spirit of St. Louis,* in Henry Ford Museum at Greenfield Village, Dearborn, Michigan. Reports say pilots looped the plane before landing at Dearborn.

United States Air Force's C-9A aeromedical airlift transport, built by McDonnell Douglas, brings jet speed and comfort to the Air Force mission of airlifting sick and injured military personnel between hospital facilities in the United States. Christened *Nightingale*, after the famed British nurse, the twinjet is produced at the Douglas Aircraft Company in Long Beach, California.

Patients in litters aboard McDonnell Douglas C-9A "flying hospital."

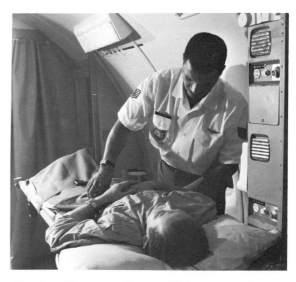

USAF C-9A aeromedical airlift transports have a special care compartment equipped with atmospheric and ventilation controls and an ultraviolet lamp system which kills more than 99 percent of micro-organisms in the compartment's outlet air. Here, a USAF medical technician attends to a patient in special care unit.

tainability and *economy of operation."*

Proof that these goals were achieved is evidenced today by the numbers of the twin-engined jetliner that are flying with more than forty different airlines throughout the world. It is by far the most popular twinjet airliner, with planes in service totaling more than 900, all versions, military and commercial. And it has been estimated that DC-9s flying in the U.S. and internationally, over routes from 100 to 1500 miles, have carried more than a BILLION passengers and flown in excess of 5.5 BILLION miles!

Five basic versions are flying, designated Series 10, Series 20, Series 30, Series 40 and Series 50. Several models in each series provide a wide range of designs tailored for maximum efficiency under diverse combinations of traffic density, cargo volume and route distances. Convertible cargo-passenger designs are included in all series. A business executive-type model is also available, featuring non-stop, trans-ocean range capability.

In addition, the United States Air Force and Navy have ordered specially-designed versions of the DC-9 Series 30 aircraft. The Air Force models are designated C-9As and are called the *Nightingale* because their prime mission is to transport sick and injured servicemen and their dependents between military medical facilities. The Navy model is the C-9B, a logistics support transport. A special Air Missions version, the VC-9C, is in service for Government VIP transport.

Smallest of the DC-9 Series is the DC-9 Series 10 with a wing span of 89.4 feet and a fuselage length of 104.4 feet, capable of carrying up to 90 passengers. Largest of the DC-9s *in service* is the Series 50 with a fuselage length of 133.6 feet and a wingspan of 93.4 feet. The latter is capable of carrying up to 139 passengers in a high-density seating arrangement.

Starting with the Series 30 a specially designed wing, incorporating a high-lift wing system of leading edge slats, was employed to give the aircraft excellent short-field performance. In normal operations all versions of the DC-9 can take off on a 600-mile flight with passengers and baggage from a runway of less than 5,000 feet, and make two intermediate stops without refueling. Turnaround time at intermediate terminals is often less than 15 minutes, made possible because the DC-9 carries its own boarding stairway for access to the cabin floor. The stairway is electrically operated from a control panel inside the cabin or by ground crews from another station outside.

Maximum gross weights of the various models range from 78,000 pounds to 140,000

The Series 30 version of McDonnell Douglas Corporation's twinjet DC-9 carries up to 115 passengers in commercial airline service, 25 more than the Series 10 and 20 models. Series 30, which is also offered as a business aircraft, is 119 feet long, has a 93-foot wingspan, and has a short-field takeoff capability due in part to increased lift from slats along leading edge of wings.

pounds with payloads ranging from 19,000 pounds to 40,000 pounds. Cruise speeds average about 500 miles per hour. Operating altitude is 37,000 feet.

All DC-9 powerplants are Pratt & Whitney JT8D series fanjet engines ranging in thrust from 12,250 pounds up to 16,000 pounds. Engines are located one on each side of the fuselage in the tail, a distinctive recognition along with the very high vertical fin and horizontal stabilizer, the so-called "T" Tail trademark.

The DC-9 in operation seldom flies that high. The most popular version, DC-9 Series 30, averages about six hours flying time a day over routes from as short as 45 miles to 1500 miles. Flight durations average 50 minutes, flight lengths average 290 miles and DC-9s average 10 takeoffs and landings per day. Dispatch reliability is almost 99 percent, the highest ever attained by any airliner, jet or non-jet.

The first DC-9 Series 10 flew on February 25, 1965. Not even those who designed and built her believed she would become such a versatile aircraft and soar to such popularity. The production line at Long Beach is still going fourteen years later.

But coming on is a new member of the DC-9 family—The *Super 80*—scheduled to make its first flight in 1979, leading to its airline debut in 1980.

Development of this new version of the highly successful DC-9 began in 1976, and the aircraft was ordered into production in the fall of 1977. Designed to ease the severe economic, environmental and energy problems faced by the airlines, the *Super 80* will carry more passengers, will be significantly quieter and more efficient than its predecessors.

A blend of new and mature technology, the DC-9 Super 80 will be the quietest commercial jetliner in service with major airlines. It will meet all current United States noise standards as well as the more stringent regulations proposed by the International Civil Aviation Organization (ICAO) for new aircraft designs.

In addition, with its increased payload and range capabilities, the *Super 80* will have the lowest operating costs per seat mile of any aircraft in its class and the lowest fuel consumption per passenger for any commercial jet. It also will have the advantage of proven systems which have helped the DC-9 achieve the lowest delay rate of any jetliner.

The *Super 80* is longer and will have a

Sleek, twinjet, DC-9 airliner is this Series 10. Capable of carrying up to 90 persons, the versatile short- to medium-range transport brought jet speed and comfort to many routes served previously only by propeller-driven aircraft. DC-9 has excellent short-field takeoff capability.

The Super 80 was designed to meet the environmental, economic, and energy problem of airlines now and in the next decade.

longer range than DC-9s now in service. A 14-foot lengthening of the fuselage to 148 feet and a 20 percent greater wing area will enable the new aircraft to carry 137 passengers in first class and coach seating more than 2000 statute miles or 160 passengers in an all-coach arrangement more than 1500 statute miles. Its maximum seating is 172 passengers.

Powering the *Super 80* will be Pratt & Whitney Aircraft JT8D-209 or -217 turbofan engines, with a higher bypass ratio than earlier JR8D engines. A product of advanced technology, the JT8D engines will provide more takeoff and cruise thrust, yet will be noticeably quieter on takeoff and will consume less fuel.

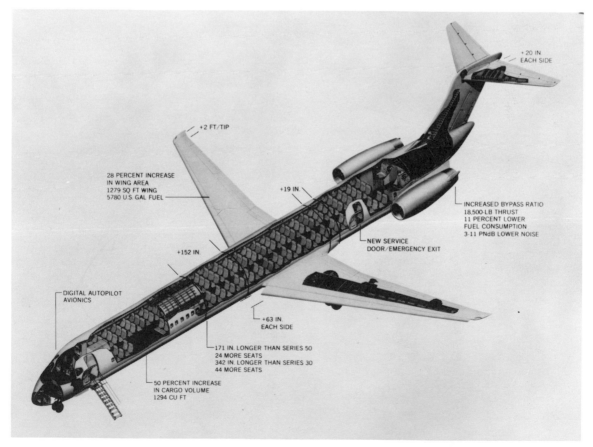

The Super 80, the sixth and largest version in the popular DC-9 series, is scheduled to enter airline service in 1980.

Other design improvements include the use of improved metals and materials technology to increase the structural life of the DC-9 Super 80 by about 20 percent beyond that of earlier DC-9s to more than 50,000 landings.

In addition, the *Super 80* will have the most advanced digital flight guidance system in commercial aviation, the first such system to be integrated with an automatic pilot and go into airline service. Benefits of the high-technology cockpit include improved aircraft performance, reduction in fuel consumption and a lower pilot workload.

The cabin will be spacious and comfortable, with the familiar DC-9 three-and-two seating pattern permitting wider passenger seats than in six-abreast interior arrangements. Enclosed baggage racks will hold up to 50 pounds of hard or soft luggage per compartment. Moreover, cabin noise will be less than in competitive aircraft, and increased cooling and air flow capacity will provide a more pleasant cabin environment.

A proposed new version of the Super 80 is designated the *Super 80SF* (Short Field). It would accommodate 120-139 passengers in a fuselage about 20 feet shorter than the standard Super 80. The versatile *Super 80SF* could utilize 4000-foot runways, or be operated at gross weights as high as 140,000 pounds and carry sufficient fuel to achieve long DC-9 ranges of more than 2000 statute miles. Using the JT8D-209 or -217 engines, the short-field version would be equipped with the same advanced wing and cockpit and would be as quiet or quieter than the *Super 80*.

Perhaps, the greatest tribute to the DC-9 is that it has been called "the hottest product since the DC-3."

Although in the beginning the DC-9 got off to a shaky start with the company losing, at one time, up to $500,000 on each aircraft it sold (Price tag: $3,300,000), the future today looks bright.

The DC-9 Super 80, the sixth basic model in the DC-9 family, was designed to confront environmental, economic, and energy problems of airline operations. It was scheduled to make its first flight in the fall of 1979 and enter airline service in 1980. By June 1979, more than 1050 DC-9s had been ordered by the world's airlines.

MR. MAC knows from experience what it means to *not* break even in the jet transport field. He doesn't like to talk about it because, like the "Doodlebug" in earlier days, McDonnell Aircraft's venture into the design and development of a jet transport simply didn't pan out as expected. Before it was over the company had invested millions of dollars and millions of creative man-hours to build Model 119, a four-engine jet aircraft suitable for business executive transportation.

The project began early in August 1956, when McDonnell, along with other leading members of the aircraft industry, received an invitation from the Air Force to submit a flight evaluation entry in a four-engine, UCX, utility-cargo-transport aircraft competition. Mr. Mac decided to enter the competition and budgeted $10,000,000 for that purpose. He also had in mind, after studying the domestic market, that the UCX could be adapted as a business jet transport. If McDonnell won the Air Force competition, it would have a good design position to go ahead with the corporate jet—and at that time this market was wide open. The Air Force, however, put up no development money. In this respect Mr. Mac was taking a mighty big gamble. Each company had to design and build an airplane with its own money and then submit it for government evaluation, with the government in no way obligated to buy.

The McDonnell entry was designated the Model 119. It was later changed at the suggestion of Mr. Mac to Model 220 to commemorate his company's second 20 years in business. Preliminary design studies were started in the spring of 1957 and continued through 34 different configurations before a final profile was adapted. It was decided that Model 119/220 would be a swept-wing, low-wing aircraft with four, pod-mounted jet engines. The airplane was designed as an all-weather aircraft to meet Air Force specifications for utility cargo use.

The aircraft was designed to cruise at more than 450 knots per hour at an altitude of 45,-000 feet, and fly 2200 nautical miles against a 70 knot headwind. Its total gross weight with fuel for such a flight duration was 43,000 pounds. With sleek trim lines, a tricycle gear, dual wheels, the McDonnell entry had a wingspan of 57 feet, a length of 66 feet and a height of 24 feet. A proposed intercontinental version with turbo fan engines, thrust reversers and additional fuel tanks had a maximum cruise speed of 490 knots and was capable of utilizing small fields with 5,000-foot runways. There were some who persisted that it might become the true replacement for the DC-3 but, of course, it never happened.

Model 119/220 was rolled out of its factory nest on January 30, 1959. Less than two weeks later, with Experimental Test Pilot George S. Mills at the controls and F.H. (Buck) Rogers as co-pilot, the airplane made its first flight. At that time and during additional flight testing the aircraft used Westinghouse J-34 engines awaiting the newer, more powerful Pratt & Whitney JT-12 engines programmed for future models. If the aircraft were to go into production phase. Which it never did.

After extensive evaluation by the Air Force, the decision came down that Lockheed Aircraft Corporation had won the UCX competition with its *Jetstar* entry.

Continued efforts to market the McDonnell jet transport type as a bombardier and navigator trainer, a high altitude electronics countermeasures trainer, as an airways and air communication service aircraft, an advanced interceptor radar navigator trainer, a "flying hospital" and priority troop carrier and personnel transport resulted in "sales zero." At one time the picture brightened when Pan American and McDonnell Aircraft appeared close to a 170-plane deal, which fell through when Lindbergh, a Pan-Am director and technical advisor, favored the French Dassault *Mercure* design. On the famous flyer's recommendation, Pan Am opted for the French plane, which became the backbone of Pan Am's Business Air Transport, Pool-Leasing and Charter Service, a subsidiary operation of the big pioneer international flag carrier, Pan American World Airways.

The sales effort also encompassed many proposals for the Model 119/220 as a commercial transport for the smaller airlines. The plane, incidentally, was the first business, non-airliner type aircraft ever to receive a Class I Provisional Type Certificate which would permit it to operate as a scheduled airliner.

With no direct business the result, McDonnell finally decided to give the Model 119/220 to the Flight Safety Foundation in Phoenix, Arizona. Gracefully and generously he bowed out of the air transport business—but not for long.

It was March 1965, and within two years the McDonnell Aircraft Corporation of St. Louis would merge with the Douglas Aircraft Company of Santa Monica to become the McDonnell Douglas Corporation whose DC-8, DC-9 and DC-10 jetliners are leaders around the world in jet transportation.

Interior of McDonnell Model 119/220 when it was converted into a business executive aircraft. It never could penetrate the business flying market, although many said it was one of best designed and most economical of corporate jets in its era, the early 1960s.

McDonnell Model 119/220, which lost in UCX competition to the Lockheed *JetStar*. It was McDonnell Aircraft Corporation's first commercial jet design, although company had been building jet fighters for almost two decades.

DC-10 flying over Catalina Island off the coast of Southern California.

Cutaway of McDonnell Douglas DC-10.

The spacious and luxurious first class interior of DC-10.

McDonnell Douglas DC-10 coach section.

This DC-10 galley can provide food for up to 250 people in an hour.

DC-10 cockpit and instrumentation.

McDonnell Douglas DC-10AF (All Freighter Concept), the first trijet in an all-freighter configuration.

USAF/McDonnell Douglas KC-10, the flying tanker and cargo aircraft.

DC-8 Super 63 is the largest member of the DC-8 family.

Subassembly of DC-9.

Final assembly for DC-9.

F-15 *Eagle*, world's finest air superiority fighter, with speed in excess of Mach 2.5.

Air Force/McDonnell Douglas YC-15.

F-18 *Hornet*, used by both Navy and Marines.

U.S. Marines/McDonnell Douglas A-4M *Skyhawks* used as tactical aircraft on close support missions.

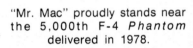

"Mr. Mac" proudly stands near the 5,000th F-4 *Phantom* delivered in 1978.

YAV-88 advanced V/STOL fighter.

Model 3104 *Delta* on lift-off. The *Delta* plays an important role in satellite communications program.

Artists rendering of *Mercury* spacecraft.

Edward H. White in his famous walk in space from *Gemini* IV in June 1965.

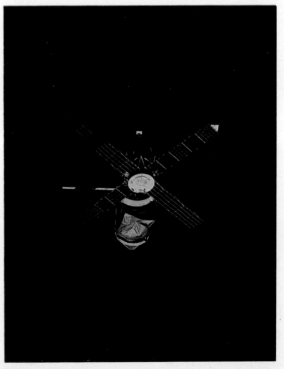

Skylab tested man's ability to live and work in outer space.

McDonnell Douglas Advanced Supersonic Transport (AST) concept.

DC-2000 hypersonic transport concept.

Long Beach, California, headquarters of the Douglas Aircraft Company division of McDonnell Douglas Corporation.

Donald W. Douglas (second from right), chairman of the Douglas Aircraft Company, accepts a check for $68,700,000 from James S. McDonnell, chairman of the McDonnell Company, as payment of 1,500,000 shares of authorized but unissued Douglas common stock. Looking on are David S. Lewis (left), at that time president of McDonnell, and Donald W. Douglas, Jr. (right), president of Douglas. This stock transaction on January 25, 1967 resulted from an offer that was part of the proposed merger of the two firms into the McDonnell Douglas Corporation.

Chapter Eleven

Urge To Merge

WHEN HE ABANDONED THE MODEL 119/220 project, McDonnell had no idea of giving up on the idea of getting into the commercial airliner market. He had set up within the McDonnell Aircraft Corporation a new Air Transport Division, and he had hired one of the nation's foremost authorities on jet transportation to head the group. The man he hired was Robert E. Hage, who before his retirement was Executive Vice President-Marketing for the Douglas Aircraft Company division of McDonnell Douglas Corporation. It was Hage who helped in the design and the development of the Model 119/220, which just about everybody agreed was one of the cleanest small jet transports ever built, even though it did lose out to the Lockheed Jetstar in the Air Force competition. And it was Bob Hage, probably more than anyone else, who advised McDonnell on how to get into the commercial transport business.

"I'm not sure that today he (Mr. Mac) would call my advice, good advice," Bob Hage told the author. "From a financial standpoint, it is very difficult in this field to get a good return on the dollar."

Born in Seattle, Washington, Bob Hage was graduated from the University of Washington with a B. S. Degree in Aeronautical Engineering, and later obtained an M. S. Degree at the Massachusetts Institute of Technology. Out of M.I.T., he went back to the University of Washington as an Instructor in Aeronautical Engineering until World War II came along and he joined the Air Corps assigned to Wright Field, where he became Chief of the Aerodynamics Branch, Aircraft Laboratory, and attained the rank of Major. In 1946, he returned to civilian life, and for the next 12 years held key engineering and sales positions with the Boeing Airplane Company in Seattle, his hometown.

At Boeing, Hage worked as Preliminary Design Engineer in the Pilotless Aircraft Division, Sales Engineer on military products, and Preliminary Design Engineer on earlier jet transports, bombers and missiles. During this period he authored a book, *Jet Propulsion in Commercial Air Transportation*. In 1958 Hage left Boeing to become Vice President-General Manager of the Transport Division at McDonnell Aircraft in St. Louis. One of his first assignments, in addition to work on the Model 119/220, was to come up with a specific design aimed at the commercial airliner market.

Bob Hage recalls: "Our experience trying to sell the Model 119/220 as an executive aircraft seemed to indicate that this market wasn't too good, so it was decided to take a serious look at what we could do for the commercial operators. At first I spent about a year looking at where we could take this concept of a four-engine jet and apply it commercially. We started out with the concept of a four-engined

40-passenger jetliner. Then, we went from the four-engine configuration to a two-engine configuration with the engines in the tail. We kept blowing it up and up and up—more seating capacity—because the cost per seat mile of a 40-passenger airplane didn't indicate it would pay off as a money maker. Finally, we got up to an 80-passenger with twin powerplants in the tail similar to the Boeing 727, only it was a twin and not a trijet. We called it the T85. The design looked good and was pretty well fixed, so we took the on-paper proposal around to the various airlines to feel out their interest.

"I talked to Braniff Airways and to American Airlines and some other domestic operators, and then I went to Europe and presented the idea to the airlines over there. People listened, but there was no real serious interest. At the time, there was a lot of interest in the French *Caravelle* twinjet, and the Douglas sales people were everywhere with their Model 2011, a twinjet with the engines in the tail, which would become the DC-9. We were up against strong competitors. The big difference was we were newcomers in the transport business. They were old pros with a worldwide reputation for the design of commercial airliners."

The end result was that the T85 died before it had a chance to be born, The role it would play—behind the scenes—probably was far more important in the light of future developments than if it had gone into production to join the growing family of jetliners around the world. For one thing, it brought McDonnell Aircraft Corporation and the Douglas Aircraft Company very close to merger status long before the ultimate consolidation.

IT WAS NO SECRET. Word travels like the speed of light inside the aerospace industry, and the word was out early in the design stage of the Model T85 that the plane McDonnell Aircraft was working on and the Model 2011 (DC-9) that Douglas Aircraft was working on were both on the same wave length. Bob Hage puts it this way: "The two aircraft were as much alike as two peas in a pod."

"Both McDonnell and Douglas had been doing independent work," he points out, "and we both had arrived at the same conclusion, namely, that the minimum number of passengers we could get by with was 80, and that we ought to use a couple of the JT8D Pratt &

Whitney powerplants. Moreover, both designs had the engines mounted in the tail, and configuratively they could be twins. It was very much a duplicating effort . . .

"After a lot of discussions, McDonnell decided that it seemed a waste of a lot of money and effort for both companies to not get together and put the program on a 50/50 basis. So, we had a meeting out here (Long Beach) with Jack McGowen, President of Douglas, and his people, and during the discussions McDonnell had several talks with Mr. Douglas, Sr. along the lines of a cooperative effort. The outcome was left hanging for a while, but Douglas finally decided to go it alone with the DC-9 program."

McDonnell, recalling these early discussions, explained—"I actually think Old Doug was leaning very strongly toward our working together on the program.

"Actually, we had had discussions before this, and we had joined forces in a program that involved some studies on a supersonic transport. Our people and the Douglas people worked very closely together on several different categories in SST research for the Federal Aviation Agency. The partnership proved to be a very amicable one, profitable to both companies.

"During this period, Doug and I had opportunity to talk very candidly with each other, and I remember pointing out the fact that our industry was getting into a historical trend similar to what had happened to the automotive industry in the past. It seemed very significant to me that in the early decades in the auto industry there were several hundred companies, but in the final shakedown only Ford, General Motors and Chrysler survived, winding up with 95% of the business. Doug agreed that with skyrocketing costs and the cutthroat competition in aerospace the same thing could happen. We talked at great length about ways we could work together, and several times the subject of merger came up. But we finally decided that at that time it was impossible."

There is the story that the real reason the merger talks broke off was because the two Scotsmen "misunderstood" each other as to who was going to merge with whom. Would McDonnell take over Douglas, or would Douglas take over McDonnell? They parted: friends, but not the best of. And it is alleged Mr. Douglas made the remark, referring to

"Mr. Mac"—"He'll be back again!"

That was back in the spring of 1963 when McDonnell and Mr. Douglas got together in Palm Springs. A short time later working relations between Douglas and McDonnell were suspended. It was about this time that Douglas decided to go ahead on its own with the DC-9, and McDonnell decided not to go ahead with the Model T85 jet transport. According to Bob Hage: "The airlines simply weren't the least bit interested in dealing with McDonnell, which had no expertise or background in the commercial transport business.

"We just dropped the idea of the commercial," Hage explained. "Then, I became Vice President for Advanced Product Planning, and I remember McDonnell called me in and very strongly emphasized that his desire was not only to double sales in the traditional lines, with traditional customers, the Army, Navy and Air Force on fighter aircraft, but he also wanted to develop commercial products in the field of aeronautics so that they would be 50 percent of the company's total business. I told him there was only one way this could be done, and that was to build large commercial transports to get the dollar value up. I honestly didn't see how we could do this alone after our experience with the Model T85, and I told him so.

"Obviously, he had an idea of his own, because in addition to my other duties he told me to keep a close eye on Douglas!

"So, during this time, then, from 1963 to 1966, I continued to update all the info that we could get on the Douglas company, and how the McDonnell products and the Douglas products would be complimentary but not competitive in the missile and space and fighter business. This was so that if we ever could get together with Douglas, we would be able to convince the Department of Justice that there was no monopoly or restriction of competition.

"I remember about every three months McDonnell would call me in and want to know just where Douglas Aircraft Company stood. He kept close track. And in the fall of 1966, when the Douglas company began to experience financial difficulties, we were right there."

FOR THE DOUGLAS AIRCRAFT COMPANY, in the spring of 1966, everything seemed to be coming up roses. At least that was the impression given by management, riding a crest of optimism. At a shareholders meeting in April, both Chairman of the Board Donald W. Douglas, Sr. and President Donald W. Douglas, Jr. gave glowing reports that reflected the company had a bright future. There was pie in the sky.

Indeed, there were reasons for the flowery presentation. The company had reported earnings of more than $14,000,000 in 1965. Common stock had hit a high of $112 a share. Both commercial and military programs were "going well" and there were exciting new programs ahead.

A closer look showed that sales of the DC-9 and DC-8 were escalating. There were new versions of the *Skyhawk* in the offing for the Navy. The Air Force Manned Orbiting Laboratory project, a billion-dollar-plus contract signed in 1965, was in full swing. The company was producing *Nike* missiles for the Army, and new missile programs were just over the horizon. There were also plans to introduce a new member of the DC family, a wide-bodied trijet transport—the DC-10—whose finalized design concept had already been approved.

Such was the picture, bright and clear. Then, suddenly and shockingly, things started to take a turn for the worse. The picture became fuzzy and blurred. By June, there were rumblings and rumors that Douglas was losing money at an alarming rate. A second quarter report showed losses in excess of $3,000,000. By the end of the third quarter, a loss of over $16,000,000 was forecast. The deficit forecast kept growing and growing. Douglas was running out of money to keep its programs going. There was trouble raising needed capital. Banks had turned skeptical. Investment brokers took the same attitude. On the financial seismograph the "rumblings" registered earthquake warnings. Losses might hit as high as $75,000,000! The word was out that Douglas was "unbankable."

In desperation, the Douglases hired one of the big New York investment houses, Lazard Freres, to look at the situation and try to come up with a solution. The investment people sent one of their top trouble shooters, Stanley de Jong Osborne, and a team of associates out to Santa Monica, Douglas headquarters, to put the problem under a microscope.

157

It was Thanksgiving weekend when Osborne arrived and began going over the books. By the time all the turkey scraps were gone, Osborne had his report ready. He called a meeting of the Douglas Board.

The verdict was in. Osborne bluntly told the Board Members that the company was "bankrupt!"

Nobody could believe it. Here was a company of worldwide repute, almost fifty years in the business of building some of the finest aircraft ever built both for the military and commercial market, a pioneer in the missile business, and with billions of dollars in backlog orders—and it was *going broke*.

What in the world had happened?

A lot of reasons came to light in subsequent investigations: (1) Suddenly, the result of an aggressive sales campaign, orders for the DC-9 and DC-8 jetliners came like an avalanche and Douglas had to expand its production facilities to meet the demand. It set up two separate production lines at Long Beach—one for the DC-9, one for the DC-8—and costs "ran wild" in an escalating economy. (2) Skilled workers needed for the job were virtually impossible to find. Millions had to be spent for special training programs to get production workers. The time it took slowed down the production of the jet transports to a snail's pace. Deliveries suffered long delays, and disappointed customers (the airlines) held back otherwise available monies. (3) Subcontractors and suppliers, pushed to the limit manufacturing hardware for our military forces fighting in Vietnam, simply couldn't meet deadlines for engines, needed systems, tires, electronics, and out-of-plant structural components. (4) Plagued by its financial problems, even if it could get parts and labor, Douglas was running out of cash to keep things going. It was tough even to meet payrolls. (5) On top of all this, there was the expressed feeling among the financial community that Douglas had been using "pencil and paper bookkeeping practices in a computerized world." The old fashioned methods simply had not flashed warning signs in time.

Perhaps no one was really to blame. Management certainly was entitled to its optimistic viewpoint. After all, it had been chiefly responsible for getting the company more business than it ever had had before. Its products were meeting and surpassing all of the requirements expected of them,

performance-wise. Nobody questioned the integrity of Douglas designs and technology, or the Douglases themselves, who had built the company and successfully weathered many storms. And who was to blame for the Vietnam war? That would be for historians to try to place the blame.

But that's the way it was in the waning months of 1966. The Douglas Aircraft Company was going down the drain. The big question was: What could be done to save it?

The investment people who had been hired as "doctors" came up with the recommendation that the company look around for a healthy partner to merge with. It was the only way to get bankers and investors to volunteer for a cash blood transfusion that might save the dying patient.

The result was that in early December the Douglas Board of Directors met in emergency session and voted to send out bid invitations to possible merger prospects. By Christmas there had been received applicants from six seriously interested parties. These included: General Dynamics, North American Aviation, Signal Oil & Gas Company, Fairchild-Hiller Corporation, Martin-Marietta Corporation and McDonnell Company. A special negotiating committee had been set up by the Douglas Board to study the applicants. For the bidders, it was to be no penny-ante poker game. To get the company on solid ground, it had been reported, would take about $400,000,000, a big hunk of immediately available cash, plus an impeccable credit rating to underwrite needed future loans. It would be a New Year, or No Year for Douglas.

By the end of the first week in January, the special negotiating committee began hearing the individual presentations of the interested merger prospects in closed meetings. Martin-Marietta had dropped out. But the other five contenders, one by one, presented their proposals with their respective top-management teams appearing before the committee. McDonnell made his own presentation. His was a strong bid that lifted a lot of eyebrows. But the competition was tough.

Finally, it narrowed down to two favored potential partners—North American Aviation and McDonnell Company.

There was a strong feeling that North American would win the day. It was a close neighbor, with its big North American plant located only about ten miles away. Moreover, its Chairman and President, R. J. (Lee) Atwood, was a long-time close friend of Don Douglas, had in fact at one time worked as a top engineer on the "team" which had designed and produced the famous DC-3. And North American was fat and rich. According to *Fortune* Magazine it was a "sound, conservatively run corporation with over $2,000,000,000 in sales and over half a *billion* in assets. But McDonnell also had an ace in the hole: He reportedly owned about 300,000 shares of Douglas stock and, although he never used this as a bargaining lever, undoubtedly it made him fight all the harder in jockeying for the takeover. After all, he stood to lose a lot if Douglas went under.

Making a final play, he upped his offer agreeing to buy 1,500,000 shares of Douglas common at $45.80 a share—in poker parlance, a $68,700,000 raise. In addition, he made a bold proposition: He agreed to buy the stock even at the risk that the Justice Department might not approve the merger because of conflicting interests of a monopolistic undertone. After all, McDonnell Company and Douglas Aircraft Company were *both* big builders of fighter planes, missiles and aerospace vehicles for the government. The Justice Department had to give its blessing or the whole deal would fall through. No merger.

North American didn't want to take such a risk. And on Friday the thirteenth, January, 1967, the negotiationg committee unanimously recommended a McDonnell and Douglas merger.

When the decision was finally reached, McDonnell was back in St. Louis minding the store. But on that date, he received a phone call in mid-afternoon from Donald Douglas, Jr. The President of Douglas Aircraft Company told the Chairman of the Board of the McDonnell Company that he had won the day. The Douglas Board had accepted McDonnell's bid.

It marked the beginning of a new era.

There were a lot of "doubting Thomases" who weren't too sure the merger would work.

In Washington, after a lot of touch and go arguments, then Attorney General Ramsey Clark announced the Justice Department's approval of the merger. It was April 26, 1967, when McDonnell was notified that the Justice Department would not oppose the merger, and the amalgamation was legally consummated as of the close of the business day on Friday, April 28, 1967.

The new McDonnell Douglas Corporation opened for business the following Monday. There were approximately 125,000 employees, and the new company's facilities were located in 14 states and Canada. It had a multi-billion dollar backlog of orders for fighters, missiles and spacecraft for the Army, Navy, Air Force and NASA, plus an almost equal amount of business building commercial jetliners for the airlines of the world.

AT THE TIME of the merger, the McDonnell Company (the name had been changed from McDonnell Aircraft Corporation) was primarily engaged in the design, development and manufacture of the *Phantom II* for the Air Force, Navy, Marines and foreign air forces and of sophisticated space exploration systems for NASA, the National Aeronautics and Space Administration. It was also engaged in various activities associated with aeronautics, astronautics, electronics and automation. Its headquarters were in St. Louis, Missouri, and it employed approximately 45,000 persons. McDonnell also had a multi-billion dollar backlog of business and, remarkably, the company had consistently shown a record of splendid business management, year after year, showing a growing margin of excess monies, most of this being poured back into the company, It was regarded as one of the best run of all aerospace corporations, with a healthy employee-employer and shareholder relationship. Mr. Mac and his "teammates" had demonstrated clearly that they knew how to work together and get the jobs done.

The new corporate "teammate" at the time of the merger, Douglas Aircraft Company, was headquartered in Santa Monica, California, with offices at 3000 Ocean Park Boulevard. Its business, however, was conducted through two operating groups, the Aircraft Group and the Missile and Space Systems Group. The Aircraft Group was headquartered at Long Beach, California, and major supplemental facilities were located at Torrance, Lomita and Palmdale, California, and Tulsa, Oklahoma. The Space Systems Group was headquartered at Huntington Beach, California, with major supporting production and test facilities located at Santa Monica, Newport Beach, Culver City and Sacramento, California, and Richland, Washington.

The Douglas organization had four subsidiaries: the Douglas Finance Corporation, the Douglas Realty Company, Inc., Douglas Aircraft Company of Canada, Ltd. located in Malton, Ontario and Douglas Aircraft Company of Japan located in Tokyo. Douglas also owned 95.3 per cent of the stock of the LaFleur Corporation in the Los Angeles area, which was engaged in the development and manufacture of cryogenic equipment for the production of liquified gases. It also controlled 50% of the stock of Douglas United Nuclear, Inc. located in Richland, Washington.

Primarily, Douglas was engaged in the design, development, manufacture and sale of commercial jet transports and military aircraft, as well as missile and space systems for various government agencies. At the merger, Douglas employment totaled about 80,000 persons.

When the two—Douglas and McDonnell—got together, the merging of talents and resources created one of the world's leading aerospace firms. The take-over did not come like a tornado. Rather, the transition was effected in a gradual and evolutionary manner with a minimum shifting of personnel. Below the top executive level, there were few outwardly visible signs of any shaking of the timbers. Engineering personnel and production workers felt the changeover very little. As "team-mates" they found they could work together even though miles apart, with revitalized effort, common goals and amid a whole new atmosphere relieved of many tensions that had previously slowed down incentives. It was nice to know where the next paycheck was coming from, and that there was money in the bank.

There were, of course, certain reorganizational changes to promote efficiency and growth. Mostly, these changes occurred at the top executive level, involving transfers and promotions.

Mr. McDonnell, as expected, became Chairman of the Board and Chief Executive Officer of the McDonnell Douglas Corporation. Donald W. Douglas, Sr. was named Honorary Chairman, with Donald W. Douglas, Jr. transferred to St. Louis, where he was made corporate vice-president for administration and a member of the executive committee of the Board of Directors.

To be President of the new corporation McDonnell named David S. Lewis, who also was made Chairman of the Douglas Aircraft Division. Lewis, a 50-year-old South Carolinian, joined McDonnell in 1946 after a seven year stint with the Glenn L. Martin Company of Baltimore, Maryland. David Sloan Lewis distinguished himself at McDonnell, and moved up rapidly from Preliminary Design Engineer to Project Engineer to Chief of Projects to Vice President of Operations and finally to become President of McDonnell Aircraft Corporation. He held that position at the time of the merger. McDonnell was Chairman, but he leaned heavily on young Lewis to run things. Lewis went with him to make the presentations before the negotiating committee that materialized into the merger. It was no secret he was being groomed to head the new corporation.

Other management positions included: "Sandy" McDonnell being moved up to become President of McDonnell Aircraft Company (new name), one of the two chief divisions of the new McDonnell Douglas Corporation. The other division, Douglas Aircraft Company, was still headed by Jackson R. McGowen, a 30-year-Douglas veteran, with headquarters being moved to Long Beach. Dolor P. Murray, Jr., a member of the original McDonnell "team," became VP for fiscal affairs. James B. Edwards, a 40-year Douglas man, was made Vice President for commercial marketing at Douglas Aircraft Company, and Bob Hage became Vice President Engineering. Significantly, John C. Brizendine, who had joined Douglas in 1950, was appointed Vice President and General Manager of the DC-10 program.

Brizendine's new position was indicative, perhaps, that McDonnell already had made up his mind to go ahead with the new DC-10 jetliner, a project that had been practically buried during the fiscal crisis. Now with new money available and a strong new management "team," the DC-10 became one of the priority programs. McDonnell had figured out a way at last to get into the commercial airliner business.

He owed a lot to brother Bill, William Archie McDonnell, one-time lawyer turned banker, who probably more than anyone else had guided the financial course of McDonnell Aircraft Corporation since 1945. It was Bill McDonnell who had immeasurably helped to put the McDonnell Company into a very strong dollar position to be able to make its bid for the Douglas take-over. Made a Director of McDonnell Douglas Corporation and Chairman of the Finance Committee at the time of the merger, Brother Bill was expected to do the same for the new company. He came through with flying colors.

The first order of business was to get the newly merged giant some fresh working capital. Bill McDonnell was very familiar with the problems involved. He had been studying the wavering Douglas position all along, advising younger brother, Mac, and he was by the latter's side during all the negotiations. Now, he came forward, putting together a financial package involving ten major banks that gave the new corporation a $300,000,000 revolving credit fund. McDonnell Douglas Corporation was ready to forge ahead and "damn the torpedoes!"

BY THE END OF 1968, the new corporation's first full fiscal year of operations, net earnings were more than 94 million dollars. Sales had hit an all-time high—more than $3.6 BILLION. The company had delivered 102 of its DC-8s (stretched versions) and 193 of its DC-9s. Production was returning to schedule. All programs were beginning to run smoothly.

Perhaps, most satisfying to Mr. Mac was the fact that in a short time he had approached that 50/50 balance between government business and commercial business.

A breakdown for 1968 showed 46.5 per cent in commercial aircraft sales; 34.8 per cent military sales; 15.3 per cent for spacecraft and missiles; and 3.4 per cent sales in automation, electronics, nucleonics and optics. Forecasts indicated the picture might be even brighter next year, maintaining about the same ratio. There was good prospect that commercial aircraft sales and other non-military or space business in the years to come might even overshadow government business. It was a healthy sign.

To do this the corporation was banking heavily on its new DC-10 trijet design. On April 25, 1968, almost one year to the day after the merger was approved by the Justice Department, McDonnell Douglas Corporation officially announced it was "going ahead" with its new wide-bodied jetliner.

It was a bold decision. Lockheed was already well along with its own trijet, the L-1011. Boeing was showing proposals for a smaller 747 that would be a heavy competitor. And the French Airbus Industries had announced it was building a wide-bodied twinjet "Airbus," the A-300.

To get into the race now was a billion dollar gamble.

Donald W. Douglas, left, and James S. McDonnell, the founders of the companies that became McDonnell Douglas Corporation.

Chairman of the Board.

Donald W. Douglas

Sanford N. McDonnell

MDC corporate headquarters (3-wing building at left) and other divisional company facilities alongside Lambert—St. Louis International Airport.

Robert E. Hage

William A. McDonnell

Douglas Aircraft Company facilities at Long Beach.

C-5A, world's largest airplane.

Chapter Twelve

Race To Catch The Airbus

SECRETARY OF DEFENSE Robert S. McNamara, speaking before a group of U.S. defense contractors, warned that the "situation in South Vietnam has unquestionably worsened." In the same speech delivered on March 26, 1964, the Secretary said that the U.S. was determined to give South Vietnam increased military and economic aid. He spoke with full authority of the White House and the State Department. The address was regarded as a "white paper" on President Johnson's policy toward Southeast Asia. The future role of the U.S. in the far-off troubled area would have far-reaching effect on both the Douglas Aircraft Company and McDonnell Aircraft Corporation, already producing combat fighters that were being sent to Vietnam. Strangely, the greatest impact of all on the two companies would have direct bearing on a peacetime aircraft development that would proudly bear the name—McDonnell Douglas DC-10.

Obviously, any buildup of U.S. forces in Vietnam posed a big problem of long-range logistics supply. As was true in the Korean action, with similar distances involved, a great portion of this load would fall upon the Air Force's Military Airlift Command, providing an aerial lifeline across the Pacific.

In Mr. McNamara's Pentagon, USAF planners were "thinking big" about a super, king-sized jet cargo plane. The program even had a

name—CX-HLS, Cargo eXperimental Heavy Logistics System. The prime mover, designated the CX-4 (later it would become the C-5A), was roughly thought of to be a subsonic cargo plane in the weight category of 700,000 pounds capable of carrying a fourth-of-a-million pound payload. The design had to be sized to carry all items organic to Army combat divisions at 550-plus mph-speeds with a max range of 6,000 miles.

In the summer of 1964, the Air Force let contracts to the "Big Three"—Boeing, Douglas and Lockheed—to go ahead with detailed design studies for the giant cargo plane. About the same time, the Air Force asked the powerplant manufacturers to develop a 40,000-pound static thrust jet engine. The stakes were high—amounting to billions of dollars—for the winner in both the airframe and engine competitions.

It was about a year later, in September 1965, that the Air Force announced the winners. Lockheed Aircraft Corporation at its Marietta, Georgia, plant would build the C-5A. And General Electric would build the engines. Altogether the airframe and engine contracts amounted to more than $2 billion.

Boeing Airplane Company and Douglas Aircraft Company had lost out in the competition. Yet, paradoxically, both *losers* were big *winners.* At Boeing, out of the technical know-how gleaned from the design studies for the

C-5A project would come the vaunted 747 Superjet. At Douglas, engineers applied the technology to designs for a passenger version that would become the DC-10 trijet.

According to Jackson McGowen, then president of Douglas Aircraft—"We thought that a new "DC" model might be made out of our C-5A design. Our studies showed that under typical airline conditions, such a plane could carry more than double the DC-8 cargo load over intercontinental ranges. We made layouts of passenger versions which could carry more than 1,000 people. The airplane was so big that we thought of it as a flying ocean liner . . . "

The so-called "BIG plane concept" in its initial stages centered around a cargo-type since it was believed that the growth of air freight services was mushrooming at a gold rush clip. Hence, early Douglas designs, which ultimately resulted in the DC-10, concentrated on air freighter configurations. As McGowen pointed out, the transportation industry—truck, rail, ship and air transport—had been trying to commonize shipping containers to permit moving a container from mode to mode without repackaging the contents. The standardized container, as a result of this movement, was a box—eight feet high, eight feet wide, with lengths in multiples of ten feet. The DC-10 designs were being "packaged" in *this all-purpose* box.

"When we reintegrated our C-5A engineers into commercial programs, a number of DC-10 studies were started," McGowen explained. "We dropped our sights a little, but we were still preoccupied with cargo, and many of the studies were closely related to the heavy military transport.

"All our DC-10 designs were tailored to take the eight-by-eight box,"

"We really didn't give up easily on that eight-by-eight requirement," McGowen says. "But when we did decide that—for this airplane—passengers were more important than cargo, we were free to size the DC-10 strictly for passengers. It made a tremendous difference. Triple seats could be eliminated, once we stopped letting cargo dictate the size of the cabin cross-section. Two wide aisles allowed us to lay out a coach section with four pairs of seats across the cabin, the center pairs separated by a convenient little table. Furthermore, we could now redirect our whole concept to *an airplane for people.* Doors, windows, ceilings, bulkheads, baggage racks, seats, lighting, service systems—all these things could be incorporated without compromising their single purpose: passenger comfort and utility."

It was about this time, in the spring of 1966, that something happened which changed everybody's thinking. The story really began a few miles north of Long Beach at Burbank, California, home of the Lockheed Aircraft Corporation. Before it was over (if it is) Lockheed and Douglas were "going at it" with no holds barred.

WHAT HAPPENED WAS that Rudy Thoren, Lockheed Chief Engineer, one day got an unexpected call from Frank W. Kolk, his counterpart at American Airlines. Kolk said he wanted to come out and talk to Lockheed about, maybe, building a plane which American could operate as a kind of "shuttle bus" over its heavy-traffic, New York to Chicago segment. Thoren set up a date and Kolk came out, and over lunch they discussed American's desires and needs.

William M. "Bill" Hannan, who was Chief Engineer on the Lockheed L-1011 in its early design phases, was present at the meeting. In the author's book, *L-1011 TriStar and the Lockheed Story*, Bill Hannon describes what took place. It is pertinent here, because what happened in Burbank "boomeranged" in Long Beach.

"Frank Kolk," Hannan remembers, "had with him a little document that he called a requirement. It was a description of what he had in mind, a little bit on the performance and so forth. He wanted a 'box' (fuselage) that could carry a maximum number of people at a minimum cost per seat mile. To him this meant two engines, not three or four. He didn't want the plane to be too big, not like the 747 project which Boeing had talked to American about. He had heard about the big new fan engines, too, and he thought they might do the trick.

"There was one thing, though, that he insisted on. American had a decided advantage over other carriers because of their close-in LaGuardia Airport terminus where the airline had millions invested in facilities. But LaGuardia had certain geometric constraints. The terminal was already fixed, the finger satellites were fixed, the turning areas were fixed. And there was a pier under one of its runways which, at that time, was only *approved to carry 270,000 pounds gross weight either taxiing or taking off.* Frank was determined that the airplane he wanted had to be designed right up to those limits, no more. Even the overall length of the airplane was a firm constraint." Did Lockheed have any ideas to meet such a requirement? Could they stay within the fence of the 270,000-pound gross weight limitation?

After lunch was over the group went back to Hannan's office,where he took out of the safe some sketches of a twin-engined, high-wing, wide-bodied design which they had been "playing around with," although nothing ever had been done about it. They called it "the little big twin" because in their C-5A program it was apparent that the more powerful engines were coming along, and a pair of the big turbo fans seemed just the ticket for the design which called for 250-passenger capacity. According to Hannan, they had talked about it during the lunch.

"We got out the drawings," Bill Hannan recalls, "and we pasted them on the wall in Rudy Thoren's office. Frank Kolk showed a lot of interest and excitement. He confessed this was something close to what he had in mind. And he told us that he thought it was a good opportunity for Lockheed, if we'd seriously like to start some work on the design, or something in a like category.

"Before he left, Frank said that he was going down to Long Beach and talk to Douglas to see if they weren't also interested.

"Nobody took it seriously right at that moment, but the race to build the so-called *Airbus* was starting."

Nobody liked the name *"airbus"* and nobody still does, but the name has stuck. It was not new. Back in 1911, Louis Bleriot, the Frenchman who was first to fly the English Channel, named one of his pusher-type monoplane designs the *Aerobus.* And he set a new record for carrying passengers in a heavier-than-air flying machine when he took six brave souls aloft for a bird's-eye view of the French countryside. The aeroplane was no longer a two-seater. It was a *bus* with wings.

WHEN FRANK KOLK approached the Douglas people in Long Beach, he talked very favorably about a twin-engined design, large capacity—200-300 passengers—capable of one-stop coast-to-coast service, meeting the

restrictions of American's LaGuardia terminus. As might be expected, Douglas engineers had also been looking at a twin-engined design, a short-haul, 250-350 passenger airliner which had a number (C9-5C) and was also built around the availability of the high thrustpower engines which the C-5A had forced into being. Frank Kolk was equally impressed, as he had been with the Lockheed twin. He likewise encouraged Douglas to "go ahead."

It was small wonder he went back to New York in a happy mood. He had both Douglas and Lockheed working on proposed designs that would be just what American wanted. But what about the other carriers?

There was the "key" to the third-engine concept. The other big carriers like Eastern, United, Trans World Airlines, Delta, Braniff and Northwest had different needs than did American. All flew over-water routes. All liked the idea of a smaller-than-the-747, wide-bodied airliner capable of carrying 200-300 passengers, but most balked at the idea of only two engines. They needed more range for trans-continental and intercontinental operations. And they wanted the third engine for over-the-ocean flights, if for no other reason than *three* engines sounded better than *two,* especially if you were a first-time air traveler about to fly long distances over water. Testing the market, both Douglas and Lockheed decided to go the three-engine route.

"The whole damn thing was rather ironic," recalled Jackson McGowen. "We could look back at the first Douglas DC airliner, the DC-1, and remember how Jack Frye and TWA had approached us to build an airliner with specifications favoring a trimotor configuration. As it turned out, the DC-1, which ultimately became the DC-3, emerged as a twin-engined airliner.

"Then almost four decades later, along came Frank Kolk favoring a twin-engined configuration which ultimately wound up as a trimotor!"

Unfortunately, the initial concept of the trijet and the accompanying specifications and proposal—as detailed as possible—went into the safe gathering dust.

Only the McDonnell Douglas merger saved the DC-10.

SHORTLY AFTER THE MERGER, as we

THE MCDONNELL DOUGLAS STORY

already know, the DC-10 project was revived. McDonnell Douglas engineers and production groups started burning the midnight lamps, setting the gears in motion to turn the "paper airplane" into reality. There was plenty of experience among the "teammates" to get the engineering, design and technical work accomplished; plenty of production "know-how" to program assembly lines and schedules. And there was optimistic talk that the first DC-10 would be flying by the summer of 1970. There was only one big hitch. The sales people had to get out and sell the product.

Never before inside the aircraft manufacturing industry was there such a battle to get customers to sign on the dotted line. Boeing had dropped out of the *airbus* race with its proposal of a smaller 747. That left Lockheed and McDonnell Douglas in contention to get the juicy plum which could mean, ultimately, business in the billions. Estimates said there was a potential market to sell hundreds of *airbuses*. With air travel increasing at an alarming rate, and congested traffic posing a new danger in the sky, airlines the world over admitted the need for the high-density new generation short-haul, medium-range airliner.

McDonnell Douglas and Lockheed salesmen "tailed" each other around the world. Wherever one turned up in an airline office, the other was not far behind. Competition was cut-throat. Each went out on the limb with promises to meet the specific needs of the air carriers, at home and abroad. A whole book could be written—and probably will be someday—on the tricks, trysts and triumphs.

The first round went to McDonnell Douglas when on February 19, 1968, at a joint press conference held in New York City, American Airlines ordered twenty-five DC-10s and placed options for 25 more. The firm order was a $400,000,000 bonanza.

Round two went to Lockheed on March 29, 1968, when Dan Haughton, Lockheed's Chairman of the Board, signed an agreement for delivery of 144 of the L-1011 *TriStars*. The dollar-value of the unprecedented order was $2.16 BILLION—fifty of the planes to Eastern Airlines, forty-four to Trans World Airlines, and fifty to Air Holdings, Ltd., a British firm which would market them worldwide.

Then, a few days later, Delta Airlines and Northeast Airlines announced orders for twenty-eight more *TriStars*. The total of $2.58 BILLION in orders and options was enough

for Lockheed to go into production.

McDonnell Douglas had not yet committed itself to production. With the prospect of facing a billion dollar cost to design, develop and deliver its DC-10, it simply wasn't good business to go ahead with less than half of the amount coming in from sales to date. More orders were needed.

Two airlines were the targets, United Airlines, the nation's largest air carrier, and Northwest Airlines, now flying transcontinental and routes to Alaska and the Orient. McDonnell Douglas had to get these giants into the fold—or the DC-10 might have to wait.

Almost a month to the day after Lockheed's multi-billion dollar announcement—April 25, 1968—George E. Keck, president of United, made public an order of thirty DC-10s with options for 30 additional aircraft.

Then, on October 29, Northwest Airlines announced it was buying 14 of the DC-10 Series 20 (later changed to Series 40) trijets and took options that would double the order.

The Series 20 was a long-range version of the basic DC-10 design capable of flying non-stop 5,000 statute miles with 268 passengers and their baggage.

Trans International Airlines, on November 25, ordered three of the McDonnell Douglas long-range trijets.

Suddenly, the DC-10 was very much alive, the front runner in the Great Airbus Race.

JOHN C. BRIZENDINE, whom "Mr. Mac" had made General Manager of the DC-10 program, and who today is President of the Douglas Aircraft Company division of McDonnell Douglas, has pointed out that one of the reasons for the success of the DC-10 program was that the original concept was geared for growth. "Right from the start," Brizendine recalls, "the DC-10 was born into a family of three basic models, the dash 10 domestic version and the Series 20 (later redesignated Series 40) and Series 30 Intercontinental versions. It had the unequalled flexibility for economical operation over the whole spectrum of short to medium to long-range routes."

Writing about the DC-10 in one of his company's publications, John Brizendine said, "To me the DC-10 is many things—advanced technology commercial transport, wide-body luxury jet, multi-range high performance jetliner, and even a jumbo jet."

168

He predicted: "The DC-10 will become the backbone of the commercial air fleet in the next decade. It will take the place of many of today's three- and four-engine jetliners most effectively on the greatest number of commercial routes.

"Our primary goal with the DC-10 is to provide the airlines with an aircraft that will help solve many of the problems they face in the years just ahead—problems born of rapid air traffic growth, such as congestion in the air and on the ground, community noise, and the creeping profit squeeze. Landing capability will minimize schedule delays and re-routings. Improvements in reliability and main-

tainability will keep the airplane in operation more, with less time and expense for maintenance. Eight passenger loading doors and our design for maximum efficiency in ground servicing will minimize the time spent at terminals. The benefits to the airlines and to airport operators are clear: They can move more people with less equipment and with greater cost-effectiveness.

"For the air traveler, the DC-10 will provide more room and more comfort than any of today's transports, and less inconvenience from delays caused by weather or mechanical difficulties."

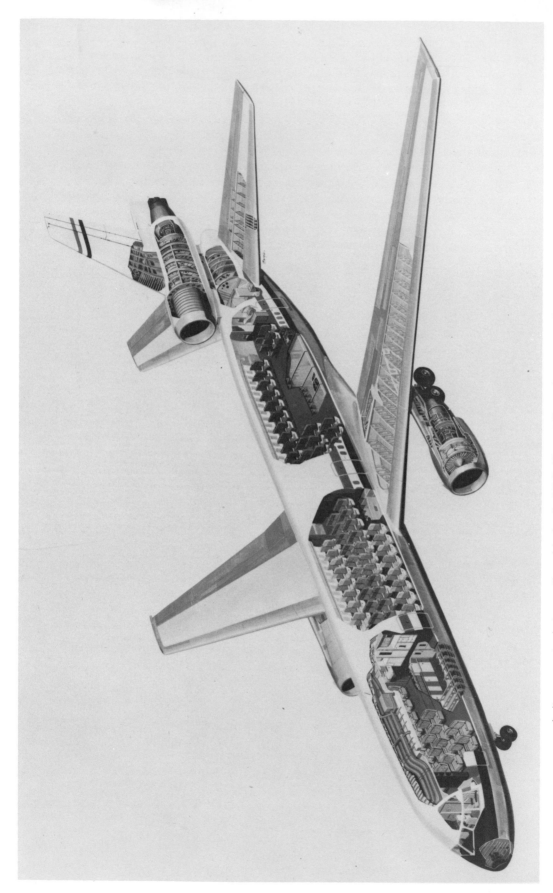

In its conceptual stages, the wide-bodied DC-10 went through many configurations. It finally emerged as a trijet, with two engines, one under each wing mounted in conventional pylons, and one engine in the tail. Cut-away shows early DC-10 with interior arrangements.

Chapter Thirteen

New Dimensions

THE FIRST DESIGN consideration for the DC-10 wasn't a trijet. It was a "twin"—to meet Frank Kolk's needs—and what it really was emerged as a commercial version of one proposal Douglas had for the coveted C-5A competition which the company lost. The passenger version had three decks. It was a high-wing, a big turbofan jet engine under each wing, with a "hump-back" forward section like a 747 profile. When the two-engine concept fell through, for reasons we have already explained, this idea was dropped, and nobody ever mentioned it as a DC-10 again!

The first DC-10 model by name, likewise, wasn't a DC-10 at all, but rather another DC-8 stretch version. Designated the DC-8 Series 83 (DC-8-83), it was a longer version (19-foot fuselage extension) of the DC-8-63 with a wider cabin. Salesmen called it the DC-10 to make it sound like a "new offering." It didn't fool anybody; the air carriers snubbed the idea. One potential airline customer, seeing the extremely elongated fuselage, quipped—"It looks like the Holland Tunnel with wings." Douglas dropped the idea, and turned to another concept that would have been even bigger than the 747—with a maximum capacity of more than 500 passengers. To say the least, it was a radical departure from previous airliner configurations. Some called it "unique." Others called it a "monstrosity." Its longest "flight" was from one drawing board to another.

What made it so different was its "double-bubble" figure "8" fuselage. One engineer described it "like putting two DC-8 fuselages together, one on top of the other." It was true, but then it wasn't quite true, either.

The upper part of the figure "8", the smaller circle, was indeed about the diameter of a DC-8 fuselage, but the lower part was wider. This lower section was then split in half with the upper part being a passenger cabin, the bottom section the cargo hold. The whole idea raised a lot of eyebrows.

The double-decker idea was all right. And it wasn't really new. It was in its favor, after all, a quick means to achieve a high-density seating arrangement. At the time that was the name of the game, to come up with a "competitor" for 747, which was no longer on paper but going into production after a big launch order from Pan American World Airways. There was, however, a big objection to this type of fuselage from the airlines.

Boeing had run into it with their Model 307 *Stratocruiser,* propeller-driven airliner which had a stairway going down to a lounge compartment in the lower part of its fuselage. Passenger reaction was adamant: No one wanted to be there when and if there had to be a ditching.

The DC-10 "Double Bubble" burst.

After that there were numerous paper airplanes (DC-10s)—a variety of shapes and sizes, different wings, different powerplants,

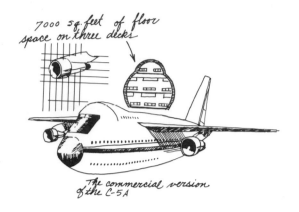

7000 sq. feet of floor space on three decks

The commercial version of the C-5A

two, three and four engines, different interiors, passenger and cargo arrangements. Some reached the model stage, went into wind tunnels for thousands of hours of testing. But finally, there emerged in early 1967 a prototype design that resembled the DC-10 of today.

THE DC-10 PROTOTYPE was to be a trijet, one engine mounted under each wing, a third engine in the tail. The fuselage would be 181 feet 5 inches, nose to tail—fifty feet shorter than the Boeing 747. Wingspan would be 155 feet 4 inches with a total wing area of 3,550 square feet. From ground level to the top of its vertical fin, she would measure 58 feet one inch, about the height of a five story building. She would carry through with the wide-body concept—a cabin 18 feet 9 inches in cross section, an eight foot high ceiling, the spaciousness of a living room. Her design gross weight would be 430,000 pounds with a maximum payload of 103,321 pounds—265 to 350 passengers, crew and cargo. She would be

powered with General Electric high bypass turbofan engines. The "front office" (cockpit) would accommodate three crew members—pilot, co-pilot and flight engineer. She would have a tricycle undercarriage, dual nose wheel, two main gear resting on four-wheeled trucks. She would be designed to adapt the latest avionics systems. She would in every sense be an advanced technology trijet.

This was the "on paper" airplane that Douglas salesmen sold to the airlines to launch the DC-10 into production. There was really only one thing wrong with her. She looked so damn much like the Lockheed L-1011 that the two companies almost got into a legal confrontation.

The likeness is still there. Even today—after both designs have been in service for almost nine years, the average air traveler can't tell the two apart, although he could probably care less. Both are good aircraft.

There IS a big difference, and it centers around the third engine in the tail. On the L-1011 the rear engine is mounted directly atop the aft fuselage. On the DC-10 it appears to be mounted on the vertical stabilizer (rudder) splitting it in half. It isn't. This is an illusion. The DC-10's third engine is also an integral part of the fuselage. The "difference" in simple terms is the way the engines kick their jet thrust out the tail. The DC-10 arrangement is probably the most efficient to get the most thrust. The L-1011's arrangement is the most widely used, common with the other trijets, the Boeing 727 and the British *Trident*.

According to Eugene Dubil, Chief Design Engineer for the DC-10 (now Vice President Engineering for the Douglas Aircraft Com-

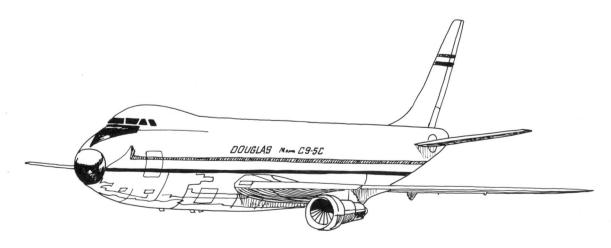

DOUGLAS Norm C9-5C

pany) in the conceptual stages of the DC-10, both arrangements were wind tunnel tested and tested again. "It was one of our toughest decisions," he recalls. "We had a lot of hassles over it. There were two reasons for going the way we did. One was to take advantage of a straight-through airflow; the other was because this arrangement gave us more seats in the aft cabin area."

What occurs is this: With the DC-10 arrangement, the third engine operates the same as the other two engines on the wings. Its big fan sucks in air, which goes through the compressor stages and burners and blasts out the tailpipe. It is a *straight-through flow.* With the L-1011 arrangement, the air is ducted through an S-turn to the engine in the fuselage, with the jet exhaust in the center of the aft fuselage. Making the turn, the air slows down a little. This is one reason, perhaps, why the DC-10 is a few knots faster than its L-1011 competitive trijet. Also, it is why the DC-10 has a longer cabin section.

The latter "additional revenue" was purposely built-in when designers figured out a new engine mount for the engine in the tail. The last three formers—cross members of the fuselage—before the tail cone were designed "banjo-shaped" which, with the circle part below (cabin cross-section) allowed the three vertical members to form the rear engine pylon. Definitely, it is part of the fuselage and not the vertical tail.

The "banjo-shaped" formers, incidentally, are machined out of a solid aluminum forging weighing about 5,100 pounds. In its final shape the "Banjo" fitting weighs only 425 pounds! The shape has changed but it is still one solid piece!

Dubil, who joined Douglas Aircraft Company in 1948, a specialist in structural engineering, and who later was also chief design engineer on the DC-8 program, told of another tough decision that affected the DC-10's profile during its design stages. "Because we were dealing with a very big aircraft," he pointed out, "we took a long look at possibly using the DC-8 wing in a slightly modified version. The DC-8, after all, was our largest airframe to date. Then, we realized that the DC-8 wing was of a vintage almost ten years old. There had been a lot of new technology in wing design since that time. Our own DC-9 (vintage 1963-64) only a few years behind the DC-8 was a good example.

"Particularly the DC-9-30, which had a new leading edge slat arrangement and new trailing edge flaps which had proved highly efficient, seemed to offer many advantages. The more we thought about it, the more we leaned toward going this route. In the end we did."

Consequently, the DC-10 emerged with a king-sized DC-9 wing. By comparison it has a wingspan that is approximately 60 feet longer than the DC-9's and almost three times the wing area. The major difference is in the sweepback, 24-degrees for the DC-9, 35 degrees for the DC-10. The sweepback of the DC-10 allows it to have a greater cruise speed, close to Mach 0.85, in long range operation.

Although the DC-10 would introduce a new jumbo trijet to the air traveler, the aircraft itself was no new radical design. Certainly, it was not the same as the technical design revolution that occurred when jet propulsion power plants replaced the piston engines, when the jetliner replaced the prop-driven airliner. Nothing like that happened. But in the case of the DC-10, there were a lot of things that were new which had to be taken into consideration during its design stages.

The state of the art in airframe technology made available to the designer many advanced techniques. There were new metals such as corrosion resistant aluminum alloys and titanium. The latter "wonder metal"— lighter than aluminum, stronger than steel— had been reduced in price to permit more widespread use in certain airframe parts. Many new plastic materials for panels, fairings and other interior parts were on the market. And there were new machines which could do things that never could be done before, giving the designers a new flexibility. Thus, the DC-10, taking advantage of all of these things, resulted in a really "new" aircraft. One must also add that it was "new" because it was the largest airliner design to come out of the Douglas shop!

And it was "new" in other aspects.

Never before in a Douglas airliner was there a passenger cabin like hers. Two aisles (not one) ran the length of the cabin, which was separated into three "room-like" sections. The aisles and seats were wider than those on the DC-8 transports.

There were three pairs of wide, luxurious lounging chairs per row in the forward first class section. With four pairs of seats across in the coach section, no passenger would be more

DC-10 coach section.

The first class section of a DC-10 wide body jet transport is spacious and luxurious.

Cockpit of wide-body DC-10 has ample space for normal crew of three—pilot, co-pilot, and flight engineer (at right foreground)—plus two observers, as demonstrated in this photograph taken during a development flight with a Douglas Aircraft Company crew. Large windshields provide exceptional visibility, particularly during approaches and landings and for ground maneuvering. Crew seats are designed to minimize crew fatigue during long flights.

than one seat from an aisle.

The DC-10 would provide passengers with 30 percent more window area, in proportion to total size, than any other jetliner. Closed compartments above the windows provided storage space for personal effects and carry-on luggage.

An advanced air conditioning and cabin pressurization system provided separate automatic temperature controls for the three main cabin sections and for the cockpit and lower galley, assuring optimum comfort for all passengers regardless of variations in load density in the different areas. Three separate air conditioning systems circulated draft-free, fresh air at the rate of 20 cubic feet per minute for each passenger.

The cabin pressurization system was designed to maintain sea level pressure in the DC-10 at flight altitudes up to 22,000 feet and a cabin altitude of less than 7000 feet at flight altitudes up to 40,000 feet.

Up front, the Flight Deck was designed for a three man crew plus two observers. It was to be one of the roomiest cockpits of any airliner. It had large windows which gave pilots a visual area greater than even in the bigger 747 cockpit. Crew seats, developed by McDonnell Douglas, featured an electric-powered adjustment system for individual positioning and comfort. Pilots love them.

Control systems were of the most advanced type. But the DC-10 not only had a back-up system for each control function, it had a back-up system for the back-up system. One pilot, an Air Force-type turned four-striper, who helped in the human-engineering of the cockpit remarked — "It reminds me of Pentagon paper-work, everything is done in triplicate."

The DC-10 would also have something else—very modern. It was designed to have two types of food service facilities. There would be a lower galley or a conventional main cabin galley system. For the first time an airliner had elevators in it!

The lower galley system had the food prepared below deck and carried by means of two elevators to a mid-cabin galley service center located between the first-class and tourist sections. A beverage bar is located at the aft end of the passenger cabin.

Space exists in the lower galley for seven modules capable of carrying 28-tray, liquor and/or entree carts, plus a freezer compartment module. These facilities can accom-

This spacious, elaborately equipped kitchen, designed to provide food service for up to 250 people in an hour, is actually a lower-deck galley of a McDonnell Douglas DC-10 trijetliner. Food can be prepared below deck and carried on carts via two elevators to a mid-cabin galley service center, then rolled along the aisles to serve passengers. The DC-10 is also offered with a conventional main galley system, adding below-deck space for cargo.

modate over 600 hot meals, which is sufficient for two complete meal services on a single flight. These modules can be unloaded from the airplane and loaded back into the airplane in less than 7 minutes.

A typical main cabin galley arrangement has galley units conveniently located to provide three service areas: one for the first-class section and two for the tourist section of the aircraft. Space and facilities in the galley units are sufficient to handle two complete meals easily. Enlargement of the first-class section can be made by removing the divider partition in the forward section and allowing the galley units at the second door to separate the passenger compartments. Incorporation of an upper galley system allows an operator an increase in the belly cargo volume from 3,045 cubic feet to as much as 4,670 cubic feet in trade for a modest reduction in seating capacity.

So it went. Design this. Design that. A different cockpit. An upstairs-downstairs galley. Control redundancy. New wing. More spacious cabin. New interior environmental system. Improvise here. Improvise there. Use old proven ideas; adapt new ones. And all the while keep in mind, whatever was done, it had to be done within a configuration and framework that would permit the DC-10 to use the new propulsion powerplants that were now available — the turbofan, high-bypass engines.

EVER SINCE THE Wright Brothers decided to make their glider into a power-driven flying machine, the selection of a propulsion system has been a kind of engine enigma. The Wrights had it toughest of all. When they turned to the still new automobile manufacturers for a gasoline piston engine, the automakers, including Henry Ford, "didn't want anything to do with such a crazy notion as a flying machine." The Wrights designed their own motor. They didn't have any other alternative.

Fortunately, sixty years later when the DC-10 was ready for her powerplants, there were three engine manufacturers — Rolls Royce, General Electric and Pratt & Whitney — offering new turbofan engines. The first airlines to order would make the choice. The big question was—which one would they choose for their new trijet?

If there was anything really "revolutionary" about the DC-10, and it applies to the L-1011 and the 747 as well, it would have to be the advanced engine technology that produced the turbofan engines.

Briefly, the turbofan (or fanjet) engine has a large diameter (about eight feet) fan in front that sucks in the air. This air then divides into two streams. One stream flows through the compressor, combustion chambers and turbines of an enclosed turbojet engine. The turbojet engine has two turbines, one to drive its compressor, the other to drive the fans. Final-

The DC-10 series 10 and series 30 models are powered by General Electric CF6 engines; the series 40 by Pratt & Whitney JT9D engines.

ly, the two airstreams meet at the nozzle or tailpipe, and the compressed hot gases, like a blow-torch, emit a powerful jet blast to generate energy we call *thrust*. At low speeds, the turbofan engine generates more thrust than the smaller diameter turbojet engines because the big fans suck in greater amounts of air. It was the advent of the big turbofan engines that made possible the larger aircraft.

Essentially, the three engines available for the DC-10 were all about the same size and all rated at about the same thrust—in the neighborhood of 40,000 pounds!

The first DC-10 was to be powered with the GE engines.

General Electric's CF6-6 commercial turbofan engine, built at its Evendale, Ohio plant, was an advanced concept in jet engine technology — one which combined high bypass ratio with high component efficiency and increased turbine operating temperatures to produce low operating costs, low sound levels, non-visible smoke emission, and high performance.

The engine's basic components included a large front fan, an advanced gas generator (core engine) and a low-pressure turbine.

The CF6 had a dual rotor and variable stators. Its front fan and single stage low pressure compressor was driven by a five-stage, low-stress, low-temperature turbine through a shaft concentric with the core engine. The fan supercharged the gas generator, which consisted of a variable stator, 16-stage axial flow compressor, an annular combustor, and a two-stage, air-cooled turbine.

The Federal Aviation Administration certified the CF6-6D for airline service with 40,000 pounds thrust.

With the engine selection made, the DC-10 design phase was now complete. It was almost three years after the first sketches and drawings had been submitted. Three years of change and contradictions, of sweat, blood and tears. But now she was ready.

On April 25, 1968 — almost one year to the day after the merger — McDonnell Douglas Corporation announced officially the DC-10 program was "all systems GO." One year and two months later, June 23, 1969, work began on the first DC-10 nose section at the Douglas Aircraft Company plant in Santa Monica.

Let it be pointed out this was also the site of the birthplace of the DC-1 which launched Douglas into the commercial aircraft business.

Assembly of DC-10 number 1 officially begins at Santa Monica June 23, 1969. John Brizendine, left of nose secton and Jack McGowen to the right.

Chapter Fourteen

The Making Of The DC-10

THERE ARE 210,000 parts in the McDonnell Douglas DC-10, exclusive of the engine components. In the airframe alone there are 1,750,000 fasteners, 1,250,000 aluminum alloy rivets, 400,000 locking bolts and 100,000 screws and shear bolts. The electric wiring, consisting of 30,000 strands attached to 60,000 terminators, laid end to end would stretch across Lake Michigan at its narrowest point, about fifty miles. Tons and tons of aluminum, titanium, steel, rubber, plastics and other materials are used in the fabrication of one aircraft. All of these things had to be source-located, contracted for, and a smooth-flow supply system set up before assembly lines could be set in motion.

Accordingly, when the decision was made to put the DC-10 into production, a Supplier Symposium was held in Long Beach with more than 700 representatives of various companies in attendance. Shortly thereafter more than 2200 suppliers were selected.

G. F. Spradling, Director of Procurement and Material, stated: "The DC-10 procurement package was probably the most extensive purchasing package in company history. In cost figures it amounted to well over $1 billion!"

Most of those selected had been doing business with Douglas Aircraft or McDonnell Aircraft for years. There was no question as to the integrity or quality of their products. The supplier line-up included a majority of the leaders in the aerospace equipment manufacturing field.

"Benefiting from past experience and assisted by computer-based procurement programs," Spradling pointed out, "we set up a supply line that would (hopefully) insure that the necessary parts and materials would be timed to on-dock readiness all along the DC-10 production line."

That line, incidentally, stretched from California to Massachusetts; from Long Beach to Toronto, Canada, to Gloucester, England, to Naples, Italy, to Nagoya, Japan. The DC-10 would be as international in body as she would be in operation, when flying the world's skies.

Besides McDonnell Douglas Corporation's own divisional companies, other principal suppliers and subcontractors and the components they contributed to the DC-10 are listed below. Each is a "corporate teammate" in the process of building the world's first jumbo DC-10 trijet.

Company/Location	Component
Abex Industries of Canada Ltd. Aerospace Division Montreal, Canada, and Oxnard, California	Nose Landing Gear Center Landing Gear
Aerfer Industrie Aerospaziali Meridionali Naples, Italy	Vertical Stabilizer and Rudders
Aircraft Mechanics, Inc. Amimech Division Colorado Springs, Colorado	Flight Crew Seats

Company/Location	Component	Company/Location	Component
Aluminum Company of America Cleveland, Ohio	Vertical Stabilizer Spar Forgings	Omark Industries Briles Aerospace Fasteners El Segundo, California	Fasteners
Bendix Corporation Navigation and Control Division Teterboro, New Jersey	Flight Guidance System	Parker-Hannifin Corporation Irvine, California	Spoiler Actuators
Bertea Corporation Irvine, California	Flight Control Actuators	Reynolds Metals Company McCork, Illinois	Wing Skin Panels
General Dynamics Corporation Convair Division San Diego, California	Fuselage Sections	Rohr Corporation Chula Vista, California	Engine Pods
Dowty Exports, Ltd. Dowty Rotol Division Gloucester, England	Nose Landing Gear	Sperry Rand Corporation Sperry Flight Systems Division Phoenix, Arizona	Auto Throttle/Speed Command System
Garrett Corporation AiResearch Manufacturing Company Los Angeles, California Phoenix, Arizona	Air Conditioning System Cabin Air Pressure Control System Auxiliary Power Unit	Sundstrand Corporation Sundstrand Aviation Division Rockford, Illinois	Constant Speed Drive
Garrett Corporation Air Cruisers Company, Division Belmar, New Jersey	Evacuation Slides	UOP Aerospace Mineola, New York	Forward Service Center Aft Beverage Bar
Sargent Industries, Inc. Pico Division San Francisco, California		Westinghouse Electric Corporation Aerospace Electrical Division Lima, Ohio	Generators
Goodyear Tire & Rubber Company Aviation Products Division Akron, Ohio	Anti-Skid Control Wheels, Brakes, Tires	Wyman-Gordon Company Worcester, Massachusetts	Pylon Fittings, Flap Hinge Fittings
Gull Airborne Instruments, Inc. Smithtown, New York	Fuel Quantity Gaging System		
Hardman Aerospace Los Angeles, California	Cabin Attendant Station, Pilot-Observer Seat		
Hi-Shear Corporation Torrance, California	Titanium Fasteners		
Honeywell, Inc. Minneapolis, Minnesota	Performance and Failure Assessment Monitor		
Hughes Aircraft Company Hughes Newport Newport Beach, California	Multiplex Passenger Entertainment/Service System		
Koehler-Dayton, Inc. Dayton, Ohio	Waste Tank Assembly		
Ling-Temco-Vought, Inc. LTV Aerospace Corporation Dallas, Texas	Horizontal Stabilizer and Elevators		
Luminator, Inc. Plano, Texas	Interior Lights		
Martin Marietta Corporation Baltimore Division Baltimore, Maryland	Bonded Honeycomb Structures		
Menasco Manufacturing Company California Division Burbank, California	Main Landing Gear		
Cleveland Pneumatic Company Cleveland, Ohio			
Metal Improvement Company of Canada Toronto, Canada	Wing Skin Forming		
Mitsubishi Heavy Industries Nagoya, Japan	Tail Cone Assembly		

The task would be easier with such an array of partners. Each knew its job well. The "corporate teammates" were good to have for another reason — gearing up for the DC-10's components program they helped share in the cost. McDonnell Douglas didn't have to take all the risk.

ALTHOUGH THE MANY different parts and pieces were to be built in so many different places, the end of the "line" was at Long Beach, where final assembly of the DC-10 would take place. The various components would be shipped by sea, by land and by air. Preparing to receive them was an expansive and expensive process. There had to be a lot of changes made at the Douglas Aircraft Company Long Beach facility. They had to make room for the new member of the DC family coming, hopefully, for a long stay.

There were two new final assembly buildings to be built, adding about 600,000 square feet of work space. Plus there was to be a new Engineering Development Center building. Investment in new facilities, it has been said, represented another billion dollars. It cost, for example, $150,000,000 to install new numerically-controlled, computerized machinery.

The "chips began to fly" and even the final assembly process was set in motion long before the new buildings were ready. It was a matter of using what they had in Long Beach, Torrance, Santa Monica, St. Louis, Tulsa and Toronto, Canada. They were all one now— McDonnell Douglas Corporation—and the DC-10 program was top priority.

One of the first operations took place in a seldom heard about "in shop" shop. Teammates at Long Beach jokingly refer to it as "The Artisan Well." It's no joke, really. As one writer called these particular teammates— "they are the Michelangelos and Rodins of the aerospace industry."

Actually they are skilled artisans whose sculptured works in plaster create the master patterns for different assemblies. They turn blueprints into body.

The precise shapes they turn out — their accuracy checked by laser beams — become the working molds for the development of installation tooling, trim fixtures, bonding jigs.

It is the initial step in shaping new wings. The size of the DC-10 made it a giant step.

Michelangelo and Rodin would have gaped with bewilderment at the size of such sculptures. A wing fillet of plaster of Paris 60-feet long. The eight-foot diameter ring for the DC-10's aft engine intake duct.

So it began . . .

There followed — as materials and components began to arrive — important dates to remember.

January 6, 1969—DC-10 fabrication begins with milling of cockpit window-frame forging at the Torrance, California plant.

January 23, 1969—Assembly of first DC-10 starts with fastening of cockpit window-frames at Long Beach.

January 9, 1970—First DC-10 fuselage section arrives at Long Beach from Convair division of General Dynamics in San Diego, California.

February 1, 1970—First wing set arrives at Long Beach from McDonnell Douglas Canada Ltd., in Toronto, Ontario.

March 2, 1970—The best of good news! First flight of General Electric CF6-6 engine on B-52 test bed at Edwards Air Force, California.

March 30, 1970—All fuselage sections and wing of first DC-10 joined at Long Beach.

April 2, 1970—Three complete engine pods arrive from Rohr Corporation, Chula Vista, California.

It was all coming together. . .

Like shade trees lining a city street, DC-10 main landing gear struts stand in rows at McDonnell Douglas commercial aircraft assembly plant in Long Beach, California. These massive struts are manufactured from forgings of an exceptionally tough steel alloy and designed to withstand the stresses of thousands of takeoffs and landings. Each strut is nine feet, and its widest diameter is 14 inches. Fully assembled, with brakes, tires, and four large wheels, each main landing gear weighs three tons.

PUTTING IT ALL TOGETHER was a masterful achievement. Watching it all come together—as we did at several DC-10 plants and in the huge new final assembly buildings—is a fascinating sight. It is difficult to describe with words. The reader, however, can see it for himself in the accompanying pages of photos that show the DC-10 in various stages of final assembly. There are some things, however, the pictures can't tell. It is best, perhaps, that we should point up a few. The DC-10, for example, changed the whole complexion of aircraft fabricating techniques, using advanced technologies that will be around for a long time.

"We tried a new technique in aircraft assembly on the DC-10 line," explained William T. Gross, who was Deputy Manager, then Manager, of the DC-10 program. "It is called the *modular mode.* Previously, electrical wiring, hydraulic tubing, aircraft system components and insulation were installed in completed fuselages. It was like that with the DC-8 and the DC-9, but on the DC-10, using the

First wing box for DC-10 is removed from big jig at McDonnell Douglas Toronto plant. Wing box is 90 feet long, has a maximum width of 12 feet, and is 4 feet deep at the fuselage end.

First DC-10 fuselage section arrives at McDonnell Douglas in Long Beach from Convair in San Diego. Section is being moved out of Super Guppy which flew it to Long Beach Municipal Airport, January 9, 1970.

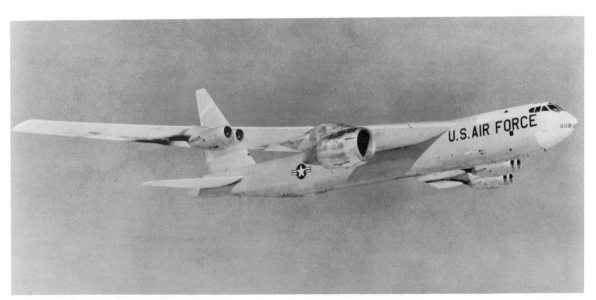

40,000 pound thrust CF6-6 turbofan engine produced by General Electric Company for use on Series 10 version of DC-10 undergoes flight testing on a B-52 aircraft leased from U.S. Air Force. CF6 engines are built at General Electric's Aero Engine Divison, Evendale, Ohio.

modular method, these elements, as well as decorative wall paneling, are installed *before* the four major manufacturing units of the 20-foot wide fuselage are joined.

"This system provides easier access to both upper and lower sections of the fuselage, and permits more work in less time than was formerly needed, speeding up the production tempo."

When we met Bill Gross in 1976, he had just been appointed Vice President Program Management for Douglas Aircraft Company division, McDonnell Douglas Corporation. At that time we talked about some of the future plans for the DC-10, including a stretched version, an all-freighter, a DC-10 tanker, which we will acquaint the reader with in a later chapter. And we talked about some of the things that were unique in the early days of DC-10 production. Bill recalled, as only one who had been very close to the whole program could, some of the high-points which he believed contributed most to the DC-10's success. There were in 1976 more than 200 DC-10s roving the world's skies.

"I think another big thing in the program was the widespread use of computerized tooling," Bill Gross pointed out. "Simply translated it means that once a part has been sized and fitted and tested, this data is fed into computers that in turn tell machine tools how to precisely duplicate the part, maybe hundreds of times. It adds up to why the tail

cone manufactured in Japan fits perfectly when it is put in place in Long Beach 5,000 miles away. The chance of human error is reduced to pushing a button; the computerized tool does it all."

How the tail cone and thousands of other parts got to be a "perfect fit" in the first place is another interesting process which Gross explained. "We built what we call a development fixture, a life-size model of the DC-10 which was never meant to fly . . .

"It is an earth-bound DC-10 used as a tool for transforming engineering design into production know-how. We design a part—say, the tail cone—it is fabricated and fitted to the development fixture. When everything is just right, it gets the go sign to go into production. It doesn't matter much where it is manufactured, when the production item comes back, we know it will fit . . ."

All of these things and many other advanced technology techniques we saw first-hand when we watched one DC-10 come together in the big new final assembly buildings.

The DC-10 assembly sequence begins with manufacture of the center wing box and the tail section, which includes the fuselage aft body, the eight-foot diameter straight-through air duct for the aft engine and the engine support pylon. The center wing box, a rugged structure approximately 20 feet by 20 feet in area and some four feet deep is the structural

DC-10 wing sections are joined to center wing box; fuel tank installations are complete.

Nose and forward fuselage section of DC-10 are joined.

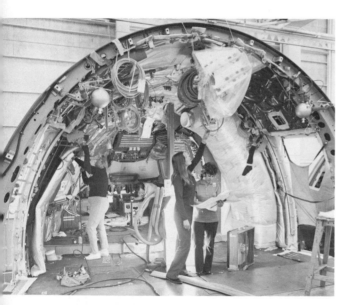

Assemblers work on interior of DC-10 nose section. Insulation, wiring, and environmental components are installed here.

As a major subcontractor on the DC-10 program, the Convair Aerospace Division of General Dynamics produces 128 feet of the 180-foot fuselage—all but the nose and tail section. The five sections produced at Convair are a maximum of 20 feet in diameter and are assembled at the company's facility in San Diego.

Wing is raised by overhead crane and moved toward joining position.

184

DC-10 wing moves into final assembly area.

Aft fuselage sections of DC-10s, with aft engine air ducts attached, line subassembly area in Long Beach. Double-decked production line permits simultaneous access to upper and lower portions of the fuselage sections. Upper areas are visible in open ends of aft fuselage sections.

DC-10 aft fuselage section dangles from overhead crane as it is moved into position for joining to center fuselage section at left.

Huge "banjo frame," a vital sructural part of DC-10, is moved by overhead crane toward numerically controlled profiler in background for final machining. Work on the aluminum part, 17½ feet long and 9 feet in diameter, is done at McDonnell Douglas facility at Torrance, California. Four of the "banjo frames" serve as the main vertical spars in the tail, supporting the aft engine and framing the large duct through which air travels to the engine's turbofan. Rough aluminum forgings from which these large frames are produced originally weigh more than 5100 pounds. Machining reduces the finished parts to about 425 pounds.

DC-10 aft fuelage section is moved into position for joining to center fuselage section. This was the first DC-10 Series 30.

Assembler carefully hand-trims polished metal of DC-10 engine pylon section to achieve precision fit essential to meet stringent specifications. Task is performed in early phase of DC-10 assembly.

Eleven DC-10s are shown in final assembly at Douglas Aircraft Company division at Long Beach, California. In this building, forward, center and aft fuselage sections and wings are joined before the wide-cabin trijets are moved to another building for installation of the vertical stabilizer and engines.

DC-10s move through final assembly.

link between the right and left wing halves and connects the completed wing to the fuselage.

In another assembly line position, assemblers are working on nose sections. Here they are installing the pilots' flight controls, the instruments, miles and miles of wiring, cockpit insulation, environmental components, the flight engineer's station, main radio avionics and other internal equipment.

The main fuselage is next. It arrives in three sections. Each segment is positioned in the subassembly building, where interior fittings are installed along a double-decked assembly line which provides simultaneous access to the upper and lower cabin sections. When this is done, at this spot on the line, the nose section and the tail cone are joined to the front and aft of the long main fuselage section—now one, not three parts.

Now come the wings to be joined to the center wing box. Already the fuel tank installations have been completed, control linkages and engine pylons have been installed, and the main landing gear is attached. From here on the DC-10, far from complete, moves along the line on its own wheels! It moves through additional assembly line positions for completion of interior fittings, installation of the horizontal stabilizer and wing control surfaces, pressure-testing and painting.

After painting, the DC-10 is towed to the final assembly and functional checkout facility. Here, the upper vertical stabilizer is attached, control cables are rigged and engines are installed. Passenger seats are installed in the cabin, and all aircraft components and systems are thoroughly checked out by company and customer inspection teams as the airplane progresses through the six final assembly positions.

The completed DC-10 rolls off the assembly line to a pneumatic test area before it is weighed and delivered to the Douglas flight ramp, where crews conduct hydraulic, electrical and fueling tests and engine run-ups in preparation for flight. Inspectors follow each step in the procedure, certifying that the airplane passes each test successfully or that any necessary corrective action is completed.

The airplane then is turned over to flight crews for taxi tests and at least three long-duration (approximately four hours each) flight tests which prove out all systems in actual operation.

Delivery of the new jetliner is made after a final test flight by a crew from the customer airline which accepts it for service.

THAT'S THE WAY it works. This is the DC-10's final assembly line in motion. In this atmosphere one finds himself in a world apart. A place of strange noises, strange sights, strange

DC-10 is towed out of final assembly building. Next stop is the paint hanger.

Shrouded to protect metal during painting.

Workman "touches up" Sabena name on DC-10 in paint hangar.

smells. The *rat-a-tat, rat-a-tat-tat* of a hundred rivet guns. Deafening. The loud *bang-slam-bang* of giant hydraulic presses—up and down, up and down. Whirring machines, buzzing voices, shouts, horns.

Overhead a sight to behold. The horizontal tail section, elevators and horizontal stabilizer—almost the wing span of a DC-3—is "flying," by itself, for the first time. Well, not really, but it *is* airborne, hanging from a giant crane that is moving it into position to join the rest of the fuselage.

Smells? Inside the giant paint room—they call it the "Studio"—it is like going into a hospital operating room. The odor of ether—an ingredient in the quick-drying paint used by the hundreds of gallons—is so strong you almost "go under." Some do.

Indeed, the place where the DC-10s are born is a world one is not soon apt to forget. Nor desire to. The picture comes back again and again every time you ride in the quiet, luxurious cabin of a DC-10. Somehow, it seems like a miracle that they could put it all together. Perhaps it is!

When we saw the assembly line in motion, we were told they were turning out a DC-10 complete at the rate of about one every seven days. The rate can be speeded up or slowed down depending upon new business.

The first DC-10 was about a year—from June of 1969 until June of 1970—in the final assembly.

On July 23,1970, it was introduced at a roll-out ceremony at Long Beach.

ACCORDING TO the *Douglas News,* a corporate publication, the DC-10 rollout was a gala event. A special edition of the paper, published the next day tells the story.

"The McDonnell Douglas DC-10, first of the wide-bodied tri-jet transport aircraft, made an auspicious public bow yesterday during colorful roll-out ceremonies here.

"On a signal given by Vice President Spiro T. Agnew, honor guest and speaker for the occasion, the gleaming new jetliner taxied under the power of its own engines from behind the massive final assembly hangar into position before more than 1000 guests of the McDonnell Douglas Corporation gathered in one bay of the building.

"When Mr. Agnew spoke, he posed the question, 'Why do so many of us from all areas of the world gather for the roll-out of a single plane? Let me suggest an answer. It signifies the contributions of the aeronautics industry. And it signifies the struggles and success of two men.'

"After his address, the Vice President

In a rollout unprecedented for commercial transports, the DC-10 taxis into view of guests during ceremonies in Long Beach on July 23, 1970. In a traditional debut, aircraft is towed out of assembly building. Fifty bagpipers (at right)—one for each year of the fiftieth anniversary of the company—saluted James S. McDonnell, chairman of McDonnell Douglas, and Donald W. Douglas, honorary chairman.

At special ceremony at Long Beach plant, the first DC-10 was the star of an unusual rollout performance. Under its own power, it taxied around in front of a hangar where over 1,000 guests had gathered for the occasion. Vice President Spiro T. Agnew (center) joins James S. McDonnell (left), chairman of McDonnell Douglas Corporation, and Donald W. Douglas, honorary chairman, in advancing an aircraft-type throttle to signal the start of the rollout of the corporation's new trijet.

First delivery of DC-10 transports to American Airlines and United Air Lines at Long Beach on July 29, 1971.

FULL FLIGHT RAMP—Nine McDonnell Douglas DC-10s, scheduled for delivery to five airlines, line the flight ramp at Douglas Aircraft Company division of McDonnell Douglas Corporation at Long Beach, California. Included are Series 10 transcontinental versions for American Airlines, Continental Airlines, National Airlines and United Air Lines and an intercontinental model for Northwest Airlines. A McDonnell Douglas DC-9 twin-jet is at the far end of the ramp.

joined Mr. McDonnell and Mr. Douglas in advancing three DC-10 throttle levers mounted on a pedestal as a signal for the roll-out to begin.

"Musical entertainment was provided by the Long Beach Symphony Orchestra under the direction of Alberto Bolet.

"Symbolizing the 50th anniversary of the corporation, a band of 50 kilted Scottish bagpipers paraded in front of the airplane as it moved into view, its white fuselage sparkling in the sun. A broad red stripe extended along the fuselage above the window line, with a parallel blue stripe below. Above the stripes on the forward fuselage was the name, McDonnell Douglas DC-10."

Bagpipe band salutes McDonnell Douglas at rollout of DC-10 on July 23, 1970 at Long Beach as DC-10 taxis into view in background.

Engineer makes adjustments to DC-10 model in subsonic wind tunnel at Long Beach.

Chapter Fifteen

Wings Under Test

THERE PROBABLY never was and there probably never will be a more rigid, rugged and more extensive test program than that which the DC-10 endured. It began as far back as November 1966 with wind tunnel testing that ultimately dictated the basic design of the new trijet. It progressed through thousands of hours of fatigue and static tests, applying loads simulating 84,000 flights and 120,000 flight hours. It moved to the sky—the DC-10's element—where five of the aircraft for months performed in all kinds of weather and under all kinds of conditions peculiar to airline operations and government safety standards.

Wind tunnels and model airplanes may not sound very important to the layman, but to the aerodynamicist or aeronautical engineer they are important tools of his trade. Perhaps, it might be well to remember that the first successful airplane—the Wright Brothers' machine—owed much to what they learned in their improvised wind tunnel. Orville called it his "wind box." The box, about two feet square, had a fan at one end driven by a small gasoline engine. The fan blew a stream of air through a series of vanes or "straighteners" and the air flowed under controlled conditions over various sizes and shapes of airfoils (wings) the Wrights were trying out. In this way, they derived the first set of basic tables that enabled every airplane designer ever

since to determine proper wing surfaces for a given design. If it hadn't been for their wind tunnel tests the Wrights might not have designed and built their successful machine. The data they collected proved to be right; others had been wrong.

Today, engineers have fashioned great tubes of steel that bend snake-like around laboratory buildings, and they have harnessed the power of electrical giants which whirl fan blades the size of giant windmill vanes to produce airstreams more powerful than hurricanes. They are simulating aircraft speeds in the supersonic range, or in subsonic wind tunnels such as that used to test DC-10 models. They can simulate every known attitude of flight and its effects on various surfaces.

The DC-10 program involved more than 22 models, large scaled-down models and scaled-down components, which were "flown" some 12,000 hours in wind tunnel tests. "These provided us with data on wings, the high lift system, nacelle and engine performance," explained one engineer. "Special configurations provided realistic propulsion simulation to determine engine effects, including thrust reverser. Other detailed studies of performance and flying qualities included tests of fuselage, nose, engine thrust reverser, control surfaces and aft-end components.

"We knew the DC-10's flying potentials

Large model of DC-10 with related equipment was used to study most efficient loading and unloading methods for both freight and passengers. Results dictated doors, hatches, and other items, with respect to on-the-ground operations.

before the first actual aircraft was ever out of the jigs."

The models, themselves, are no playthings. Some of them cost ten times as much as did the first DC-3s.

The reason why is because these are precisely built models to exact scale, and they are highly instrumented. Telemetrics in one model, alone, cost more than three Cadillacs.

Wind tunnel models of the DC-10, we were told, were worth their weight in gold. Indeed, they helped make the DC-10 one of the "Cadillacs" of its winged world.

Another type of model—a metal-sheathed, one-tenth scale version of the DC-10—was placed high atop a 40-foot tower in a remote corner of the Long Beach plant. This particular model was used to simulate antenna characteristics of the actual aircraft. All in-

strumentation was contained within the model, which simulated an aircraft in flight. Still other models were used by the Antenna/Radome engineers to evaluate radiation pattern characteristics, as well as other antenna systems under development.

FATIGUE TESTING STATIC TESTING. To most of us *fatigue* means "getting tired" and *static* is some words we hear from each other or the interference on the radio. To the aeronautical engineer the meanings may be the same, but they have definitely more meaning when translated relative to aircraft structures. For example *fatigue* means the weakening or deterioration of metal or other material occurring under load, especially under repeated cyclic, or continued loading. *Static testing* on the other hand means, as the

This busy airport terminal layout may look like child's play, but far from it. Note different models of jetliners. All are exact scale, as is terminal docking area. Models enabled engineers and planners to determine "rules of the road" for handling DC-10 on the ground and how big trijet would fit into terminal operations with smaller airliners.

word implies, holding a structure (i.e. wing, tail assembly, fuselage part) in a stationary or hold-down position to verify structural design criteria, structural integrity, and the effects of limit loads.

The DC-10 fuselage and other assemblies underwent fatigue and static tests the equivalent of 30 years "flying" time. Because of the size of the new trijet, special test machines had to be designed and built. The four machines are among the world's largest fatigue testers.

Writing in a company publication, *DC-10 Progress,* one writer described them: "They stand tall and forbidding in a hangar-like working area in the huge Douglas facility at Long Beach. To the layman, their function is incomprehensible; they loom merely as wondrous offspring of a new technology. But their function is well-known and respected by the teams of technicians which daily swarm around the machines and concern themselves with such terms as *static strength, fatigue life* and *fail safe.*"

When the author visited the area one test engineer explained—"These machines can apply cyclic loads to handle the largest DC-10 test panels. They have a loading capacity of 1.5 million pounds in *fatigue* testing and 3 million pounds in *static* load. This loading spectrum allows the test specimen to undergo much more punishment than any strains it would receive in flight."

Such loads and/or stresses are effected by

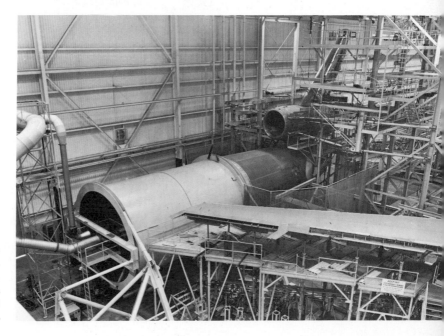

Big bend demonstrates strength in DC-10 wing under 2.5G load during structural proof testing. Double exposure shows wing in normal position (lower) and at maximum deflection of 90 inches at tip (upper), with full test load applied by giant hydraulic jacks.

Tail section of DC-10 gets "the works" in fatigue test rig. Computers applied cyclic loads simulating takeoff, taxiing, landing. Fuselage was cut into three parts for test.

powerful hydraulic jacks that push and pull, applying tremendous forces on the structure under test. In one test, a DC-10 wing was deflected upward 90 inches. Then it was bent downward 51 inches. The structure showed no ill effects, and the test was repeated several times.

In another test they cut a complete aircraft structure into three sections, each of which was mounted in a steel jig where loads were applied until structural failure occurred. Controlled by computers, the fatigue test program applied loads at the rate of one cycle every two minutes, simulating the aircraft's takeoff, climb, pressurization, cruise, maneuver, descent, landing and taxi operations.

After a year of such treatment, FAA (Federal Aviation Administration) observers, always present at the tests, pronounced the DC-10, structurally, had met or exceeded all their requirements. All of this done *before* the first DC-10 came off the line and rolled out of the final assembly hangar.

Any weaknesses or suspected weaknesses discovered in the extensive test program had been remedied and the corrective measures built-into the production aircraft. Changes made in No. 1 aircraft and all others to follow assured she was ready to try her wings.

Before "first flight," however, another test fixture located in the new nine-story-high development center building made sure the aircraft would have excellent control characteristics. They called it the *iron bird,* a heavy, structural iron framework in which every cable, bracket, pulley, hydraulic line and actuator of the DC-10 flight control system was installed exactly as in the airplane itself.

Through this sophisticated simulation, engineers had a head start on developing and debugging the stability and control features of the new trijet before first flight. Likewise, pilots who "flew" the *iron bird* had opportunity to familiarize themselves with all the aircraft's control functions. In the "cockpit" of the *iron bird,* pilots, through computerized simulated forces, got "the feel" of actual flight.

By the time the first DC-10 was ready for its maiden flight her flight test crew had already "flown" her for many hours

WHO WERE THEY? These men who would take the prototype DC-10 aloft for the first time. There was to be a four man crew: pilot, co-pilot, flight engineer and a flight test engineer. The latter's duties—to tend the myriad of test recording equipment that would

Members of the first flight crew for DC-10's maiden flight confer prior to takeoff from Long Beach Municipal Airport. Clifford L. Stout (left), DC-10 project pilot, was captain for the flight. Other crew members are (from left) Harris C. Van Valkenburg, deputy chief engineering pilot, as first officer; John D. Chamberlain, flight engineer, as second officer; and Shojun Yakawa, flight test engineer.

Cliff Stout, Douglas director of flight operations (left), confers with Lyle Wright (right), Douglas Director Design, commercial projects, and John Brizendine (between them), Douglas Aircraft Company President, prior to DC-10's first flight.

be on board, 25,000 pounds of it! The men selected were: Clifford Lee Stout, pilot; Harris Clifford Van Valkenburg, co-pilot; John Dean Chamberlain, flight engineer; and Shojun Yukawa, flight test engineer. This "front four" had a combined 80 years of design, engineering and flying expertise. Each had been involved in similar duties on the DC-8 and DC-9 programs. They were well Douglas-oriented.

Cliff Stout, born in Asheville, North Carolina, raised in southern California since age six, had joined Douglas Aircraft Company in 1956 as a test pilot on the DC-6 and DC-7 programs. At that time he brought with him more than 15 years of stick-and-rudder experience in everything from a Piper Cub to fighters, bombers and transports as a World War II Air Transport Command ferry pilot. When Douglas got into its commercial jet programs, Cliff was assigned to the DC-8 and DC-9 projects as engineering test pilot.

With a math, physics and science college background, he contributed much to the design and development of the DC-8, DC-9 and DC-10 cockpit designs and functionary controls and instrumentation. Many of the DC-9's automatic landing capabilities were his reponsibility. He also shouldered the responsibility for the DC-8 and DC-9 all-weather Category II flight programs. When the DC-8 Super 63 series aircraft made its maiden flight, April 10, 1963, Cliff Stout was in command. At that time the DC-8-63 was the world's largest commercial jet transport.

When the DC-10 was in its design stages, and all during mock-up, Cliff was in charge of the cockpit design and arrangement. "I spent more time inside that cockpit mock-up than I did at home," he once remarked. "A lot of us did, Douglas pilots and airline captains, and I think for the first time because of the pooling of our ideas, the DC-10 has a front office that will set the standards for many future aircraft. Since at this stage (mock-up) it was all ground time, I couldn't wait until we had a chance to try it out in the sky."

Harris Clifford Van Valkenburg, co-pilot and second in command, was born on March 22, 1924 in Sydney, Nebraska. He got his wings in 1942 when he signed up for the Naval Aviation Cadet Program at Livermore Naval Air Station in California, age eighteen. He soloed on Christmas Day, little more than a year after Pearl Harbor.

A short time later, assigned to the Marine Corps, he got his first introduction to the Douglas family—flying the Douglas SBD *Dauntless* on dive bombing missions in the Marshall Islands during World War II. "I was so impressed with the way the *Dauntless* responded and with the punishment it could take," Van confesses, "that I made up my mind someday I would like to join the company that made an aircraft with such in-

DC-10 takes off from Long Beach Airport, adjacent to plant where she was built, on first flight, August 29, 1970. Flight was longest "maiden flight" for any aircraft.

tegrity."

After completing his tour with the Marine Corps, Van attended Salinas Junior College and San Jose State College and in 1950 received his Bachelor's Degree in Aeronautics. That same year he was back in the Marines again flying F4Us on recon missions in Korean skies. After Korea, he worked as a civilian wind-tunnel project engineer for the California Institute of Technology. Then, in 1954, came the opportunity to join Douglas Aircraft Company as a production test pilot at the Douglas El Segundo facility.

Later, Van was involved in the DC-8 production and development program as a pilot and co-pilot. He was pilot for the MARS and LEM simulator studies, the C-133A Apollo Module Drop Program and DC-9-10 development flight testing.

Altogether, he brought 28 years of aircraft flying and industrial experience into the DC-10 cockpit for its initial flight. Like Cliff Stout, he "couldn't wait" to get the big bird airborne.

Another "cornhusker", John Dean Chamberlain, born July 27, 1930 in Plattsmouth, Nebraska, would sit behind Cliff and Van in the flight engineer's station. John would be senior Douglas family man aboard, having joined the company at age 20 in 1950 as an electronic technician. A series of promotions and in 1958 we find him a qualified flight engineer at Douglas with duty assignments that included the parameters of customer flight training, experimental test programs, production test programs, ground school activities and performing as a radar navigator systems engineer.

In 1965 he served as flight engineer instructor at the DC-8 and DC-9 ground schools. Aside from carrying on his duty as an instructor for company and customer flights, he also participated as a Flight Engineer in production flight test programs on the DC-8 Series 61 and 63 and subsequent aircraft.

Two years later he was promoted to the position of DC-10 project flight engineer. Like both Stout and Van Valkenburg, he virtually "lived" with the DC-10 from its concept.

Fourth member of the crew, Shojun Yukawa was born in Tacoma, Washington, a *Nisei* American who at age 21 enlisted in the U.S. Army where he found himself in the Intelligence Group assgned to duty in Japan. "It was interesting," Yukawa says, "but I

Chase plane (top) on DC-10's maiden flight was a Navy F-4 *Phantom II*.

always wanted to get into aviation field, but never did get a chance to be a pilot."

After being discharged from the service, Yukawa decided upon a career in aeronautical engineering—"at least, I felt I could become a part of aviation in this way. . ." He was graduated in 1958 from the University of Michigan with a Bachelor of Science Degree in Aeronautical Engineering.

Tired of Michigan's cold winters he headed for California country and sunshine, and reaching Los Angeles hired on with North American Aviation as a flight test engineer. After 18 months, he joined Lockheed Aircraft's Special Projects Group as a dynamicist. In September 1960 he rejoined North American, where he worked on the B-70 bomber until 1964 when he joined Douglas' Flight Development and Engineering Group at Long Beach.

After that, as a Flight Development Engineer—responsible for establishing test procedures and test equipment supervision— he was involved in both the DC-8 and DC-9 programs. His job would be the same on the DC-10 flight test program.

Such was the caliber of the men selected to fly the DC-10 on her first flight. The crew was ready. So was the aircraft by the last week in August, and the date was set, August 29, 1970.

Test console in DC-10 during flight development phase.

Part of on-board test equipment Shojun Yukawa had to monitor during first flight. Test equipment aboard weighed more than 25,000 pounds. Signals were sent back to flight control center.

THE DAY DAWNED bright and clear, but it was still dark outside when they rolled the DC-10 out of her hangar nest. As the sky brightened with an orange sunrise, a swarm of mechanics, engineers and others crowded around the aircraft, checking last minute details. "I came out to the aircraft at about 0500," Cliff Stout recalled, "and John (flight engineer) was already there well into an inspection sequence, checking every minute detail with the eye of an eagle . . ."

Four hours later, it was a different scene. Some 20,000 spectators, most of them team-mates who had helped build the DC-10, had gathered to witness the takeoff. There were cheers as the big plane rolled out to the end of the runway and into position. Inside the cockpit the front four went through last minute check lists. It was now precisely 10:00 A.M.

Cliff Stout released the brakes, pushed forward on the trio of throttle knobs, and DC-10 *Number One* started to roll. She rolled and she rolled, faster and faster, for almost a mile (4890 feet to be exact) over the concrete runway and then her nose lifted, and the next

DC-10 lands at Edwards Air Force Base, California, after completing highly successful first flight.

Test pilot H. H. (Nick) Knickerbocker (standing, center) serves as test controller in automated flight test data center at Long Beach, during a DC-10 developmental flight. With large TV-type consoles, Knickerbocker and test engineers could view computer-processed data from instruments in the aircraft while it was in the air. The test controller, in direct voice contact with the air crew, helped direct flight maneuvers to obtain maximum information on aircraft performance from each test mission.

instant she was airborne.

McDonnell Douglas' newest DC liner took wing and headed out over the Pacific Ocean. There was a chase plane, a McDonnell Douglas F-4 *Phantom II* and a photographic plane to record the flight. Inside the photo ship, a cameraman, when he saw the F-4 and the DC-10 in his lens remarked—"what a symbolic sight!" It was: For in one frame was the F-4 which had made McDonnell Aircraft Corporation of St. Louis famous and the latest of the DC airliners which had made Douglas Aircraft Company of Santa Monica and Long Beach world reknowned.

Cliff Stout may have had other thoughts. Like "how close is that chase plane?" But he was too busy. Climbing out over Catalina Island Stout levelled off at about 10,000 feet. There he did a few banks and turns and some other test maneuvers. Then he cycled the gear and the flaps for the first time. Everything was functioning beautifully.

The flight plan had called for maneuvers to evaluate stability and control characteristics up to 20,000 feet, but the plane was performing so well Stout took her up to 30,000 feet, in an element where she was designed to strut her stuff.

Up there, almost six miles above the earth, Stout, Van Valkenburg, Chamberlain and Yukawa carried out the many tasks that had been assigned them, performing and monitoring the various tests called for in the day's flight plan. These included: testing of all systems, stability and control in a series of all flight maneuvers, flying qualities evaluations, structural/aerodynamic damping tests up to speeds of 300 knots, low speed handling tests and sundry others. Before they realized it they had been "up there" for over three hours.

Usually a first flight doesn't last over an hour. It was an endurance record for the first flight of any commercial transport when at 1:26 PM the DC-10's wheels touched down at Edwards Air Force Base in the Mojave Desert of California where she was scheduled to begin a week long series of tests. Her maiden flight had lasted 3 hours and 26 minutes.

On the ground, interviewed by reporters, Stout paid this tribute to the DC-10—"Without reservation, I can say that the DC-10 is the finest airplane I have ever flown. . . The airplane handles magnificently despite its size, and control response is fast and absolute. . ."

He added: "My confidence in the airplane is such that I would have no second thoughts about taking my family up on the very next flight. It has the maneuverability of a fighter and the grace of a swan!"

Some seven years later, when we talked with Cliff Stout, he reiterated his feelings about that first flight. "There's one thing, though, about that flight that people often overlook," Cliff pointed out. "It was not just a test of an advanced technology aircraft, it was a test of an advanced technology in the whole state of the art of flight testing."

He went on to explain that McDonnell Douglas had set up at Long Beach in its new Engineering Development Center building a Data Acquisition Center which made possible by complex computer telemetry "almost instantaneous recording and interpretation of data accumulated during the various tests."

During the first flight, the Data Center was the focal point of all activity outside of the airplane itself. From there, George Jansen, Chief Engineering Test Pilot, controlled all ground aspects of the flight. In short, the pre-programmed tests to be performed by Stout and crew as they were actuated could be viewed instantaneously on five graphic displays similar in appearance to TV screens in the Ground Control Room. It was like seeing the whole flight pattern "live" instead of on film.

"In this way," Jansen explained, "if we didn't get the exact kind of data we wanted from a specific maneuver or test, we could run it again until we got the info we wanted. In constant communication with Stout, I could tell him what the test results looked like, and we could do our own reruns. Always before, it was necessary to wait for films and tapes to be processed. Then, maybe, we could run the test again next day, or next time . . ."

Using the new Data Acquisition Center's complex of computers tracking capabilities (telemetry signals were relayed from a tracking station atop 8400-foot Frost Peak, north of Los Angeles and from the aircraft itself and its on-board electronic monitors), results of tests could be obtained in hours, not days. Because of the 800 channels that can be monitored and recorded on any given flight, more components could be evaluated, resulting in an aircraft more thoroughly tested than ever before.

THE COMPLETE flight test program for the

DC-10 involved five aircraft each assigned to different missions. The program lasted more than thirteen months and before it was over the five planes in the "test fleet" had flown 929 flights following the first flight of No. 1 aircraft. In all, the planes accumulated more than 1500 hours of flight time. According to Jackson McGowen, then President of the Douglas Aircraft Company division of McDonnell Douglas, it was the most thorough testing and development program ever conducted by the company. In addition, the DC-10 had to pass tests that no other commercial airliner had been subjected to—new federal regulations pertaining to noise levels.

Briefly, the five planes and their respective test objectives were: Ship No. 1 to be the primary stability and control airplane. It flew tests for verification of longitudinal control during configuration changes (landing gear retracted and extended, various wing flap positions used), checked out both trim and mistrim configurations, and made crosswind takeoffs and landings. Lateral control in banked turns as well as dynamic longitudinal lateral and directional stability were also evaluated.

Ship No. 2 was used to evaluate automatic pilot, automatic throttle and automatic flight performance. Tests were conducted in various modes and flight configurations relevant to speed, altitude and Instrument Landing System approaches.

Ship No. 3 was the performance evaluation aircraft. Engine installation evaluations were completed and engine compartment cooling on the ground and during takeoff and climb were demonstrated. Other engine tests included evaluation of the engine fire detection system; airstarts at various altitudes and speeds; climb performance in various flight segments; rejected takeoff stopping distances; minimum control flight speed, two-engine inoperative en route climb performance; two-engine takeoff acceleration; and takeoff time and distance verification.

Ship No. 4 was used to test air conditioning and pressurization systems, communications and navigation equipment, de-icing equipment, flying into actual ice storms, and the auxiliary power unit, under contingency as well as normal operations. She was also designated as the plane to face the new noise tests.

Ship No. 5, the eighth production airplane, was charged to fly 150 hours of functional and reliability tests. She was to be "fitted" into the airline operational pattern. In short, do

The 181-foot-long DC-10 dwarfs a 28-foot replica of the *Spirit of St. Louis,* the Ryan monoplane in which Charles A. Lindbergh made the world's first solo flight across the Atlantic from New York to Paris in 1927. The wide-bodied DC-10, called the *Spirit of St. Louis*—1971 for its trip to the Paris Air Show, is shown parked on the McDonnell Douglas flight ramp in St. Louis prior to leaving for Paris. Both aircraft were products of Southern California and both stopped at St. Louis en route to Le Bourget airport.

The license to fly.

The United States of America
Department of Transportation
Federal Aviation Administration

Type Certificate

Number A22WE

This certificate issued to McDonnell Douglas Corporation
certifies that the type design for the following product with the operating limitations and conditions therefor as specified in the Federal Aviation Regulations and the
Type Certificate Data Sheet, meets the airworthiness requirements of Part 25 of
the Federal Aviation Regulations.

Model DC-10-10

This certificate, and the Type Certificate Data Sheet which is a part hereof,
shall remain in effect until surrendered, suspended, revoked, or a termination date is
otherwise established by the Administrator of the Federal Aviation Administration.

Date of application : 26 December 1967 – original date of application for DC-10
                       20 January 1969 – amended application for DC-10-10
Date of issuance :   29 July 1971

By direction of the Administrator.

(Signature) Robert H. Stanton

(Title) Chief, Aircraft Engineering Division

This certificate may be transferred if endorsed as provided on the reverse hereof.

Any alteration of this certificate and/or the Type Certificate Data Sheet is punishable by a fine of not exceeding $1,000,
or imprisonment not exceeding 3 years, or both.
FAA FORM 8110—9 (7-67) SUPERSEDES FAA FORM 331

Amid pomp and ceremony, DC-10s in American Airlines and United Airlines markings were officially
turned over to the first two carriers.

everything an airliner must do in routine scheduled flying. Part of her test time was done at Los Angeles International Airport where she was just another airliner, coming and going.

No. 5 made history of a sort when she flew non-stop from St. Louis, Missouri, to Paris, France, a distance of 4,518 miles in the record time of 7 hours 45 minutes. Cruising at flight levels of 33,000 to 37,000 feet at a long-range cruise speed of Mach 0.82, she still had 4800 gallons of fuel left when she touched down at LeBourget Airport to become the star of the 29th International Paris Air Show in June 1971.

The author, attending the Air Show, saw the DC-10 for the first time. He decided then and there to one day write this book. One thing impressive about her was the quietness of her engines during takeoff, as compared to the thundrous roar of the SSTs—the Russian TU-144 and the French/British *Concorde*, also present for their public debut.

About the same time that *No. 5* was getting ready to go to Paris, DC-10 No. 4, was en route to the Federal Aviation Administration's National Aviation Facilities Experimental Center (NAFEC) near Atlantic City, New Jersey. The big trijet had undergone the usual static and flight tests on its way to receiving FAA approval of its airworthiness, but this was something new—a special series of trials leading to *noise certification*.

ON DECEMBER 1, 1969, the FAA had enacted Part 36 to the Federal Air Regulations that set noise standards for all new type subsonic aircraft. The new rule responded to Congress' passage of Public Law 90-411 giving the FAA broad authority to set standards for aircraft noise and develop regulations for its control. The new FAA law (Federal Air Regulation Part 36) gave the agency authority to withhold certification of an aircraft that failed to meet the prescribed levels. In this case that meant specifically the DC-10—she was the first of the new subsonic airliners required to pass the test.

The DC-10 had three sound levels to meet during the tests at NADEC in Atlantic City. The plane had to demonstrate that it would generate no more than 105.3 effective

American Airlines DC-10 takes off from Long Beach with American crew on board. It was appropriate for American Airlines to have the honors (United was right behind), because American was first to order DC-10 and launched the program.

perceived noise decibels on takeoff and 106.9 EPNdB in the sideline and approach modes. That was the standard Part 36 called for.

McDonnell Douglas engineers in cooperation with the FAA range officers established the certification measurement stations—in accordance with FAR Part 36—at a point one nautical mile from the runway threshold on centerline for approach; one quarter of a mile to the sideline of the runway; and three-and-a-half miles from the beginning of takeoff roll for the takeoff measurement.

Thus the stage was set for the first noise certification test measurements ever taken at NAFEC, with the DC-10 ready for a busy two-day schedule of flying the acoustical range.

During the testing at NAFEC, the DC-10 made the required number of passes, permitting engineers to obtain a minimum of at least six measurements of the approach and six sideline and takeoff noise levels. After the tests the aircraft was certified as meeting all three specific sound level requirements.

According to John H. Shaffer, the Federal Aviation Administrator—"The DC-10 demonstrated noise levels *below* the standards we had set."

"The advanced technology that has produced the DC-10," Shaffer added, "offers our greatest hope in solving the environmental problems of today and tomorrow."

On May 24, 1971, three years and one month almost to the day (April 25, 1968) when McDonnell Douglas announced the commitment to build the DC-10, the FAA issued a provisional type certificate for the DC-10. She was now just not a new trijet; she was now a *new trijet airliner.*

Then on July 29, 1971, the two DC-10s on the ramp at Long Beach, were the center of attraction at a special ceremony. One proudly wore the colors of American Airlines, the other was all decked out in United Airlines markings. Officially, the two planes were turned over to representatives of the two carriers. Both ships were flown away to the home bases of the two airlines for crew indoctrination in preparation for entering scheduled service.

On August 5, American Airlines' Flight 184, a DC-10 took off from Los Angeles on a round-trip flight to Chicago. It was the first time the DC-10 carried paying passengers on a scheduled flight.

United was not far behind. It inaugurated DC-10 service nine days later flying from San Francisco to Washington, D.C. The decision to make the DC-10 trijet proved she was capable of transcontinental trips as well as medium or short-hauls.

Even so, it was just the beginning. In the nest back at Long Beach a whole new family of DC-10s with intercontinental range capabilities was already being hatched.

Artist's rendition shows McDonnell Douglas KC-10A Advanced Tanker Cargo Aircraft (ATCA) refueling F-15 *Eagle* in flight. MDC has order for twenty of flying gas stations for USAF. KC-10A will be flying in 1980s.

Chapter Sixteen

Another "Rubber" Airplane

THERE LONG HAS BEEN inside the airframe manufacturing community a tongue-in-cheek expression about Douglas airliners. It goes like this: "Don Douglas builds *rubber* airplanes." Anyone knows, of course, this is not true in a material sense. The DC-ships aren't made of rubber, except maybe for the tires and some sealants. But in a "rubber band sense" which stretches and snaps back, there is a certain truism in the phrase.

Certainly, it was true of the DC-1 which was stretched to become the DC-2 and stretched again to become the famous DC-3 and again to become the *Super Three*. Likewise the DC-4 was stretched and stretched and stretched again until there emerged the DC-7C, largest of the propeller-driven commercial airliners. Then came the DC-8, originally with a fuselage length of 150 feet 6 inches to 186 feet 5 inches in the elongated DC-8 *Super Sixty-Three*. About the same "stretch ratio" can be applied to the DC-9 family, culminating with the Super DC-9-80, which is 43.5 feet longer than the first DC-9-10 and capable of carrying 172 passengers as compared with 90 passengers in the original version.

From its very concept the DC-10 was geared for growth. There was to be a DC-10 *Series 20* (later changed to *Series 40*) and a DC-10 *Series 30,* which were intercontinental range aircraft. It was probably this decision to offer a whole family of trijets—medium and long-range—which enabled McDonnell Douglas salesmen to capture the lion's share of a worldwide market. By the end of 1970—six months after the first DC-10 made its maiden flight—the corporation had more than 120 firm orders plus an almost equal number of options from seven U.S. airlines and eleven overseas carriers.

Although there are three versions of the DC-10 plus a DC-10CF (convertible freighter) all have a high degree of commonality. All are identical in arrangement and aerodynamic configuration. Because the long-range *Series 30* and *Series 40* are direct outgrowths of the medium-range DC-10 *Series 10,* no unusual modifications were required to increase the takeoff weight from 430,000 pounds to 555,000 pounds for the DC-10-30 and 572,000 pounds for the DC-10-40. There were, however, some changes made.

The *Series 30* and *Series 40* aircraft emerged with an added three feet to each wing tip. No change was made in the wing planform, but an increase of more than 1100 square feet in wing area provided added lift. There was also added an extra set of dual wheels in the fuselage centerline. Provision for the extra undercarriage had been made in the original DC-10-10 concept. Likewise the aft engine position had originally been sized to accept larger diameter engines that were known to be coming along. And did, in time to power the *Series*

First long-range DC-10 version (Series 20 designation was later changed to Series 40) soars over California's Sierra Nevada mountains during maiden flight. The intercontinental model is designed to transport a full passenger load nearly 6,000 statute miles. Three Pratt & Whitney JT9D-15 turbofan engines, each generating 47,000 pounds of takeoff thrust, powered the DC-10 on its successful 4-hour and 10 minute flight.

DC-10-30 takes off on maiden flight. Series 30 and Series 40 aircraft were designed for inter-continental range. Each has larger wing than DC-10-10 and upgraded engine thrust.

Both DC-10 Series 30 and Series 40 have additional centerline gear to spread added weight on runways and taxistrips.

30 and *Series 40* aircraft.

It is in this area, the powerplants, that the *Series 30* and *Series 40* differ. The former uses the General Electric CF6-50C engines, the latter is powered with the slightly larger diameter Pratt & Whitney JT9D-59A engines.

With these modifications, the *Series 30* and *Series 40* provided further operational flexibility by increasing the DC-10's range to over 5,500 nautical miles. Such performance characteristics make the DC-10 capable of accommodating 99 percent of the world's air travel market.

According to Bill Gross, this range increase was accomplished with about a 14,000-pound increase in structural weight of the aircraft. Equally important, Bill pointed out that it took little more than six months to develop the basic changes to upgrade the DC-10's flexibility.

A fourth member of the trijet family is the DC-10CF, a double-duty trijet designed to carry either passengers or cargo loads. Except for an 8½ by 11½ foot cargo door which swings upward on the left side of the forward fuselage, the DC-10CF closely resembles passenger versions of the transport. The convertible DC-10 is available in the middle-range DC-10-10, and the intercontinental-range *Series 30* and *Series 40* models.

The DC-10CF can accommodate as many as 380 passengers and their baggage, or up to 156,000 pounds of cargo. Total usable cargo space is more than 16,000 cubic feet, with more than 12,000 cubic feet in the main cabin.

In passenger service, the "convertible" can be arranged in various combinations of first-class and economy-class seating.

Travelers ride in luxurious comfort of the conventional DC-10 wide-bodied cabin. But for cargo service, airline mechanics, overnight, can remove seats, carpets, overhead baggage racks, food service modules and other passenger accommodations, leaving 2200 square feet of unobstructed floor area in the main cabin with ceiling heights of eight feet for cargo space.

With special livestock pens set up in the cabin, the DC-10CF can carry up to 385 head of 300-pound cattle on flights between major beef production areas—a fast-developing new market for air transport operators.

Having such versatility, the DC-10 family by the summer of 1979—nine years after the first DC-10 flew—was serving a total of 44 different airline customers.

Customers included: American Airlines, Continental Air Lines, Laker Airways Ltd., National Airlines, Turkish Airlines, United Air Lines, Northwest Airlines, Japan Airlines, Aeromexico, Air Afrique, Air New Zealand, Air Zaire, Alitalia, Ariana Afghan Airlines, Balair, British Caledonian Airways, Condor Flugdienst, CP Air, Finnair, Garuda Indonesian Airways, Iberia Airlines of Spain, Jugoslovenski Aerotransport, KLM Royal Dutch Airlines, Korean Air Lines, Lufthansa German Airlines, Malaysian Airline System, Nigeria Airways, Pakistan International Airlines, Philippine Airlines, Scandinavian Airlines System, Singapore Airlines, Swissair, Thai Airways International, Union de Tran-

Big difference between intercontinental DC-10-30 and DC-10-40 jetliners is in powerplants. The DC-10-30 is powered with General Electric turbofans while DC-10-40 uses Pratt & Whitney turbofans. The P&W engine necessitated slightly larger diameter nacelle.

DC-10CF convertible freighter model can carry up to 380 persons in an all-passenger arrangement, more than 155,000 pounds of cargo in an all-freight configuration or a combination of the two. As a cargo carrier, DC-10CF has a cabin 121 feet long, with total volume exceeding 16,000 cubic feet.

sports Aeriens, VARIG Airlines, VIASA, Wardair and Western Airlines, with Loftleidir Icelandic, Martinair Holland, Sabena Belgian World Airlines, Seaboard World Airlines, Spantax, Trans International Airlines, and World Airways users of the DC-10CF on world routes.

Plans for a DC-10 stretch version long have been on paper, much model testing has been done, and the "Stretch Ten" has generated a great deal of buyer interest from many poten-tial airline customers. Few people doubt that the DC-10 Stretch will go into production as a direct competitor with the high density standard 747, both having about equal passenger capacity.

"With air traffic, passenger and freight, maintaining a steady growth rate," one Douglas sales executive explained, "We've simply got to push for a growth version to keep the DC-10 family the leader that it is in the air transport market. Otherwise, that company

Peering into the capacious cabin of a cargo-carrying DC-10CF is like looking into a New York subway. The DC-10CF houses 30 standard 88x108-inch pallets of freight in its 121-foot-long and almost 19-foot-wide cabin. Interior has an area of 2200 square feet and volume of more than 16,000 cubic feet, equivalent to space available in four 40-foot class railroad freight cars.

up north will grab off a juicy plum."

He added: "Our surveys show a potential market for the king-size airliner of the DC-10 Stretch and 747 class to be 700 to 800 aircraft over the next ten to twelve years!"

According to DC-10 program planners, the "rubber airplane" philosophy would apply to all three of the now in-service DC-10 family— the DC-10-10, DC-10-30 and DC-10-40 jetliners. Although maintaining the original DC-10 profile, the DC-10 Stretch would embody, besides dimensional increases, the latest advanced technology in materials, aerodynamic design, and powerplants. Definitely, it would be a *second generation* for the famous DC-10 family.

A closer look at the proposed DC-10 growth versions describes some of the modifications made to the basic models of the trijet family.

Fuselage length on all models (DC-10-10, DC-10-30 and DC-10-40) will include a 21.7 ft. extension, accomplished by "plugs" fore and aft of the wing. The stretched DC-10 will have a fuselage length of 203 feet 3 inches as compared with the original lengths—181 feet 5 inches for Dash Ten and Dash Thirty models and 182 feet 1 inch for the Dash Forty model.

The basic DC-10-10 will keep its original wing dimensions, but the DC-10-30 and DC-10-40 will have extensions bringing the wingspan to 165 feet 4 inches as compared with the original 161 feet 4 inch wing. The new dimensional wing will have new nacelles with longer ducts for improved noise characteristics. It will also include some update aerodynamics, new flap arrangement and use of more composite materials for weight reduction. Wing planform will follow the basic DC-10 outline.

For power plants the DC-10-10 Stretch will use General Electric CF6 series engines uprated to 46,500 pound thrust, an increase of almost 5,000 lb. thrust per engine. The DC-10-30 will also use GE power plants, but with increased thrust ratings upwards of 50,000 lb. thrust. Pratt & Whitney JT9D engines of 50,000 lb. thrust, standard in the DC-10-40 models, likely upgraded in power ratings, will go into long-range intercontinental DC-10s.

Translated into some general performance figures, the DC-10 Stretch versions will produce increased payloads, seating, cargo and range extension. The DC-10-10 Stretch, for example, will have a gross takeoff weight of approximately 470,000 lbs., an increase of some 30,000 lbs. over the standard model. In mixed class seating arrangement the longer DC-10-10 will be capable of carrying 342 passengers as compared with 264 in the original concept. In range it will have an increase of

A proposed intercontinental version of extended fuselage DC-10 would carry 353 passengers in a mixed class cabin on nonstop flights of more than 6000 statute miles. Aircraft would have five-foot tip extensions on the wings and would be powered by three 52,000 to 55,000-pound-thrust engines housed in long-duct nacelles. This aircraft would consume less fuel and offer lower operating costs per seat mile.

about 200 nautical miles.

In the DC-10-30 and the DC-10-40 stretch versions, gross takeoff weights will be about 603,000 lbs. Seating will be increased to 352 as compared to 275 in the standard models. With full passenger load, the stretched versions will have a 5400 nautical mile range.

With such capabilities, the new family of "stretched trijets" will be comparable to standard 747 performance—plus the advantage of three engine economy.

IF THE DC-10 could be stretched, it could also be made smaller. Like a rubber band, the "rubber airplane" philosophy had to have snap-back properties built in. Consequently, Douglas engineers took a long look at several smaller DC-10 concepts. Most seriously considered was a DC-10 Twin, an almost exact copy of the standard DC-10 in profile, but minus the third engine in the tail, with a shorter fuselage, but a larger wing. The Twin idea was dropped, and there came into being a whole new design, the DCX-200, another twin-engine design, but incorporating many advanced features, even though still having, in general, a commonality with the basic DC-10 family. The DCX-200 also never got much farther than the drawing board. Although (pardon, no pun intended) it is still in the wings.

Originally, the DC-10 Twin was the solid choice to be the next member of the DC-10 family. Its fuselage was almost identical to the DC-10-10 but ten feet shorter in the forward section. The cockpit, however, was the same. Gone from the empennage (tail) was the straight-through-flow third engine. Added were larger vertical and horizontal stabilizers.

Essentially, the wing was the same as that of the DC-10, but with three foot wing tip extensions. By comparison the original DC-10 had a wingspan of 155.3 feet, while the Twin had a wingspan of 161.3 feet. Actually, in profile and size, it looked so much like the European Airbus Industrie A-200B coming on that one wag called it "Les Frenchman's Folly."

At that time (1972-73), neither the French Airbus nor the DC-10 Twin "caught on" with the airline market. Both, it was said, were too large and too expensive to operate. The airlines, surveys showed, were more interested in a wide-bodied twin with 180 to 200 passenger capacity. The DC-10 Twin had a seating

capacity of 265. Efforts were made to scale down the Twin, but it still came out too BIG, too costly.

One engineer put it this way: "With only two engines, there was no way we could get away from the larger wing. When we looked at a new wing, the DCX-200 design emerged. Before we knew it, we had a new wide-body concept going."

The DCX-200, originally it was Model D-969N-18D/18F, was aimed at the then airline needs, with interior arrangements in a mixed class version for 18 first class passengers and 180 economy class, total 198. There was also a high density seating arrangement for a total of 226 passengers. It was also programmed for a growth version, 248 passengers. There was no secret; it was designed to be the American competitor with the French Airbus. Douglas officials preferred to say, however, that it was designed to replace larger DC-9 models and Boeing 727s. As it turned out, DCX-200 never got the chance to prove its intended purpose.

To some degree, the DCX-200 was common to the DC-10, and in all fairness, should be considered an offspring of the family. Certainly, it could be called a "first cousin."

Cockpit, the forward fuselage section, aft fuselage section, and engine nacelles were identical to the DC-10, with the exception of the shorter fuselage. Fuselage length was 140.5 feet, ten feet shorter than the DC-10 Twin, twenty feet shorter than the DC-10 original. There, however, the likeness stopped. The wing was something very new.

Eugene Dubil, whom we met earlier as Chief Design Engineer of the DC-10, and now Vice President Engineering for Douglas, relates it this way: "We had done a lot of extensive wing experiments to develop the supercritical wing for our YC-15 Advanced Medium STOL transport (See Chapter 19) and it seemed natural to use this background in the development of the wing for the DCX-200. For one thing, we were sure it would give the aircraft good short field capability, bringing the wide-body airliner into service for smaller communities where long runways do not exist."

He pointed out that the supercritical wing would mean a much smaller wing area, a different sweepback angle, increased thickness, flaps on both the leading edge and trailing edge providing a vastly "improved high lift system." Such features, it was said, would permit higher cruise speeds while at the same time having greater lift potential in the slow speed range.

Propulsion for the DCX-200 involved consideration of new king-size turbo fan engines being developed by General Electric, Pratt & Whitney and Rolls Royce, and ranging from 40,000 lb. to 53,000 lb. thrust. Neither airframe nor engines got to a finalized acceptance stage when the DCX-200 project was cancelled. At least, for the time being.

Probably the main reason for the "drop out" was the sudden upsurge of orders for the European Airbus A300 and its successor A300B. For the first time in years, one major U.S. air carrier had ordered a foreign-built airliner. And it seemed likely that the European airlines, once a stronghold for Douglas, would turn to the Airbus. Competing against the government-financed European industry with private monies seemed to many, at least — and, perhaps rightly so—a kind of one-sided gamble. Playing against a stacked deck.

Perhaps another influencing factor in the cancellation of the DCX-200 program was that Lockheed was offering a 220-230 passenger medium range version of its L-1011 TriStar. The L-1011-400 was about to make its first flight when, in mid-summer 1978, Douglas announced plans to abandon the DCX-200 project.

Boeing also was in on the act with the announcement of its 767-200 medium range transport. Moreover, Boeing had some firm orders for its 197-passenger version (United Airlines) with other customers waiting in line.

The DCX-200 remained, unfortunately, an unknown.

Douglas turned to the development of other DC-10 derivatives. "It seemed the better way to go," explained Douglas Aircraft Company President John Brizedine. "It would cost a billion to a billion and a half dollars to successfully launch a new medium range aircraft program."

McDonnell Douglas, however, as we shall see, has other plans for the day after tomorrow.

MEANWHILE OTHER VERSIONS of the DC-10 are making their debut. There is, for example, the DC-10 All Freighter, and the new KC-10 flying tanker. Both programs have assured the DC-10 family a long life. And who knows? Like its distinguished and famous "grandmother," the DC-3, which saw combat in Vietnam skies as a gunship, the DC-10 could one day become an airborne missile

Proposed new wide-cabin jet transport under study in Long Beach was designated the DCX-200. A twin-engine aircraft, the DCX-200 was proposed as a replacement for narrow-cabin short-to-medium-range jetliners. As envisioned by McDonnell Douglas engineers, the twinjet would carry about 200 passengers in a cabin almost 19 feet wide, same as the DC-10. Fuselage would be 138 feet long, and wingspan would be 150 feet. Tail height would be 52 feet. Advances in the DCX-200 would include a supercritical wing and advanced high-lift system. DCX-200 would offer considerable improvement over narrow-cabin jets in terms of fuel economy, passenger comfort, and cost of operation.

launcher.

The DC-10 All Freighter. Derivatives of the basic DC-10-30 and DC-10-40 series line of convertible freighters have produced a new family member that Douglas calls the DC-10 All Freighter. Exterior dimensions of the All Freighter are the same as the DC-10-30CF, the major outer profile change being the elimination of all cabin windows. Indeed, the DC-10 All Freighter is a huge flying boxcar, not a passenger car or Pullman.

Replacing the windows are huge cargo doors on each side of the aircraft. There is a forward cargo door (104 inches x 66 inches) on the right side just ahead of the wing. On the left side to the rear of the cockpit is a larger main cargo door (120 inches x 140 inches) plus a center cargo door (104 inches x 66 inches) on the right side just aft of the trailing edge of the wing, and a bulk cargo door (30 inches x 36 inches) on the left side just forward of the horizontal stabilizer. These huge doors permit rapid loading and unloading of a variety of cargoes. The All Freighter is adaptable to carry all standard sized pallets and containers.

Powered with the General Electric CF6-50J engines or the Pratt & Whitney JT9D-59A engines, the All Freighter has a payload capability of from 177,000 pounds to 182,000 pounds. Domestic versions have a range of 2500 statute miles with maximum payload, while the international versions have a range

DC-10 ALL FREIGHTER

More than 91 tons of cargo could be transported from New York to London or from Anchorage to Tokyo in the proposed DC-10AF. Jetliner would be powered by either the General Electric CF6-50J or the Pratt & Whitney Aircraft JT9D-59A advanced turbofan engines.

Cut-away drawing shows DC-10 All Freighter's pallet-carrying capability. Lower hold takes standard freight packages and/or bulk shipments.

of 3500 nautical miles. Total cargo space available is 17,714 cubic feet for main deck and lower holds. DC-10AF is the first of the trijets in an all freighter configuration. There is likelihood that it will join the airline fleets in the 1980s.

The KC-10A ATCA (Advanced Tanker/Cargo Aircraft). Powered by three General Electric CF6-50C1 turbofan engines, the KC-10A tanker can deliver 200,000 pounds of fuel to a receiver 2200 statute miles from the home base and return, or it can carry a maximum cargo payload of 170,000 pounds a distance of 4370 statute miles. Unrefueled ferry range of the KC-10A is 11,500 statute miles.

Design fuel capacity is 356,065 pounds, including a maximum of 238,565 pounds in the standard wing tankage and a maximum of 117,500 pounds stored in seven fuel cells below the main deck.

For its cargo-carrying assignments, the KC-10A has a total usable cargo space exceeding 12,000 cubic feet in its spacious cabin. The cabin has a maximum width of almost 19 feet, ceiling height of 8.5 feet and a floor area of 2200 square feet.

In an all-cargo configuration, the KC-10A accommodates 25 standard 88 x 108-inch cargo pallets in the cabin with aisles down both sides, or 27 pallets with a single aisle.

Gross takeoff weight of the KC-10A is 590,000 pounds, up from 555,000 pounds for the standard DC-10 intercontinental commercial model.

Under a separate contract McDonnell Douglas is also developing an advanced refueling boom system for its flying tanker. The new system, already tested, can transfer fuel at the rate of 1800 gals. per minute!

Further, McDonnell Douglas has designed a completely new refueling station to be installed in the lower aft fuselage of the ATCA. With room for a crew of three—observer, trainee and refueling boom operator—the station will have many improvements over present jet tankers of the KC-135 class. Seats for crew members will replace the reclining couch, and the refueling station will take advantage of the DC-10's much advanced heating and airflow environment.

If the ATCA program goes as expected, the first of the new cargo/tankers will be completed in February 1980, with the first flight some time in mid-April of that year.

According to Louis F. Harrington, KC-10A program manager at Long Beach, the new

KC-10A tanker has capacity to fly out and meet other tankers (KC-135s) to replenish their supply so that smaller "flying gas stations" can rendezvous with fighters far from home bases. KC-10A would then have fuel enough to return home.

Combat role of DC-10? This is artist's concept of DC-10 as cruise missile launcher. Modified DC-10 would carry two or four missiles and launch them tailward. Because of long-range of DC-10 launcher, small "cruise" missiles with A-heads could become ICBMs (Intercontinental Ballistic Missiles).

tanker/cargo DC-10 will be integrated right into the commercial DC-10 production lines.

He pointed out these modifications to the commercial DC-10CF—Elimination of upper deck windows and lower deck cargo doors; provisions for additional crew; a flexible capability for accommodating additional support personnel; receptacle for in-flight refueling of the KC-10A itself; military avionics; director lights for aircraft being served; supplemental fuselage fuel tanks; modernized aerial refueling operator station; hose reel with drogue for refueling Navy and other probe-equipped aircraft; advanced aerial refueling boom, and an improved cargo handling system.

Describing it as "an advanced version of the intercontinental-range DC-10CF convertible freighter," Harrington outlined the missions of the new tanker cargo aircraft.

"It will refuel fighters and simultaneously carry the fighters' support equipment and support personnel on overseas deployments," he explained. "It will also refuel strategic airlifters (such as the USAF C-5 and C-141) during overseas deployments and resupply missions, and augment USAF cargo carrying capability."

"In most cases," he added, "the KC-10A will perform these missions without dependence on overseas bases, and without depleting critical fuel supplies in the theater of operations."

Some further performance characteristics of the KC-10A are described in a company brochure:

The aerial refueling capability of the KC-10A nearly doubles the nonstop range of a fully-loaded C-5 strategic transport. In addition, its cargo capability enables the U.S. to deploy fighter squadrons and their unit support personnel and equipment with a single airplane type, instead of requiring both tanker and cargo aircraft.

BEYOND ITS ROLE in the military

inventory as a "flying gas station," the DC-10 is also being considered as a missile carrier for the proposed MX advanced Intercontinental Ballistic Missile. A modified DC-10, according to McDonnell Douglas planners, could be used to air launch the new missile.

Having the lift capacity to carry two of the big ICBMs, the DC-10 could be modified to permit launching of the missiles using a rearward ejection system.

If this ever happens—and it probably won't—the DC-10 could one day be classified as a "combat aircraft."

Meanwhile, part of the McDonnell Douglas story must show that both McDonnell Aircraft Corporation and the Douglas Aircraft Company, long before the merger, were active in pioneering the design and development of a variety of missiles.

Delta 3914 launches an RCA *Satcom* communications satellite.

Chapter Seventeen

Missile Makers

IT WAS ABOUT the same time that the Davis-Douglas Company was starting up back in 1920, when a small group of men at McCook Field, Dayton, Ohio, gathered on the flight line to watch the experimental launch of a strange new kind of flying machine. McCook Field, named after Civil War General Anson McCook, at that time, was the experimental test and procurement center for the Army Air Service. Among the observers present was Charles F. Kettering, the famous inventor (self-starter, ethyl gasoline), and a young Lieutenant, George Holloman, later to become a general in World War II, killed in action, and for whom Holloman Field in Alamogordo, N.M. is named. Kettering and Holloman were the designers of the unusual aircraft to be tested that day. Both believed it would revolutionize aerial bombardment operations. The future would prove them right. What they had built was the first flying bomb—the day of the missile was born.

True, it was a crude beginning, but the principle was there—pilotless missiles carrying lethal loads of destruction.

The Kettering-Holloman "missile" was a biplane, its fuselage shaped like a fat bomb and loaded with dynamite. It was powered by a two-cylinder motorcycle engine and two-bladed steel propeller. There was no radio control or automatic guidance system. The idea was to point the "winged bomb" in the direction of a predetermined target area, fill it with enough fuel to keep it in flight until it reached the target, when the engine would quit, and it would dive to the ground (or glide) and explode upon impact. The fin-like rudder and horizontal stabilizer had "fixed" controls to effect lift-off and arrow-like flight. It was launched from a special platform like a railroad handcar running along a metal track—the track "aimed" in the direction of the target.

Several of the "flying bombs" were built and tested over short distances. But the idea was dropped for lack of interest. In 1920, even the army was tired of war-making devices.

Holloman, however, never did give up on the idea. In 1937-38, when he was Chief of the Equipment Laboratory at Wright Field, Dayton, Ohio—successor to Old McCook Field—he and a civilian electronics wizard, Ray Stout, built several miniature aircraft (models with the wing span varying from five to ten feet), and they loaded the fuselages with high explosives. Only this time it was different—they had devised a radio-control system for the models, and the "flying bombs" became our first guided missiles.

George Holloman once told this writer—"We could make these things a helluva lot larger, the equivalent of carrying a 2,000-pound bomb, and we could, by radio control, "home" them on any radio station, anywhere. They could explode on contact, or we could electronically send a signal to explode them

The Kettering-Holloman flying bomb of 1920.

amid an attacking formation of aircraft . . .''

We didn't think about it right then, but he was talking about the day of "push-button" warfare.

The threat, of course, came home with sudden frightfulness when the Nazi launched their V-1 glide bombs and their V-2 missiles against London in the latter days of World War II. And from that moment on, missile development in the U.S. became an important phase of the aircraft manufacturing industry. Both Douglas Aircraft Company and McDonnell Aircraft Corporation would become leaders in the design and development of a variety of missiles and rockets.

McDONNELL DOUGLAS has been engaged in the design, development and manufacture of missiles as long as, if not longer, than any other aerospace firm. As far back as 1940-41, *before* Pearl Harbor, the Douglas Aircraft Company in Santa Monica developed an air-to-ground, 1,000-pound rocket equipped with a homing device that directed it to ground targets. Its secret was radar detection linked to electronic controls, at a time when the word *radar* had not yet been invented. They called it *ROC-1,* purely an experimental rocket. *ROC-II,* a tactical version, came along too late to be used in World War II, but it put Douglas in the missile business.

Today the McDonnell Douglas Astronautics Company (MDAC) is the division of McDonnell Douglas Corporation which has the responsibility for the design, development and production of missiles, space boosters, and space vehicles. Its headquarters are in Huntington Beach, California, with plants in St. Louis and Titusville, Florida. Since *ROC-1,* Douglas Aircraft and McDonnell Aircraft

(now one) have produced more than 100,000 separate units of missiles and space launchers for the Army, Navy, Air Force, and the National Aeronautics and Space Administration.

These devices include air-to-surface, air-to air, ground-to-air, surface-to-surface vehicles with nuclear and non-nuclear warheads and a variety of guidance systems. They range in size from the tube-like *Dragon,* an anti-tank missile that one man can carry, to the towering *Delta* launch vehicle that stands as high as a ten story building. In addition, McDonnell Douglas is engaged in the development of underwater devices such as the ALWT program, an advanced lightweight torpedo, and *PRAM,* a propelled rapid ascent mine.

MDAC missiles have names that boggle the imagination—*Sparrow, Nike Zeus, Honest John, Bird Dog, Thor, Katydid, Gargoyle*—each with a specific mission. The list could go on and on. To describe them all would fill a Sears Roebuck catalogue, but it is noteworthy to elaborate on a few which in their own right have had strong impact on America's defense, strike potential, and space programs.

THE *Nike* family of missiles—*Ajax, Hercules* and *Zeus*—is a good example of missiles for defense. It was in the latter part of 1944, when Nazi V-weapons were first introduced, that a young first lieutenant in the Army's Frankfort Arsenal Fire Control Development Office broached his superiors with the idea for a rocket or jet propelled projectile controlled by radio commands from the ground. The Army was impressed. The idea was proposed to the Bell Telephone Laboratories, a subsidiary of Western Electric. Could Bell come up with a guidance

Katydid, an early McDonnell missile program.

KUD-1 *Gargoyle*, a radio-controlled dive bomb.

Honest John was used like a huge artillery gun.

Nike Zeus defensive missile.

Nike Hercules at White Sands test range in New Mexico.

higher speeds of new jet fighters and bombers then on the drawing boards.

Ajax emerged as a two-stage rocket, 20 feet long, one foot in diameter, weighing about 1,000 pounds with a 300-pound warhead, non-nuclear. The long telephone-pole-like missile had two sets of fins, one in the nose and one farther aft, with a vertical and horizontal stabilizer. It used both solid propellant (rocket fuel) and liquid propellant (standard jet fuel) for its propulsion systems. Inside the tube were two sets of radar, one for tracking the target, another for guiding the missile on the basis of tracking information. *Ajax* had a range of about 30 miles.

Its development did not come easy, probably because the state of the art in missile development at that time was the state of the art of developing the state of the art. It was nine years after the concept of the system, that the first *Nike-Ajax* battery became operational in December of 1953 at Fort George Meade, Maryland. After that, *Ajax* sites sprang up all over the countryside.

Nike-Hercules was next, an improved and enlarged version—27 feet long, 2.5 feet in diameter—and capable of carrying an atomic warhead. *Hercules* doubled the range, and it was 1,000 mph faster than *Ajax*. The Army said of *Hercules*—"It can fly out and attack a fleet of attacking aircraft at high altitudes and destroy them with its atomic warhead without damage to surrounding terrain." It did not say what damage might be caused by the falling debris of the destroyed air fleets.

There followed in logical order, development of the *Nike-Zeus* weapons system, designed as an anti-missile-missile. *Zeus*, a three-stage rocket using solid propellant fuel only, equipped with latest radar detection and tracking systems and linked to a computerized control system, could seek out and destroy oncoming missiles.

In tests against our own *Atlas* Intercontinental Ballistic Missiles launched from California, *Zeus* missiles on Kwajalein Island successfully destroyed the approaching missiles. For a missile developed in the mid and late 1960s, *Nike-Zeus* was far ahead of its time.

Nike batteries around strategic target areas were America's front line defense against any attack by aircraft or missiles. It was almost certain that any attacking force would suffer great losses, give us time to

system for such a weapon? Bell accepted the challenge. By December 1944, Bell came to Douglas Aircraft, already known for its role in the *ROC-1* and *ROC-2* guided bombs. If Bell came up with the guidance system, could Douglas design, develop and build the missile to accept it?

The team that gave us *ROC-1* and *ROC-2* accepted the challenge. But it was not until shortly after VJ-Day in the fall of 1945 that Don Douglas accepted the responsibility as prime subcontractor to the Western Electric-Bell Laboratories organization to build the missile hardware. They called it *Nike-Ajax*—in the broadest sense, a long-range, self-propelled anti-aircraft weapon. In Rocket Age jargon, they call it a *surface-to-air* missile. Its primary mission—to replace anti-aircraft batteries whose biggest guns could no longer reach the higher altitudes, or track the launch retaliatory attacks on the enemy. That was the name of the game in the early fifties—*retaliation*.

The idea was never to become the aggressor. But if any enemy should strike first, be able to *retaliate* with a powerful bomber or missile force and obliterate his forces. Indeed, that was Presidential policy and Pentagon policy.

Retaliate with what?

It was true we had a growing force of high flying, 600-mile-an-hour B-52 bombers capable of delivering the A-bomb and even the more deadly H-bomb. But the concept, or precept, of launching an intercontinental ballistic missile (ICBM) from bases in this country to arc into the ionosphere and drop down on enemy targets was far from reality. At this point in time, we didn't have any ICBM. Our missile force, capable of ranges of 5,000 miles or more, was still in the planning and development stage.

There were some good ICBMs abuilding, but there were none on the launching pads. Intelligence reports were alarming: They told of Russian missiles (ICBMs) with nuclear warheads being built by the numbers. In five years, the National Security Council warned, the USSR would have a commanding missile lead, and it was likely we could never catch up. The Russian ICBMs, pad-ready pointing at vital U.S. centers, posed a definite threat to peace. The so-called "cold war" could, at their will, suddenly become a very HOT one. Moreover, the Russian Bear was making growling sounds, flexing his muscles. Khrushchev, the Russian leader, was getting bolder and bolder.

Something had to be done to fill the missile gap. A step in the right direction was the decision to build an IRBM—Intermediate Range Ballistic Missile—to fill the breach until our own ICBMs could become operational.

Our IRBM was given a name. They called it *Thor* after the Norse God of Thunder. And on Christmas Eve 1955, the Air Force announced that Douglas Aircraft Company of Santa Monica, was the winner in the competition to build the *Thor* missile. Two days later, Douglas signed the contract to design, develop and deliver the IRBM as soon as possible. The game of catch-up couldn't wait.

USAF *Thor*, produced by Douglas, was an Intermediate Range Ballistic Missile which held the line until Intercontinental Ballistic Missiles came along. Here, it carries an *ASSET* vehicle, developed by McDonnell to expand the technology of lifting body reentry.

Douglas was prime contractor, responsible for airframe, systems integration and supporting ground equipment. The Rocketdyne Division of North American Aviation would build the propulsion systems. A.C. Spark Plug Division of General Motors would be responsible for the guidance systems. And the General Electric Company would build the nose cone and the warheads. It was a big "team" playing for very high stakes.

Before the *Thor* program was over there would be a whole family of *Thors*. They would fulfill their prime objective as a deterrent force, capable of instant retaliatory action, and, as well serve as launch vehicles for pioneering U.S. space satellites. Operational from bases in England, *Thors* minimized the Soviet ICBM threat until our own *Atlas*, *Titan* and *Minuteman* long-range ICBMS were in position.

There was so much urgency for the *Thor*

Mighty Thor in readiness at launch sites in England. It was our "Sunday Punch" until long-range ICBM's came along.

program that no prototype was ever built. It is also interesting to note that the basic design of *Thor* was completed in about eight months. What emerged was a missile 65 feet in length, 8 feet in diameter, with a gross weight of 110,000 pounds. *Thor* had a range of 1500 miles. The first *Thor* was launched on January 25, 1957, one year and one month from the date of the first production order.

By early 1958, *Thor* missiles were in position at bases in England. *Thor* was ready. With its deadly nuclear warhead, it could be launched in fifteen minutes, pierce the sky at ten thousand miles per hour, come screaming down on Moscow or other targets in the Soviet Union less than five minutes later. There could be little doubt *Thor* was a deterrent threat.

It has been said that when Khrushchev "got tough" with Eisenhower over the U-2 Spyplane incident in 1960, Ike quieted him down with *Thor* as his "big stick."

Perhaps, the greatest tribute of all for *Thor* is that it has been called *"the DC-3 of the Space Age!"*

THOR was the largest weapons system missile developed by McDonnell Douglas. That is strictly in the sense of being a defensive missile bomb. There is, however, a long list of smaller missiles which, one way or another, fitted into the weapons category. These include: *Sparrow I* and *Sparrow II,* developed for the U.S. Navy as an air-to-air missile. *Honest John,* a surface-to-surface missile with an atomic warhead, having a short range about equal to average artillery fire. *Genie,* an air-to-air missile, the first to have an atomic warhead. *Gargoyle,* one of the first rocket-propelled, radio-controlled glide bombs. All of these were missiles developed in the early years of the new art of missile warfare.

Today, McDonnell Douglas scientists, engineers and technicians are still busy with the development of advanced defense systems such as *Dragon* and *Harpoon* missiles, ballistic missile defense programs and systems for *Cruise* missiles. Perhaps, a closer look at programs of late 1979-80 is in order.

Harpoon is an all-weather, over-the-horizon, anti-ship missile system. The *Harpoon* serves as the U. S. Navy's basic anti-ship missile for fleetwide use. High survivability and kill probability are assured by *Harpoon's* low-level cruise trajectory, active

Harpoon missile launched from a fast hydrofoil boat.

radar guidance, counter-countermeasures, and effective warhead design. *Harpoon* may be launched from surface ships, aircraft, and submarines, and is compatible with current launch and fire control systems. A dedicated reuseable canister permits integration with existing ship and aircraft launch systems.

The M-47 *Dragon,* a medium range anti-tank assault weapon, was developed by Mc-Donnell Douglas for the U.S. Army and Marine Corps. More than 50,000 *Dragon* missiles were produced before follow-on production contracts were awarded to Raytheon by the Army at the end of 1977. McDonnell

Infantryman shoulders *Dragon* anti-tank missile.

Douglas continues to provide engineering services for *Dragon* and to build training and maintenance devices for the Marine Corps and international users, and to work with the Army on development of follow-on systems.

The *Dragon* is the Army's first guided missile system light enough to be carried and fired by one man, yet powerful enough to destroy tanks and other fortified battlefield targets.

McDonnell Douglas is also providing the navigation and guidance systems for *Tomahawk* cruise missiles under a full-scale development contract with the Joint Cruise Missile Project, as well as the navigation and guidance equipment for the Boeing Air Launched *Cruise Missile.*

The *Tomahawk* missile, for which General Dynamics Corporation is the airframe and systems integration contractor, is designed to fly at high subsonic speed and low altitude, striking land or ship targets with great accuracy.

Two distinct guidance systems are employed, one for land attack missiles, the other for antiship missiles. The guidance system for the land attack *Tomahawk* employs terrain correlation for navigation updating. At launch, the system's inertial guidance platform is provided with the location of the launch platform and the target. Operating autonomously, the guidance system directs the missile over a circuitous flightpath to the target. While flying over land, downlooking radar is used to construct terrain altitude profiles along preselected segments of the flightpath. This information is compared with computer-stored digital map data to provide corrections to the missile's flightpath. With each terrain correlation update, the accuracy of the missile's flightpath is improved. Consequently, the missile achieves previously unattainable levels of target accuracy.

ANTISHIP MISSILE—The antiship version of *Tomahawk* has the basic active radar guidance system now used in the McDonnell Douglas *Harpoon* antiship missile. In addition, the *Tomahawk* version employs passive detection and identification features.

Launched in the general direction of an enemy warship, the missile flies to a preprogrammed distance where it climbs slightly to its search altitude. There the mis-

USAF Quail was decoy for B-52 bombers.

sile detects and identifies the target. At this point the missile streaks toward the target ship. Operational range of the antiship version is several hundred miles.

UNDERWATER DEVICES: The U. S. Navy selected McDonnell Douglas as one of the prime candidates for the development of the Advanced Lightweight Torpedo (ALWT). The program benefits from the McDonnell Douglas advanced technology base in hydrodynamics, acoustics, propulsion, guidance, materials, and advanced warhead design.

McDonnell Douglas won a design program for ALWT, the Navy's Advanced Lightweight Torpedo.

Another Navy underwater program is Propelled Rapid Ascent Mine (PRAM). The PRAM program was conceived at the (NSWC) Naval Surface Weapons Center. It is the first of a series of mine developments to be used against submarine and surface targets. PRAM's component parts utilize hardware compatible with the wide range of missile, guidance and warhead experience at MDAC.

The systems analysis skills of McDonnell Douglas are being applied to develop Naval threat scenarios that will help in the offense and defense of the fleet. These threats have been used in its ASW, Surface Warfare, and Air Warfare systems designs. They have been instrumental in identifying the potential Naval Systems requirements for the future.

MISSILE DEFENSE TECHNOLOGY: The U.S. Army's Ballistic Missile Defense Systems Technology Program is a research and development effort dedicated to the development of technology needed for defending the United States against all types of potential ballistic missile attacks.

As the System Engineering, Design and Integration Contractor, McDonnell Douglas Astronautics Company has direct responsibility for the operation of the Systems Technology Test Facility (STTF) at the Kwajalein Missile Range in the Marshall Islands, South Pacific. Equipped with an advanced phased array radar, data processors and related computers, this facility is used in the development and testing of new BMD elements/sub-systems in a total system context in a realistic operational environment.

Currently, the STTF is being used to search, detect and track reentry vehicles launched by *Minuteman* from Vandenberg

Harpoon missile launched from submarine.

McDonnell produced airframes and integrated ramjet engines for the Navy's *Talos*, a supersonic, surface-to-air missile.

AFB, California. Emphasis is on the Terminal Defense Mode. This is where the engagement would occur at altitudes 60,000 to 100,000 feet, usually in the earth's atmosphere. The system filters out radar return from missile tank fragments to separate them from reentry vehicles and decoys prior to track and discrimination. Discrimination then permits the distinguishing of reentry vehicles from decoys.

This development and testing is a coordinated effort of the Army Ballistic Missile Defense Systems Command and industry contractors. Working in close cooperation for many years, they constitute an important national resource.

A key defense issue facing the U.S. is the growing threat to *Minuteman.* To meet this increasing threat in the 1980s, maximum use must be made of past state-of-the-art accomplishments combined with advanced and promising new concepts.

FOLLOWING its *Thor* family of missiles, McDonnell Douglas was selected as the prime contractor to build the S-IV upper stage for the giant *Saturn* program. The program represented many advances in the areas of rocket technology, *Saturn I* being the test-bed for liquid hydrogen and liquid oxygen as a high-energy propellant combination, S-IV, it is said, made *Saturn I* the first totally successful large launch ever built.

The S-IVB stage of *Saturn IB* and *Saturn V* was a missile 21.7 feet in diameter, towering to a height of 58.4 feet, capable of developing 200,000 pounds of thrust from its bi-propellant J-2 engine using liquid hydrogen and liquid oxygen fuels. An aluminum airframe, S-IVB, later in its development, would be used to become a vital part of the *Skylab* operation (See Chapter 18). As the upper stage of the *Saturn* launch systems, the McDonnell Douglas S-IVB played a significant role in America's lunar landing program. It placed the *Apollo* and lunar modules in orbit and sent them on their way to the moon. The S-IVB participated in all the *Apollo* manned space flights, including the historic *Apollo* 11 mission that in July 1969 landed the first men on the moon.

Most famous of the McDonnell Douglas launch vehicles is the vaunted *Delta,* 116-feet in height, eight feet in diameter. A development from *Thor*, *Delta* has been in production at the MDAC (McDonnell Douglas Astronautics Company) in Huntington Beach, California, for many years.

The versatile *Delta* has launched most U. S. meteorological, communications, and scientific satellites, as well as numerous international satellites.

Delta has hurled payloads into low circular Earth orbits, into synchronous transfer orbits, into eliptical orbits extending 270,000 miles into space, and into orbit about the sun, 93 million miles from Earth. Its payloads have varied in size from the 100-foot diameter Echo 1 to the 28-inch diameter Syncom B, and in weight from the 80-pound Explorer X to the 2400-pound OSO-1.

Since its first launch on May 13, 1960, the building-block evolution of *Delta* has resulted in improved payload performance at a fraction of the cost to develop new rockets for increasingly difficult space assignments.

The first improvement was a more powerful *Thor* first stage, in 1962. A more powerful third stage was used in 1963. The first version to employ three strap-on solid motors ap-

A Saturn S-IVB stage being readied for assembly with the Saturn 1B first stage. Service tower is in foreground. (Cape Canaveral Kennedy Space Center)

The expended Saturn S-IVB stage, photographed from the Apollo 7 spacecraft during transposition and docking maneuvers at an approximate altitude of 124 nautical miles.

Full-scale mockup of the Army's *Spartan* anti-missile, a long-range interceptor for the Safeguard Ballistic Missile Defense System. *Spartan* is 55 feet long and can intercept warheads outside the earth's atmosphere. The Army tests the missile at the Kwajalein Test Site in the Marshall Islands.

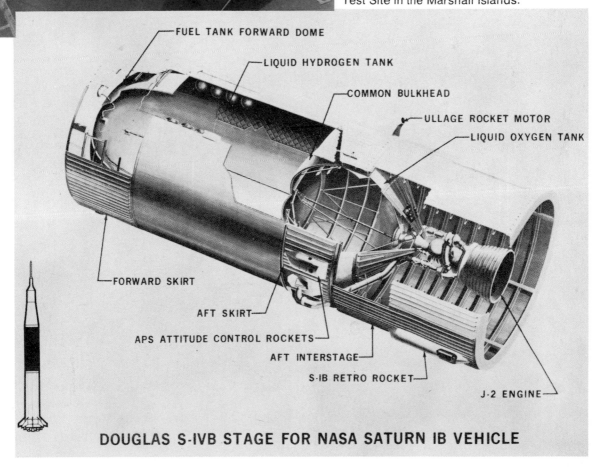

FUEL TANK FORWARD DOME

LIQUID HYDROGEN TANK

COMMON BULKHEAD

ULLAGE ROCKET MOTOR

LIQUID OXYGEN TANK

FORWARD SKIRT

AFT SKIRT

APS ATTITUDE CONTROL ROCKETS

AFT INTERSTAGE

S-IB RETRO ROCKET

J-2 ENGINE

DOUGLAS S-IVB STAGE FOR NASA SATURN IB VEHICLE

peared in 1964. A *Delta* with a larger diameter second stage was launched in 1965. The Long Tank *Delta* with a longer *Thor* first stage appeared in 1968, followed in 1969 by a version that increased the solid strap-on motors to six.

The straight-eight *Delta*, named for a configuration change that increased the shroud diameter to eight feet, and capable of placing in synchronous orbit a payload fifteen times heavier than the first *Delta*, launched the domestic satellite ANIK-1 for Telesat Canada on November 10, 1972.

Delta Model 3914, which increased payload capacity from 1550 to 2050-pounds in geosynchronous transfer orbit, was developed to meet the requirements of a new generation of communications satellites, and represented the first launch vehicle program ever undertaken on a commercial basis. Development costs were paid by McDonnell Douglas, with reimbursement from user payments in the domestic commercial satellite program. Model 3914 made its debut at Cape Canaveral

on December 12, 1975, when it placed in orbit the 1913-pound Satcom 1, the RCA Corporation's first commercial domestic communications satellite.

MDAC says that *Delta* is scheduled for launches well into the 1980s.

THE MCDONNELL DOUGLAS CORPORATION'S penetration into the field of missile design and manufacture is virtually assured of growth in the future. A good indication, perhaps, is the construction in St. Charles, Mo., of a $20,000,000 new buildings and facility complex. Here will be centered advanced design and manufacturing facilities for the *Harpoon* and *Cruise* missile programs expected to carry on well into the '80s.

Combined with the MDAC facilities in Huntington Beach which encompass almost 250 acres of buildings and facilities, McDonnell Douglas has one of the most modern and complete aerospace plants in the world, a master facility for design, development and

Delta launch vehicle in production at McDonnell Douglas Astronautics Company in Huntington Beach, California.

production of advanced missile and space systems.

MDAC is one of the best equipped aerospace firms to meet the broadening challenge in space.

Delta 3914 was developed to launch a new generation of communications satellites. It represented the first launch vehicle program ever undertaken on a commercial basis; development costs were paid by McDonnell Douglas, with reimbursement from user payments.

Delta launching a Telesat Canada domestic satellite. By August 1979, Deltas had made 149 flights since the first launch in May 1960.

229

Astronaut John Glenn (Senator Glenn, D-Ohio, today) before boarding Mercury spacecraft No. 13. Glenn was first American to orbit the earth.

Chapter Eighteen

Man In Space

WE WERE VIEWING a television documentary film on President Roosevelt's history-making career when, suddenly, the program was interrupted for a special news bulletin, It was April 12, 1961, the sixteenth anniversary of FDR's death, but it was a day to remember for a much more significant reason. It marked the beginning of man's greatest venture—the conquest of space. The newscaster's voice almost cracked with disbelief when he informed us—"The Soviet Union today announced that it has rocketed a manned spacecraft into orbit . . ."

There followed some sketchy details: "Major Yuri Gagarin, Soviet Cosmonaut, was launched into orbit from Siberia in a spacecraft called *Vostok I,* and was safely returned to earth after one circuit of the globe."

So it began—man's quest to touch a star. The Soviet Union versus the United States. And the world has never been quite the same since.

In January 1963, Mr. McDonnell admonished: "Whether we like it or not, there is a space race between the Free World and the Communist World.

"From the military standpoint we can never tell when some new discovery in space science and exploration will have the potentiality of leading eventually to military control of the earth, so we have to proceed whether we want to or not.

". . . the nature of the soul of man is such that man wants to discover and explore everything that he is able to discover and explore. Man's flights from Earth to the moon and to the planets will be the most prodigious adventure in his history. The hard work, the self discipline, and the soaring spirit of man, which have brought him to the brink of this great achievement, will not stop now. I believe it will have no end as long as man exists on Earth.

"Permeating all of this activity there will be a vast program of scientific research in almost all of the known sciences, and from both basic research and applied research there will in the end inevitably be many applications to everyday life on Earth which will be stimulating both to education and to our business economy in many ways. I am speaking not of months and years to come, but of decades and centuries to come . "

BACK IN 1946 a group of engineers and scientists at Douglas Aircraft Company conducted a study with regard to the building of a spacecraft. A paper called *"Preliminary Design of an Experimental World-Circling Spaceship"* became one of the first documents that excited interest in the exploration and exploitation of space. Nothing much ever came of it, but it was a beginning. Ever since, Mc-

Donnell Douglas has been engaged in active investigation of systems intended to explore the unknowns of space. Certainly, no individual aerospace company captured public attention more than did McDonnell Aircraft Corporation of St. Louis when it accepted the challenge in the late fifties to build the *Mercury* spacecraft which would carry the first American into orbit.

What was *Project Mercury?*

It was America's counterpart to Russia's Vostok I manned spacecraft. Under the direction of the National Aeronautics and Space Administration, *Mercury* was the program to launch man into a controlled orbit around the globe, and bring him safely back to earth. Beyond this feat itself, the program mission was to study the capabilities of man to live in the environment of outer space.

McDonnell Aircraft Corporation got into the picture in 1959 when it was selected by NASA to design, develop and construct the *Mercury* space capsule. (Mr. Mac doesn't like the word capsule: "It sounds as if we were manufacturing a pill!") The announcement on January 12, 1959, that McDonnell would build the one-man *Mercury* spacecraft, called for the building of twelve space vehicles. Additional orders were subsequently issued for eight more. The contract was signed on February 13, 1959.

America was in the space race for keeps.

The challenge McDonnell accepted was an extraordinary one for a number of reasons:

1. The program called for the design and production of hardware which pushed the state of the art. Although McDonnell's long experience in the development of aircraft and missiles had been extremely valuable, much new knowledge and many new techniques were required for the spacecraft development.

2. The spacecraft had to be designed and produced in a manner that would insure the astronaut's safety to the highest possible degree. Improvements that might increase this safety factor were incorporated at any time.

3. The spacecraft had to be developed concurrently with the research and testing conducted by both NASA and McDonnell. The development could not be carried out on a normal step-by-step basis because of the stringent time limitations.

4. Of major importance was the fact that the spacecraft, of necessity, was designed to be used with available rocket boosters rather than wait for those as large and powerful as the Russians were known to possess. This decision resulted in the design of a spacecraft that weighed only about a ton and the use of miniaturized components.

The *Mercury* spacecraft, as it turned out, was cone-shaped with an overall height of 28 feet and 6.5 feet wide at the base. It has been

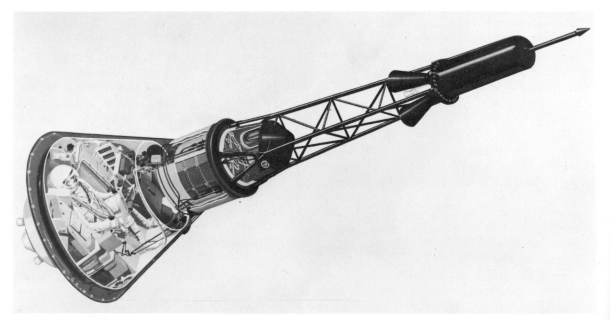

Mercury spacecraft and escape tower is shown in this cut-away drawing. Spacecraft size limitations and need for escape egress system in case of emergency were big challenge to McDonnell engineers.

described as resembling a butter churn and dasher like grandmother once used. The churn was the main body and the dasher was the escape tower. The spacecraft itself was about 9 feet high, of conical shape. The basic structural materials were titanium, beryllium, and nickel-base alloys—strong light-weight metals known to be capable of withstanding extreme high temperatures.

The spacecraft was an extremely complex vehicle in that it was designed to operate automatically, manually, and by ground control. Every component essential to the safety of the astronaut was backed by at least one other method of achieving the same result.

The *Mercury* spacecraft had three principal sections. The base of the cone formed the ablation heat shield that was designed to protect against extreme thermal conditions during re-entry from orbit. This base contained provisions for attachment to the booster through use of a special adapter. At the apex of the cone was a cylindrical section which contained the devices for recovery of the spacecraft at the conclusion of the mission. In the mid-section was the cabin and the systems for regulating flight environment, attitude data reading and telemetering, and spacecraft recovery.

Mercury's cabin was so designed that all operating and emergency provisions were accessible to the astronaut while he was restrained to his support couch. This couch was constructed of a crushable honeycombed aluminum, bonded to a fiber glass shell and lined with a protective rubber padding. This support couch, molded to the contour of the astronaut, was designed to transmit bodily loads evenly through peak accelerations and decelerations and make it easier for him to absorb the various high forces characteristic of the mission.

The instrument panel, which was 24 inches in front of the astronaut, and consoles on both sides, had a total of 165 different switches, dials, meters, toggles, buttons, and lights which the astronaut would be required to monitor and operate as required. The environmental system in the cabin was designed to provide the astronaut with environmental conditions comparable to those in military aircraft. The system had two separate controls so that one would continue to operate in the event of another's malfunction. A third emergency control was also incorporated.

The escape system was comprised of a rocket system on a 14-foot tubular tower attached to the top of the spacecraft by explosive bolts. It provided a safe means for the astronaut to abort the mission before launch or at any time during the booster-sustaining operation until the spacecraft was in orbit. During the escape sequence, the spacecraft would be disengaged from the booster as the escape rocket was fired simultaneously; the escape rocket would pull the spacecraft upward and to the side as it separated at a rate of at least 200 feet in a second. The spacecraft in flight and the escape tower would then coast until they slowed down. The tower would then be jettisoned and a normal parachute sequence landing started.

Mercury's power system consisted of small posigrade rockets integrated into the retrograde rocket housing on the face of the re-entry shield. When fired they separated the spacecraft from the booster at a rate of 15 feet per second when orbital velocity had been achieved, or when abort separation was needed.

Three retrorockets, enclosed in a housing on the blunt end of the spacecraft, provided reverse propulsion and slowed the spacecraft in orbit by about 500 feet per second speed so

A *Mercury* spacecraft is hoisted for mating to its *Atlas* launch vehicle.

Test of *Mercury's* 63-foot ring-sail main chute used to ''land'' spacecraft. Test here was done in desert. Actual flight would end over water.

Mercury spacecraft production.

Gemini spacecraft in ''clean room.''

that it would drop out of orbit. Each of the three rockets had its own prime and reserve ignition system to assure utmost reliability. In an emergency, one of the rockets could effect re-entry, but for expeditious recovery all three were used.

The landing of the spacecraft was to be achieved with a six-foot drogue parachute which opened at about 21,000 feet and a 63-foot ring-sail main parachute which would be deployed at about 10,000 feet. A reserve 63-foot parachute was also carried, and, if unused, jettisoned upon landing.

This was *Mercury,* America's first spacecraft built by McDonnell Aircraft Corporation of St. Louis. It came into being after many problems of manufacturing had been solved. In many cases McDonnell had to explore and devise entirely new manufacturing processes.

An example of this task was the development of a technique for the automatic fusion-welding of titanium spacecraft skins only .010 inches in thickness and nearly six feet long. At the outset of the program there was considerable doubt as to whether successful welds of the desired quality could be achieved with such thin titanium sheets. McDonnell manufacturing people spent many long hours on the problem, finally designed fixtures that

provided inert gas shielding for both sides of the weld plus the exact amount of chilling required to control the temperature of the material in the area of the weld. This permitted the welding to be done in room air rather

Alan B. Shepard, America's first man in space, prior to his ballistic flight beyond the atmosphere in *Freedom* 7, on 5 May 1961.

Seven original *Mercury* astronauts, with Walter Burke (left) and James S. McDonnell (third from left, standing), beside *Mercury* mockup.

than a gas chamber in which all previous fusion-welding of titanium had taken place. The weld achieved by this new technique was believed to be the highest quality yet achieved in the industry.

Another interesting example of the extent of the manufacturing job was the "superclean white room," developed for the assembling of the environmental and reaction control systems. All controls, both reaction and environmental, must function perfectly and respond accurately and immediately. They can tolerate neither dust particles to interfere with operating mechanisms, nor rust which might originate from human contact during assembly operations, and which might cause equipment failure. Under certain conditions, the smallest metal particle could cause failure of a system if not removed.

To protect against these possibilities, McDonnell designed and built a 9000 square foot "superclean white room" which incorporated an air conditioning filtration system that removed dust particles down to a .3 micron in size, maintained a temperature of 74 degrees F, and a relative humidity of not over 50 per cent to provide for worker comfort, control per-

spiration, and dimensional control of materials. The room was pressurized at all times and anyone entering the room had to wear white uniforms of dust-free nylon, nylon caps, and plastic shoes.

The "clean room" was one of many innovations designed to insure that the spacecraft was being built under the best possible manufacturing conditions.

The first *Mercury* spacecraft was delivered to NASA on April 2, 1960, little less than 14 months after the contract to build the spacecraft was signed. The rapidity with which *Mercury* came to be was probably due to the fact that more than a year *before* NASA had announced a competition to build a spacecraft (October 1958) McDonnell Aircraft, with its own funds, had set about designing a spacecraft of its own. When NASA came to McDonnell, it has been said, the McDonnell effort was so close to what NASA had envisioned that McDonnell was almost certain to get the contract.

What had led McDonnell to go it alone? That decision was probably more than anything else influenced by the Russian launch of *Sputnik I,* an unmanned spacecraft,

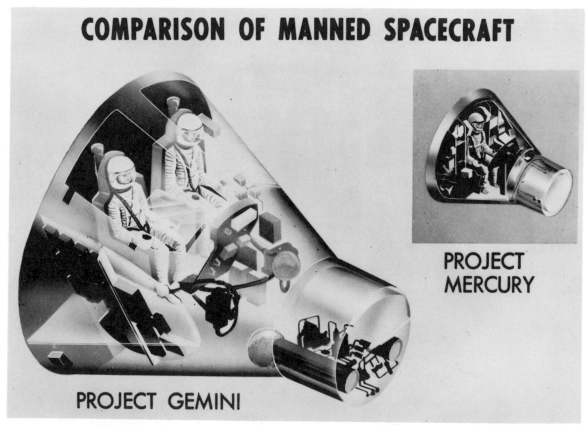

Cut-away drawings show comparison of *Gemini* and *Mercury* spacecraft.

Mr. Mac (with arms folded) inspects *Gemini* spacecraft at Cape Canaveral.

A *Gemini* spacecraft is hoisted for mating to its *Titan* launch vehicle.

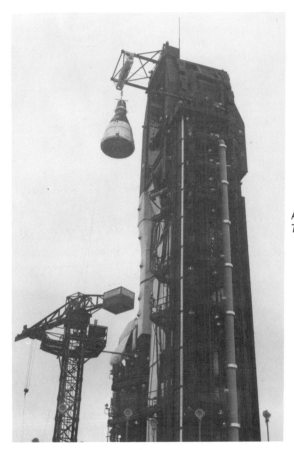

An Atlas launch vehicle, topped by the Gemini-Agena spacecraft, undergoes final preparations prior to lift-off from Cape Canaveral.

Mr. Mac and Walter Burke, McDonnell vice president responsible for *Mercury* and *Gemini* spacecraft programs, at Cape Canaveral.

Control consoles of *Gemini* two-man spacecraft.

Gemini launch from Cape Canaveral.

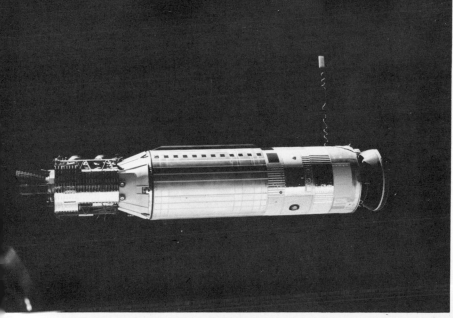

The Agena Target Docking Vehicle seen from the National Aeronautics and Space Administration's Gemini VIII spacecraft during rendezvous in space.

Edward H. White, the first to walk in space, June 1965.

Gemini spacecraft, with service module, jettisoned before reentry.

Gemini 7/6, first rendezvous of manned spacecraft.

on October 4, 1957. Anyway, shortly after that, a small group of engineers and scientists were brought together in St. Louis and the McDonnell "space team" had its beginning.

Mercury spacecraft No. 1 on May 9, 1960, was fired in an off-the-pad abort escape rocket test. There would follow many "firsts" and flights to remember.

January 31, 1961—"Ham," the 37-pound Astro-Chimp, was rocketed into space history aboard Mercury-Redstone 2. "Ham" and spacecraft (No. 5) were recovered after reaching an altitude of 155 miles and landing 420 miles downrange. Flight demonstrated ability of primate to react normally in prolonged weightless flight. "Ham" was recovered safe and well.

May 5, 1961—Astronaut Alan B. Shepard, Jr. rode Mercury-Redstone 3 into history with his ballistic flight seen by the world. The flight reached a peak altitude of 116 statute miles and was recovered 302 miles downrange.

September 13, 1961—Mercury-Atlas 4 placed the McDonnell Mercury Spacecraft in orbit for the first time. The spacecraft (No. 8) carried a *McDonnell-developed "mechanical man"* designed to use oxygen and add moisture to the cabin at the same rate as a man. The spacecraft was recovered after one orbit 160 miles east of Bermuda.

February 20, 1962—Three years and 39 days after Mercury contract was awarded, Mercury Spacecraft (No. 13) and Astronaut John Glenn aboard an Atlas launch vehicle lifted-off from Cape Canaveral. After three orbits, spacecraft and astronaut returned safely to the earth and were recovered. It is significant to note that the initial assignment of Project Mercury was completed with this flight. The spacecraft is now on public display in the Smithsonian Institution.

May 15-16, 1963—Four years, four months and four days after the announcement of the selection of McDonnell to build the Mercury Spacecraft, Astronaut L. Gordon Cooper flew his Faith 7 Spacecraft (No. 20) through 22 orbits to a touchdown 4.4 miles from the Recovery Carrier U.S.S. Kearsarge. The MA-9 mission began 34 hours 19 minutes earlier, lifting-off from Cape Canaveral only four minutes from the earliest possible launch time. Following a "textbook" insertion into orbit, the Astronaut began a series of experiments involving eating, exercising and sleeping during weightlessness; took photographs of

the earth and space; allowed his craft to drift without attitude control through most of the flight without difficulty; experimented with space vision with reference to flashing lights in space and on the ground. He passed over an area of the globe which included parts of five continents and more than 100 countries, islands and possessions. Due to an inoperative automatic stabilization system, Astronaut Cooper manually controlled the spacecraft throughout the entire re-entry and landing sequence.

About one month later (June 12, 1963) NASA officially announced the completion of the Project *Mercury* program. By now, however, McDonnell Aircraft was far along in the development of *Gemini,* a two-man spacecraft, destined to play a star role in America's second step in space exploration.

GEMINI was a two-man spacecraft built as a follow-on of the *Mercury* project. About a fourth again as large as *Mercury,* the *Gemini* spacecraft was 19 feet long (high), 10 feet in diameter and weighed about 8400 pounds. *Gemini* employed a "two-wall" structure which permitted locating many of the systems and accessories between the cabin itself and the outer skin of the spacecraft. In this way much of the confinement experienced by *Mercury* astronauts was eliminated. Things didn't have to be stacked up inside the cabin. Otherwise the cabin interior was similar to that of *Mercury* but with the addition of an extra couch, providing for two-man occupancy.

Gemini differed in another way, besides just being larger, almost twice the total volume. There was no escape tower. In *Gemini* the crewmen, in case of emergency, would use ejection seats similar to those standard in high speed aircraft.

Specific objectives of the *Gemini* program were:

Earth orbital flights of up to 14 days duration. This was accomplished with Spacecraft 7, and showed that man had complete capability in the space environment for periods up to 14 days.

Demonstrate rendezvous and docking with a target vehicle in earth orbit, using various rendezvous techniques. Rendezvous was first achieved by *Gemini* 6; docking by *Gemini* 8.

Develop spacecraft countdown techniques and operational procedures for accomplishing rapid launch pad turnaround. In order to rendezvous and dock, it was necessary to launch almost precisely on time. This objective was consistently accomplished throughout the program.

Demonstrate controlled re-entry and landing to a predetermined touchdown area. First accomplished by *Gemini* 6.

Provide a test bed for "in-space" experiments. Experiments were carried on all spacecraft, first with *Gemini* 3.

Demonstrate maneuvering in earth orbit using the Agena target vehicle for propulsion. First achieved with *Gemini* 10.

To design and build the *Gemini* spacecraft it has been estimated that more than 11,300,000 engineering man-hours and more than 7,750,000 manufacturing man-hours were spent by 5,322 McDonnell personnel, performing 138 different job tasks, to put together the more than 1,230,000 parts, including every rivet, "every everything." In the process, many new technologies were discovered and perfected which would help in all spacecraft design and fabrication in the future.

One such technique was the development of new tooling methods of forming and welding continuous magnesium-thorium extrusions.

McDonnell also developed a number of thermal coatings necessary for thermal balance of the spacecraft and its equipment. The proper coatings were selected using furnaces and vacuum chambers and ultraviolet radiation to simulate the space environment

Artist's rendering of proposed S-IVB and *Gemini* B combination for *MOL*, Manned Orbiting Laboratory program.

Skylab, floating in space, minus one of its solar panels.

for periods equivalent to two weeks.

Space walking or extra-vehicular activity (EVA) was not an original objective of the *Gemini* program, although "hatch open and stand" was. This achievement was made possible by the design of personnel hatches, contoured to the shape of the conical cabin, and located on top of the spacecraft. Mechanical latching devices on the *Gemini* hatch permitted opening and closing of the hatches manually by the astronauts from inside the cabin. It was this arrangement that made EVA possible when this requirement was added to mission planning for the first time on *Gemini* 4.

Another McDonnell innovation on *Gemini* was an early decision to fabricate the wire bundles separately from the spacecraft and make all terminations before the bundles were installed. This wire bundle technique, a carry over from F-4 *Phantom* experience, gave flexibility to change the wiring more easily as the mission planning changed on each flight.

The first launch of *Gemini* into space was on March 23, 1965. Aboard were Command pilot Virgil I. Grissom and Pilot John W. Young. The *Gemini* spacecraft made three-plus orbits of earth, and splashed down 4 hours 53 minutes later after having traveled 80,000 miles! The Grissom/Young space trip was made in the Number Three *Gemini* spacecraft.

The last flight of *Gemini* was made on November 11-15 the following year. Aboard were James A. Lovell, Jr., Command Pilot, and Edwin E. "Buzz" Aldrin, Jr., pilot. The duo of astronauts circled the earth almost sixty times, remained aloft 94 hours 34 minutes 31 seconds, and they traveled 1,628,510 miles. Their flight concluded the *Gemini* program.

Probably the most gratifying results of the *Gemini* program, which proved all its objectives during ten manned space trips, was that each crew was successfully recovered in excellent physical health. In both the *Mercury* and *Gemini* spacecraft missions, American astronauts amassed a total of 1,071 hours 36 minutes in space. McDonnell Aircraft space vehicles—*Mercury* and *Gemini*—started us a long way on the journey to the moon.

WHILE McDONNELL AIRCRAFT in St. Louis was implementing Project *Mercury* and Project *Gemini,* its partner-to-be in a few years—Douglas Aircraft Company—on the West Coast, was getting involved deeper and deeper into the space program. The project would have the name Manned Orbiting Laboratory, a USAF program. It probably had its beginning as far back as 1963, or earlier, when Dr. Werner Von Braun, then Director of the NASA George C. Marshall Space center, suggested that the S-IVB Stage (developed by Douglas, as we know) of the *Saturn* rocket launch vehicle be used as an orbital workshop.

In his book, *Space Frontier,* Dr. Von Braun wrote: "These tanks (S-IVB) are empty on arrival in orbit. After being vented to the vacuum of space, they are clean as a whistle, free of odors other propellents would leave, and pressure-tight. They may then be filled with an atmosphere of pure oxygen or any desired oxygen-nitrogen or oxygen-helium mixture. They provide ample room for a spaceman to 'pitch his tent' in complete privacy—and can accommodate a kitchen, a doctor's dispensary, a shower bath, a men's room, a library, or anything else an astronaut on a one-year stint (in space) could desire . . ."

The idea broached here by one of the world's foremost rocket experts, probably triggered thinking which led to the development of the Manned Orbiting Laboratory. At any rate, on August 25, 1965, President Lyndon Johnson gave the official go ahead. Douglas Aircraft Company (Missiles & Space Systems Group) had been selected to design and develop the Manned Orbiting Laboratory—a $1.5 billion program!

"This program," the President said, "will bring us new knowledge about what man is able to do in space. It will enable us to relate that ability to the defense of America. It will develop technology and equipment which will help advance manned and unmanned space flight, and it will make it possible to perform very new and rewarding experiments with technology and equipment."

But MOL was cancelled before it flew, NASA's Apollo Applications Program, which more closely paralleled the original Von Braun idea, was continued. This program, later known as *Skylab,* concentrated on adapting an emptied hydrogen tank of an S-IVB that would stage as an orbital laboratory and provide more space than the MOL.

It would provide an environment in which man could live and work in space under controlled conditions for long periods. Experiments conducted in the Workshop would develop data on man's physiological and psychological responses to the space environment and provide more detailed information on his abilities for extended manned flight.

A *Saturn V* third (S-IVB) stage was modified and outfitted on the ground as living and working quarters for three astronauts. The stage's liquid hydrogen tank provided a 283 cubic meter (10,000 cubic-foot) space laboratory, many times larger than any spacecraft which had yet flown.

The McDonnell Douglas S-IVB No. 212 was to be the primary flight Workshop. Another stage, S-IVB No. 211, was outfitted

Werner von Braun inspecting *Airlock* module, under development for *Skylab* program.

The *Skylab* workshop portion of the first U.S. space station. McDonnell Douglas produced the workshop, a two-floor structure that accommodated the three-man crew and many of their experiments, and the airlock module, the nerve center of the earth-orbiting cluster.

and checked out as the backup hardware.

The S-IVB converted for *Skylab* did not have an engine or other propulsive hardware. A reusable access hatch replaced an existing manhole in the forward tank dome. A personnel hatch was also added to the side of the stage to permit workmen and technicians easy access to the inside during the checkout and pre-launch phase.

Aluminum grid-pattern floors and ceilings were installed in the tank to divide it into a two-story 'space cabin.' An aluminum foil, fire-retardant liner was placed around the inside tank insulation surface, and a meteoroid shield on the stage's exterior. Two solar arrays were mounted to the stage's outer wall.

Crew quarters, one of the most important features of the Workshop, were at the aft end of the tank. A ceiling grid separated these quarters from a large laboratory area in the tank's forward end. Solid partitions divided the crew quarters into a sleep compartment, a wardroom, a waste management compartment and a work/experiment space. Lighting fixtures were mounted in the crew quarters ceiling. The wardroom and waste management compartments were sealed separately with walls and doors to retain odors and loose particles in the weightless environment.

The crew quarters were relatively large. The wardroom had about 100 square feet of area; the waste management compartment had 30 square feet of floor space; the sleep compartment about 70 square feet; and the work area about 180 square feet.

The Workshop's Airlock Module provided the thermal control and ventilation system for a habitable environment with a temperature ranging from 15.56 to 32.22 degrees Celsius (60 to 90 degrees F). Fans circulated the artificial atmosphere to keep a constant temperature.

Solar arrays on the Workshop and the ATM provided electrical power for the entire Skylab. The systems were cross-linked for flexibility in habitability in handling peak loads and for countering failure. The electrical power distribution system was installed to connect the Workshop areas with power sources in the AM and the solar cell assemblies. Light fixtures could be individually controlled, and portable lights could be used for additional illumination.

Water and food for the Skylab's operational lifetime were stored inside the Workshop. Water could be stored in tanks located in the upper experiments area. Food could be stored

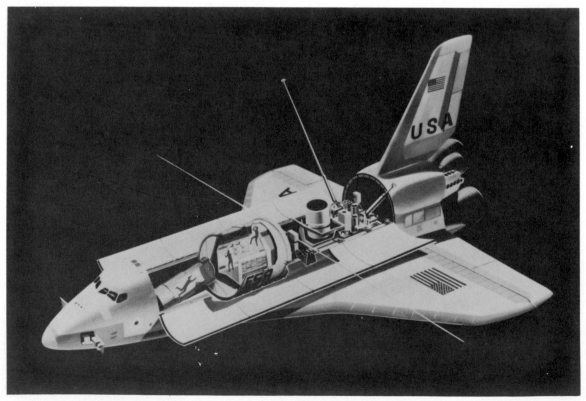

Cut-away of space shuttle *Enterprise* shows systems developed by McDonnell Douglas.

in compartments and freezers in this area and in the wardroom.

Skylab astronauts were able to look back at Earth through a wardroom window. The window, 18 inches in diameter, was located in the middle of the wardroom, facing the sunlight side of the Earth. It had doublepane glass, with heaters to keep it from fogging.

The large liquid oxygen tank on the S-IVB stage was converted into a waste container. An airlock was installed in the top of the common bulkhead so that crewmen could safely deposit waste items in the tank. Metal screens were placed in the tank to restrict the movement of the waste items.

Skylab, itself, consisted of four other components: The Command Service Module, a modified *Apollo* three-man spacecraft, designed and built by the North American Aerospace division of Rockwell International Corporation; the Multiple Docking Adapter, which provided docking facilities for arriving and departing Command Service Modules, built by the Martin Marietta Corporation; the Apollo Telescope Mount, developed by the Marshall Space Flight Center; and the Airlock Module, also developed by McDonnell Douglas.

The first *Skylab* was put into orbit on May 25, 1973, with astronauts Charles "Pete" Conrad, Captain USN, Commander; Commander Joseph P. Kerwin, Science Pilot; Commander Paul J. Weitz, Pilot. The trio remained aloft for 28 days zero hours and 49 minutes. The last *Skylab* mission was flown November 16, 1973 to February 8, 1974, a total of 84 days 1 hour and 16 minutes in space! Aboard were Lieut. Col. Gerald P. Carr, USMC, Commander; Civilian Edward G. Gibson, Ph.D., Science Pilot; and Lieut. Col. William R. Pogue, USAF, pilot.

We know now that *Skylab* experiments proved man could live and work in outer space for extended periods of time.

The new space frontier was opening wider and wider.

TODAY, FIVE programs connected with the United States Space Transportation System (STS) make the McDonnell Douglas Corporation still a major contributor to the development of the vehicles for man's next major ventures into space.

Divisions of the corporation are providing the aft propulsion system (APS) for the Space Shuttle Orbiter, building large support structures for the Shuttle's solid rocket boosters, supplying engineering and opera-

The McDonnell Douglas S-IVB performed a vital role in the success of the Apollo lunar landing program.

THE MCDONNELL DOUGLAS STORY

tions support to the National Aeronautics and Space Administration's (NASA's) Johnson Space Center and playing a dual role in support of the European Spacelab for the Shuttle.

The Shuttle Orbiter's APS is being designed and produced at McDonnell Douglas Astronautics Company (MDAC) facilities in St. Louis, Missouri, under contract with Rockwell International's Space Division. The system consists of a pair of 23-foot long external pods mounted on the aft fuselage of the Orbiter. Each pod contains a rocket motor rated at 6000 pounds thrust, with thrust vector controls for steering the vehicle in flight outside the earth's atmosphere, where its aircraft-type controls are not effective.

Orbiter pilots will fire the rockets in short bursts to maneuver the vehicle along its track around the Earth. They will use longer burns to make large changes in the orbital path and will use the APS as retrorockets to slow the vehicle and bring it out of orbit for the descent to Earth.

The McDonnell Astronautics Company in Huntington Beach, California, is building the forward and aft skirts, nose cone and other support structures for the Shuttle's solid rocket booster (SRB) motors, including the struts that attach the boosters to the shuttle. Two of the boosters, each rated at 2.65 million pounds thrust, will provide extra lift to the Shuttle during the first phase of launch.

Assembled from thick, machined aluminum plate, the SRB structures will support the entire weight of the Shuttle vehicle on the launch pad, and transfer booster thrust loads to the main vehicle during flight. The structures also provide protection and support for the burned-out rocket case as it separates from the Shuttle, parachutes into the ocean and is recovered for re-use.

McDonnell Douglas Technical Services Company (MDTSCO) at Houston, Texas, has been involved in the Shuttle program since April 1974 through a contract with the NASA Johnson Space Center. Some 300 engineers and technicians apply the expertise gained through MDC's work in the *Mercury, Gemini, Apollo* and *Skylab* programs to assist in development of Shuttle Orbiter systems and operations. They provide support in systems analysis, aid in mission planning, analysis and computer programming, and develop crew procedures and flight training.

McDonnell Douglas has been principal con-

sultant to VFW-Fokker/ERNO, developer of the European Space Agency's *Spacelab,* since June 1974. The company's extensive experience in manned space programs is supporting development of the laboratory module that will be carried into space in the Shuttle Orbiter. MDAC personnel are assigned to the European consortium headquarters at Bremen, Germany, and at the facilities of several major European aerospace companies participating in the Spacelab effort.

The MDTSCO Spacelab Division at Huntsville, Alabama, has a separate but related role in the Spacelab program under a contract with the NASA Marshall Space Flight Center. MDTSCO will provide a wide range of technical services to help assure smooth and timely integration of the Spacelab into the Shuttle Orbiter for manned flights.

Work will include systems analysis and computer software development; devising analytical methods for experiment integration in the laboratory module; performing safety, reliability and quality assurance tasks; producing Spacelab hardware and support equipment for which NASA is responsible; logistics support activities, and launch site operations, including vehicle checkout, launch preparations and refurbishing the laboratory between flights.

Where do we go from here?

Mr. Mac had some answers back in 1963: "During the next 65 years exploitation of our science and technology will permit us to undertake manned or unmanned flights to all the planets in our solar system except, perhaps, Pluto.

"Despite its tenuous atmosphere and what may be severe dust storms, Mars is the most likely first planet for manned space exploration. Some boys now in school will probably grow up to be the first human beings to visit Mars and tell us whether the seasonal change of the dark areas from brown to green does or does not mark the growth of vegetation, and whether the polar caps and the frost-like areas are composed of solid carbon dioxide, ordinary crystallized water, or some entirely different substance which cannot now be identified."

The unmanned flights have proved his point.

"Explorers to Jupiter will probably land on Ganymede, the largest of Jupiter's twelve moons," he continued. "A probe from Ganymede to Jupiter itself could conceivably

246

be made by a powered winged vehicle, a derivative of the aerospaceplane.

"If we employ a launching velocity of 96,280 fps in addition to 1 EMOS (Earth's Mean Orbital velocity around the sun), we would be able to make a flight from Earth around Neptune and return to Earth in less than ten years.

"Research on objects outside our solar system will be an almost routine matter with the Earth-orbiting telescopes that will be available during the next 65 years. If we are ingenious enough, we may be able to build larger space-based telescopes that might detect planets orbiting around other stars."

Artist's concept of passenger version of YC-15 short-takeoff and landing (STOL) aircraft. STOL airliners could bring air transportation to the people, eliminating a need for the huge, expensive airports which service major cities.

Chapter Nineteen

Vertical Vertigo

THE EMPIRE STATE BUILDING sticks its obelisk-like shape more than one-fourth of a mile straight up into the New York sky. The equivalent of the population of a town of over 35,000 people work every day in its myriad of offices, and thousands more, sight-seeing tourists from all over the world, ride the elevators to an observatory near the top for a breathtaking view of America's largest city. It is, and has been since it was completed in 1931, one of the big city's major attractions.

But to many who ride the fast elevators to the top, there are mixed feelings and emotions. Is it safe? What if you should get stranded up there? Supposing there is a fire on one of the floors below, and you get trapped above? And many persons can recall when a B-25 bomber, flying in fog, slammed into the Empire State, the point of impact 915 feet above street level.

It happened on July 28, 1945. Fourteen persons died and twenty-five others were injured in the fire and smoke, the aftermath of the collision between skycraft and skyscraper. Others were stranded for hours before they could get safely back down. There was near panic as fire fighters fought the flames, and tried to effect rescue operations.

Such a catastrophe could happen again. But thanks to a new vehicle developed by McDonnell Douglas, fire-fighting techniques and rescue operations in such cases may be greatly improved. Called the Suspended Maneuvering System (SMS), the vehicle is a flying fire engine and rescue craft designed to carry fire fighters to high-rise buildings and other inaccessible areas to deliver emergency assistance. It is being built by McDonnell Douglas in its St. Louis aircraft manufacturing facilities.

The prototype is composed of a 7 by 8-foot platform, weighs about 2,000 pounds and will transport four to eight fully equipped firemen or paramedics. It will have rescue capabilities for up to 16 persons.

The vehicle is suspended beneath a helicopter by cable. At the scene of the emergency, crewmen employ the propulsion and control system built into the vehicle to maneuver to their destination. This could be, for example, the eighty-ninth floor of the Empire State or a ship in distress at sea.

THE HELICOPTER, prime mover in the SMS (Suspended Maneuvering System) is no stranger in the family of aircraft designed and built by McDonnell Douglas over the years. To many old-timers at McDonnell Aircraft Company in St. Louis, it is more like a Godchild. Before World War II, when MAC was in its infancy, that first $20,000 Air Force contract for jet propulsion research produced a new kind of power plant system which led to the development of the world's first ramjet

249

"Flying Fire Engine" in actual test. Suspended Maneuvering System using helicopter as prime mover has many applications for rescue work.

BEACON

FAN SCREEN

POWER CONTROLLER

GUIDANCE UNIT

COMMUNICATION UNIT

BATTERY

GATE

PERSONNEL RESTRAINT SYSTEM (BUNGEE CORD AND WAIST BELTS)

ALUMINIZED INSULATION SHADE ON EACH SIDE

SUSPENSION CABLE

SWIVEL AND SLIP RING ASSEMBLY

VECTORABLE NOZZLE (4)

ENGINE

NOZZLE DRIVE (4)

FLOODLIGHT (2)

BULL HORN

TV CAMERA (2)

EQUIPMENT TIE DOWN (10)

GLASS DEFLECTOR (STOWED POSITION)

GANGPLANK (DEPLOYED POSITION)

DOCKING SENSOR

GLASSBREAKER (4)

Suspended Maneuvering System (SMS)

Mayor Jane Byrne of Chicago gets a lesson in operating the McDonnell Douglas flying fire engine which the City of Chicago plans to operate on an experimental basis. Suspended from a helicopter, the vehicle can deliver firemen to and rescue victims from highrise buildings and inaccessible terrain. Mayor Bryne said: "It is a credit to the Chicago Fire Department that it was chosen to test this equipment. I am pleased that McDonnell Douglas thinks so highly of the caliber of the personnel we have here in the Chicago department." Coaching the Mayor during a recent demonstration at Meigs Field on the Chicago lakefront is John Rychlewski, SMS operator, and Peter Simmons, right, program manager for the McDonnell Douglas vehicle. At left is Chicago Fire Commissioner Richard Albrecht.

rotary winged aircraft.

BACK IN 1939-40 Russian-born Igor Sikorsky, famous for his big flying boat designs, built and flew the world's first single-rotor helicopter, acclaimed as the first practical rotary winged aircraft. A later model, the Sikorsky XR-4, a two-place helicopter, was widely tested by the Air Forces, Maritime Commission, and the Wartime Shipping Administration as an anti-submarine weapon. At the time, in the early days of World War II, the U-boat menace was taking a heavy toll of Allied shipping. Shipboard based helicopters were used as an anti-submarine defense with good effectiveness. In the spotlight with its anti-sub role, it was soon observed that the helicopter offered many other useful purposes, such as air rescue operations, transport, artillery spotting. The sudden interest brought several new helicopter designs into being. Two aircraft manufacturers, Platt-LePage Aircraft Corporation of Eddystone, Pennsylvania, and Sikorsky Aircraft of Hartford, Connecticut, were awarded contracts by the Air Force to build their XR-1 (a twin rotor) and XR-4 (single rotor) helicopters, respectively. Both were reciprocating engine powered. The future looked bright for this new segment of the aircraft manufacturing industry.

The Platt-LePage and Sikorsky helicopters were flying with acclaimed success when McDonnell became interested and began a thorough study of available helicopters. Mr. McDonnell's approach was a shrewd one. In the spring of 1942, he bought a substantial interest in Platt-LePage. In 1943, he established a new Helicopter Research Division within the McDonnell Aircraft Corporation, and moved a cadre of engineers and other "teammates" to Eddystone, near Philadelphia, in space provided by Platt-LePage. The idea, of course, was that the "teammates" should learn all they could about helicopters. As it turned out, they did their homework very well.

Following more than a year's research in Philadelphia, the newly formed Helicopter Research Division was moved to St. Louis.

Chief engineer of the new division was Costia L. Zakhartchenko whom we met earlier as a partner with McDonnell in J.S. McDonnell and Associates in Milwaukee, which had produced the *Doodlebug*. That venture, one must recall, also involved an aircraft capable of short takeoff and landing capabilities. The helicopter, with its vertical flight sidewise and even backward flight capabilities, is perhaps the epitome in this area of flight. One can assume this characteristic sharpened McDonnell's interest in getting into the helicopter development.

McDonnell embarked upon a program to

World's largest and first twin-engine helicopter, McDonnell XHJD-1 *Whirlaway* hovers over Douglas DC-4 airliner at St. Louis Lambert Field.

251

design and develop a far larger helicopter than any previously built. By early 1946, the new Helicopter Research Division, McDonnell Aircraft Corporation in St. Louis, had designed, constructed and had ready to test its XHJD-1, the world's largest and first twin-engine helicopter.

Designated the XHJD-1 *Whirlaway* and designed to carry ten passengers, the helicopter was fitted with tandem rotors mounted on short, airfoil pylons which housed two 450-horsepower Pratt-Whitney Wasp, Jr. engines.

The counter-rotating rotors were mounted well above head level and eliminated the need for a compensating tail rotor, making the XHJD-1 exceptionally safe for ground personnel. The flight control system in the cockpit consisted of a dual arrangement of conventional control stick and rudder pedals as well as pitch controls characteristic of helicopters. The rotors, each fitted with three 50-foot blades covering a span of 91 feet, received power through transmissions and gear boxes incorporating centrifugal and over-running clutches which permitted emergency power transmission from either engine automatically.

The use of twin engines gave the XHJD-1 greater reliability for flights over rough terrain, cities or large expanses of water, as level flight could be maintained with either of the two engines, at full gross weight of 5½ tons. In addition, the power-off autorotative characteristics of this helicopter were excellent.

Though this aircraft never became a production model, it provided valuable data on helicopter performance, stability, balance and vibration characteristics under all possible combinations of situations which such a craft would encounter in flight.

After years of research, the XHJD-1 was flown for the last time in June 1951, and has since been turned over to the Smithsonian Institution's National Air and Space Museum.

After *Whirlaway* came three more McDonnell helicopter designs, each of which contributed much to the advancement of rotary winged aircraft.

Next came the world's first ramjet helicopter. Dubbed "Little Henry" by the men who designed and built it, and officially designated the XH-20 by the Air Force, the small jet-powered rotorcraft was acclaimed as a major breakthrough in the evolution of the helicopter.

McDonnell himself recalls—"We knew we had something here, but we never referred to it with the fancy title of it being an *aircraft*. We simply called it a *flying test stand* developed to prove and demonstrate a new propulsion method."

Describing "Little Henry," a company press release on the occasion of the *flying test stand's* public debut says—"It is a three-dimensional aerial motorcycle consisting of a two-blade rotor, two tip ram-jets, a small rudder and an open steel structure supporting the pilot, fuel tanks and controls.

"An important feature of 'Little Henry' is its Tom Thumb power plant—two McDonnell-developed ram-jet units weighing only twelve pounds each. The workable, lightweight ram-jet engine, long a tantalizing engineering goal, has been developed by McDonnell after several years of research and experimentation. This ram-jet is attached to the end of each of the all-metal rotor blades which are actuated by conventional pilot controls. With power applied directly to the blade tips, heavy engine parts, gear systems and transmissions are eliminated.

"Engineering ingenuity has accomplished, for the first time, the generation of power at the point of application, to produce a two-fold beneficial result: maximum efficiency and

Whirlaway and the *Phantom*. First big helicopter and the first carrier-based jet fighter.

complete elimination of torque, making the conventional (helicopter) counteracting tail rotor unnecessary.

"Weighing only 280 pounds, the XH-20 has lifted an additional useful load of 500 pounds; in the course of its flight test development it has already attained a forward speed of more than 50 miles an hour. It is the first ram-jet to carry both pilot and passenger. The flying test stand measures 5 feet wide, 7 feet high, and 12½ feet long. Various rotors, measuring from 18½ feet to 20 feet, have been used.

"The entire project was developed through the closely-knit cooperation of the Rotary Wing Branch, Propeller Laboratory; the Rotary Wing Unit, Aircraft Projects Section, Wright-Patterson Air Force Base, Dayton, Ohio; and the Helicopter and Propulsion Divisions of the McDonnell Aircraft Corporation."

The XV-1 Convertiplane as its name implies, was part helicopter, part winged aircraft. Its purpose was to combine the vertical flight characteristics of a helicopter with the speed and range of a conventional fixed-wing

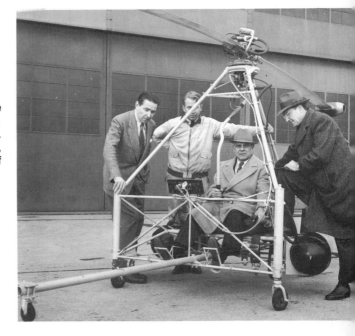

In November 1947, General James H. Doolittle visited St. Louis and tried the controls of *Little Henry,* an experimental ramjet helicopter for the Air Force. Observing are Costia L. Zakhartchenko (left), helicopter chief engineer, Charles R. Wood, Jr., chief helicopter test pilot, and James S. McDonnell.

Little Henry flying test stand was major breakthrough because of McDonnell-developed remjet engines.

aircraft. Several manufacturers had tried for years to develop a successful convertiplane, but McDonnell was first to prove the concept.

The XV-1 had a length of 31 feet 10 inches and a wingspan of 26 feet with a gross weight of 5,391 pounds. The rotor diameter was 31 feet. Its pusher propeller was 6.4 feet in diameter, driven by a 525-horsepower Continental engine.

The convertiplane had a four-place fuselage with a conventional piston engine, pusher-propeller powerplant in the rear. It had short stubby wings. Atop the fuselage was mounted a large three-bladed rotor powered with blade tip pressure jet engines—a "spin-off" of the "Little Henry" experiment.

Using the rotor, the aircraft could take off vertically and perform like a helicopter. Then, when the aircraft reached sufficient speed,

power could be shifted from the rotor to the pusher propeller to execute a flight conversion. As a winged vehicle, with the rotor "windmilling" overhead, the aircraft could achieve speeds of more than 200 mph. The fastest speed attainable with previous helicopter aircraft was approximately 160 mph.

Two of the XV-1 convertiplanes were built. Except for important research data in this strange flight realm nothing much ever came of the idea. Like the *Whirlaway,* the convertiplanes wound up in museums.

Another helicopter built by McDonnell was the Model 120, specifically designed as a cargo helicopter. This multi turbine-engine aircraft, also known as the "flying crane," was developed at McDonnell expense. A revolutionary rotor and drive system

McDonnell pioneered new flight technique with XV-1 *Convertiplane*, which combined flying characteristics of helicopter and fixed-wing aircraft. Plane could be flown as helicopter for vertical takeoff and landings, or in level flight as winged vehicle with rotor "windmilling."

pioneered in the XV-1 convertiplane—combined with a rugged type airframe of unprecedented simplicity and versatility—made the new helicopter unique in several respects.

The Model 120 had an empty weight of only 2400 pounds and a maximum takeoff gross weight of 6300 pounds. The useful load was 62 percent of its gross weight, unusually high for a helicopter.

This high useful load was achieved by using a McDonnell-developed pressure jet-powered rotor. The pressure jet burners were mounted on each of the three blade tips. Compressed air was ducted through the rotor hub and rotor blades to the pressure jets where fuel was injected and burning occurred.

These pressure jets were the result of seven years of development by McDonnell Aircraft. The unique rotor system, made possible by the use of these pressure jets, was developed originally for the McDonnell XV-1 Convertiplane.

The compressed air for the pressure jets was supplied by three Airesearch GTC-85-35 gas turbine compressors. This propulsion system eliminated the need for power shafting, gear box, clutch, and even the usual tail rotor, which substantially reduced maintenance requirements.

The three GTC-85-35 compressors afforded true multi-engine reliability, since level flight could be maintained at maximum gross weight with one engine inoperative.

The fuselage was extremely simple in design in order to minimize maintenance and to facilitate cargo loading. Cargo was carried suspended from a pilot-controlled cargo hook located immediately below the rotor. Twelve people could be accommodated on "toboggan seats" which attached to the cross member supporting the cockpit.

The Model 120 was the last helicopter built by McDonnell. It never did find many interested customers.

Although the lessons learned and the research data obtained were invaluable, McDonnell decided to get out of the helicopter business. And for good.

As late as 1978, McDonnell told the author — "We don't have any helicopters in the garage."

"Helicopters are an inefficient form of transport regarding fuel cost per ton mile," he emphasized. "STOL and VTOL aircraft are more efficient in the long run.

The experimental Model 120 "flying crane" was small but had unusual lift capabilities. It could carry a useful load exceeding its own empty weight.

"We were starters and are leaders today in this field."

MCDONNELL DOUGLAS has had an extensive STOL background. Early in 1961, McDonnell evaluated the potential STOL and V/STOL aircraft under development, considering technology, state of development, potential market, and international implications. Breguet Aviation, in France, seemed to have made the most progress with its Model 941, a deflected slipstream cross shafted STOL aircraft. Arrangements were made for McDonnell personnel to visit Breguet and work out an agreement for collaboration on a proposal for a STOL Transport.

During the remainder of 1961 and early 1962, additional engineering effort was applied in a detailed and thorough evaluation of Breguet's 94X series aircraft in preparation for an upcoming U.S. Army Tactical Transport Competition (ATTAC) requirement. McDonnell then proceeded to negotiate with Breguet for a license agreement, and concurrently to prepare a proposal to the Army, offering the Model 188 (Americanized Breguet 941S).

In June 1962, McDonnell and Breguet entered into a license agreement whereby McDonnell obtained the right to manufacture and/or sell the Model 188/Breguet production Model 941S in North and South America and the West Indies. Breguet retained the manufacturing/sales rights in the remainder of the world. Also in June 1962, McDonnell submitted a proposal on its Model 188 in response to the Army ATTAC requirement.

McDonnell 188 prototype STOL—short takeoff and landing—aircraft, tested under arrangement with Breguet Aviation in France.

The McDonnell Model 188 STOL aircraft was a production ready, flight proven assault transport having application to the support missions of the U.S. Air Force's Tactical Air Command.

The Model 188E was powered by four 1500 horsepower free-turbine engines. The propellers were interconnected by a cross-shaft system which permitted the slow speed flight required for STOL performance, and provided a flight safety factor superior to that possible with four-engine transport aircraft then available.

Proven by six years of flight development, including evaluations by the USAF Aeronautical Systems Division, the Air Force Flight Test Center and the National Aeronautics and Space Administration, the Model 188E was the only true STOL aircraft

in the "over 20,000 pound payload" class ready for volume production in the mid '60s.

The Model 188E was the first in a proposed series of STOL aircraft tailored to the needs of the USAF. The Model 188H was a larger version, with four 3400 horsepower GE-T-64 engines and a payload capacity of 25,000 pounds. Like the 188E, the 188H could operate from rough, unprepared areas. Its additional power, however, enabled it to operate from strips of less than 500 feet in length at maximum gross weight.

The 188H had a top speed in excess of 400 miles an hour (360 knots), equal to many World War II fighters.

In November 1964, McDonnell submitted an unsolicited proposal to the Air Force for procurement of the Model 188. Formal evaluation of the proposal resulted in two significant

The McDonnell Douglas revamped and improved Model 188-STOL in Eastern Airlines colors.

statements by the Air Force. The Air Force said the Model 188 provided STOL, as advertised by McDonnell, and had many features which should be incorporated into future Air Force tactical transports.

It also said that the Air Force had at that time no stated requirement nor developed operational concept for STOL or V/STOL transport aircraft.

THE AIR FORCE, within a few years would change its mind with regard to STOL operations. Taking a closer look at their in-service medium transport fleet, comprised of C-130, C-123 and C-74 aircraft—some over twenty-five years old—USAF planners decided the time had come to think about a replacement for these service-weary transports. Thus was born what the Air Force called its Advanced

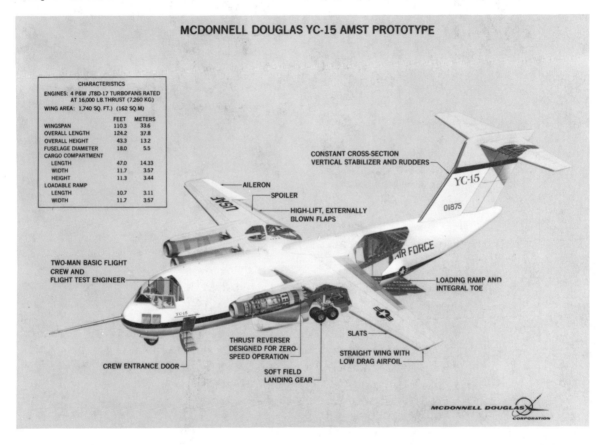

MCDONNELL DOUGLAS YC-15 AMST PROTOTYPE

CHARACTERISTICS		
ENGINES: 4 P&W JT8D-17 TURBOFANS RATED AT 16,000 LB. THRUST (7,260 KG)		
WING AREA: 1,740 SQ. FT.) (162 SQ.M)		
	FEET	METERS
WINGSPAN	110.3	33.6
OVERALL LENGTH	124.2	37.8
OVERALL HEIGHT	43.3	13.2
FUSELAGE DIAMETER	18.0	5.5
CARGO COMPARTMENT		
LENGTH	47.0	14.33
WIDTH	11.7	3.57
HEIGHT	11.3	3.44
LOADABLE RAMP		
LENGTH	10.7	3.11
WIDTH	11.7	3.57

AILERON

SPOILER

HIGH-LIFT, EXTERNALLY BLOWN FLAPS

CONSTANT CROSS-SECTION VERTICAL STABILIZER AND RUDDERS

YC-15

01875

AIR FORCE

TWO-MAN BASIC FLIGHT CREW AND FLIGHT TEST ENGINEER

LOADING RAMP AND INTEGRAL TOE

THRUST REVERSER DESIGNED FOR ZERO-SPEED OPERATION

SLATS

STRAIGHT WING WITH LOW DRAG AIRFOIL

CREW ENTRANCE DOOR

SOFT FIELD LANDING GEAR

MCDONNELL DOUGLAS
CORPORATION

McDonnell Douglas YC-15 STOL aircraft was designed and built for needs of military as possible replacement for C-130 and other cargo aircraft. Air Force wanted STOL capabilities for airlifting heavy equipment. YC-15 was in competition with Boeing (YC-14), but contract never got beyond production of two YC-15s, although there is possiblity it may be revived.

Medium STOL Transport (AMST) program, with circulars going out to various airframe manufacturers asking for their design concepts. The STOL principle was given a new lease on life, and because of its background, McDonnell Douglas was eager to get into the competition.

As it turned out, in November 1972 McDonnell Douglas was one of two aerospace firms (the other was Boeing) selected by the Air Force to initiate design and development of AMST prototypes. Authority to proceed with fabrication of two such aircraft was granted by the Air Force on December 26, 1972. It was a nice "Christmas present," the prototype contract amounting to more than $85,000,000 to McDonnell Douglas.

The first AMST aircraft, designated the YC-15, made its maiden flight on August 26, 1975, and on December 5, 1975, the second prototype was successfully flown for the first time. There followed a joint government-McDonnell Douglas flight test program at Edwards Air Force Base, California, and at MDC test facilities in Yuma, Arizona. The AMST prototypes came through with flying colors.

The YC-15 is a high-wing, wide-cabin transport built to demonstrate STOL operations from small, unimproved fields by a jet-powered aircraft large enough to haul modern military equipment.

An advanced technology aircraft, the YC-15 was the first jet transport to fly with an externally blown flap (EBF) powered-lift system, which makes use of the wing, four engines and large flaps to produce approximately twice the lift of a conventional transport.

The YC-15 also was the first jet transport to fly with a supercritical wing, designed for the utmost in aerodynamic efficiency. Selecting this low-drag, thick wing permitted a simpler design, a lighter weight and a greater fuel capacity. Span of the straight (unswept) wing is 110 feet 4 inches, and its area is 1740 square feet. During phase two of the YC-15 flight test program, a long-range wing was installed on one of the prototypes for evaluation. This wing, also supercritical, is 132 feet 7 inches long and has an area of 2107 square feet. It also incorporates the new flaps.

In the EBF system, the 32 feet 9 inch-long, double-segmented flaps are lowered directly into the exhaust from the engines, mounted two on each wing forward of the leading edge

and positioned so the air flow skims the underside of the wings. A portion of the exhaust air is deflected downward by the flaps, creating lift. Another quantity passes through the wide spaces (slots) between the flap segments and is turned downward by the Coanda effect (named after Belgian scientist Henri Coanda) to produce more lift.

The high-lift qualities of the YC-15 permit quick, 2000-foot takeoffs, approach speeds as low as 85 knots (97.8 mph) and steep glide path angles for descents and landings. It is designed to haul twice the payload into half the field length required by the majority of present USAF tactical transports.

With its advanced STOL characteristics reducing landing distances to 2000 feet for tactical missions, the YC-15 still is capable of cruising at more than 500 miles per hour on employment operations.

Another YC-15 advance is the large fuselage containing 67 percent more cargo space than the Air Force's largest tactical transport. Overall length of the YC-15 is 124 feet 3 inches, fuselage width is 18 feet and the cargo bay is 11.3 feet high, 11.7 feet wide and 47 feet long.

This increased cabin width permits the YC-15 to carry up to 40 troops and six pallets simultaneously, containers up to nine feet high or eight Army jeeps, four in each of two rows. Weaponry that could be air-lifted includes such standard Army self-propelled artillery as the 8-inch (203 mm) howitzer and the 175 mm gun, air defense vehicles such as the M48 Chaparral and M163 Vulcan dump truck. A large ramp in the rear of the aircraft facilitates vehicle loading, while a truck-bed level floor permits straight-in access.

Engines powering the YC-15s, in the start of the program, were JT8D-17 fanjets, each developing 16,000 pounds of takeoff thrust at sea level at 84 degrees Fahrenheit. The engines were the latest model of the reliable JT8D family built by Pratt & Whitney Aircraft division of United Technologies Corporation.

Two higher-performance engines were flight tested in 1977 on the YC-15. A single General Electric-SNECMA CFM-56, rated at 22,000 pounds of takeoff thrust, was installed on a YC-15, replacing one of the JT8D-17s, and a JT8D-209, with 18,000 pounds of thrust, was mounted on the other YC-15.

The YC-15 utilizes the cockpit enclosure of

the McDonnell Douglas DC-10 trijet, modified with the addition of two downward-viewing windows to meet the aerial delivery requirement for additional visibility. The cockpit is designed for a crew of two, with room for three if desired.

To land and take off repeatedly from rough fields, the YC-15 is equipped with a high-flotation landing gear system which includes a long-stroke main gear to accommodate high sink rates. Maximum gross takeoff weight of the YC-15 is 216,680 pounds and the design landing weight is 150,000 pounds. The transport will carry a maximum payload of 62,000 pounds and is designed to take off from a 2000-foot runway with a 27,000-pound load and deliver it to a destination at least 460 statute miles away. Ferry range is approximately 3,000 statute miles.

Despite the splendid performance of the YC-15 and the Boeing YC-14, the USAF advanced medium STOL program was not in the Administration budget submitted in January 1978. Neither aircraft, as late as the spring of 1979 had been given a go sign for a production contract.

According to Eugene Dubil, who was Vice President Engineering on the YC-15 project—"Its creative design could well be the predecessor of an efficient STOL jet aircraft for use in a broad variety of civil, government and military operations involving the transport of passengers and cargo."

THE FUTURE OF STOL aircraft, Mr. Mac

likewise believes, is tied irrevocably to the future of our entire air transportation system. He has pointed out that over 95% of commercial airlines' tonnage (passengers and freight) is generated from fifty large airports serving the fifty largest cities. Yet there are over 10,000 airports in the U.S. today. But because of the need for long, expensive-to-construct runways to accommodate conventional airliners, these smaller airports are virtually useless in the overall air transportation system. Thus, a great portion of our populace in the smaller cities and towns does not reap the benefits of air transport, stopping many growth potentials.

"The challenge is to bring air transportation to where the people are," declares Mr. Mac. And he adds — "STOL airliners can meet that challenge. With STOL capabilities the airliner can operate from small existing airports near city centers and from new STOL-ports which can be built in mid-town areas. No major runways are required. Any small 1500-foot strip is more than adequate. These potential new termini will also eliminate the long trip to outlying airports which often, on short hops, takes more time than that required to get to the destination."

Beyond STOL aircraft for commercial use comes the advent of VTOL airliners. With it will be the potential of taking off and landing on specially prepared surfaces atop buildings right in the center of cities. These will be much faster than large helicopters which today operate from some rooftops in major cities, mostly as "shuttles" carrying persons to

Two McDonnell Douglas YC-15 Advanced Medium STOL Transports began a year-long prototype flight test program for the USAF in 1975, but a production decision has been delayed. The YC-15 was the first aircraft to fly with an externally blown flap powered lift system, and the first large jet transport to fly with a supercritical wing.

Too large for existing United States tactical transports, a U.S. Army 155mm self-propelled howitzer travels up loading ramp into U.S. Air Force YC-15 jet prototype. Other Army equipment loaded into the wide cargo bay of the YC-15 included a "Goer" wrecker truck, a Mechanized Infantry Combat Vehicle, and an Armored Reconnaissance Airborne Assault Vehicle.

Large titanium flaps on Air Force YC-15 AMST (Advanced Medium STOL Transport) are shown in position for STOL (short takeoff and landing) operations. Additional lift is derived from the basic wing and flap and from supercirculation of air along the wing and flap resulting from jet exhaust passing through the slots between the flaps and turning downward. The total lift is designed to permit YC-15 takeoffs and landings from 2000-foot runways.

outlying airports. The VTOL will be capable of carrying large payloads and of flying long distances at jet speeds and offering jetliner comforts.

We are talking here of ten, twenty years ahead, but one thing seems assured — STOL and VTOL aircraft are here to stay. The trend will be to improve on present designs. A good example is the proposed commercial passenger version of the C-15 STOL aircraft.

Meanwhile, McDonnell Douglas is also engaged in the development of an advanced VTOL fighter, a modified and improved version of Hawker Siddeley's famous *Harrier*.

It is the latest to join a whole new breed of fighter planes built by McDonnell Douglas.

McDonnell Douglas F-15 *Eagle* air superiority fighter, it is said, can out-fly and out-fight any other fighter. The F-15 structure uses composite boron-epoxy material on control surfaces, and about 25 percent of airframe is made of titanium.

Chapter Twenty

Aerie Of The Eagle

ON MAY 24, 1978, the 5,000th *Phantom II* (F-4) Serial No. 77-0290 was delivered to the USAF. It was seventeen years and almost six months (December 29, 1960) since the first *Phantom II* was delivered to Navy Training Squadron VF-121 at the Naval Air Station in Miramar, California. Ever since, the F-4 has been a front line fighter design, in one configuration or another, flying with the air services of ten different Free World nations including the United States. Moreover, the F-4s are still in production (1979) and many others are undergoing up-date modifications at the McDonnell Douglas, Tulsa, Oklahoma facility.

Such a record of longevity and serviceability, marked by a stellar performance in both peacetime and in combat (Vietnam and the Mid East), has never been equalled in the lifetime of any other U.S. fighter design. Even though it is over twenty years old, a true "senior citizen" as aircraft go, there is still very little the F-4 can't do in the sophisticated world of modern air warfare. It does just about everything, and does it well, as is evidenced by the fact that it still is in heavy demand.

Keys among the replacements—if and when the *Phantom II* (F-4) disappears from the scene as time and technology catch up—are other McDonnell Douglas fighters—the vaunted F-15 and the multimission F-18 *Hornet*.

MOST RESIDENTS of the St. Louis area will not recall Tuesday, December 23, 1969, as anything to cheer about If they remember it at all, it might be because it was two days before Christmas, with weather to match. The temperature ranged from a high of 35 degrees to a low of 26 degrees and there was not a moment of sunshine. The winds wailed at a chilling 30 miles per hour over 5 inches of snow.

But most of the 33,000 St. Louisans who worked at McDonnell Douglas remember the date with unusual warmth and pleasure, because an event occurred which, among other points of significance, promised the difference between sustained employment levels and the potential loss of 10,000 jobs.

At about 4:30 on that Tuesday afternoon, a telephone in the office of Mr. Mac purred quietly. Brig. Gen. Benjamin N. Bellis, USAF, director of the F-15 System Program Office, was calling from Hq. USAF in Washington, D.C. to tell Mr. Mac that McDonnell Douglas had won the long and fiercely contested competition for the F-15 air superiority fighter contract, which, over the years ahead, could result in a multibillion dollar program for the corporation.

Mr. Mac beamed, thanked General Bellis, and within seconds his voice crackled over the plant wide public address system relaying the news of this great Christmas bonus to all his teammates.

No one stopped work, and if they had, it

would have been the first halt in years for those directly assigned to the F-15 program. Mr. Mac's announcement was the capstone of a massive team-building effort that began before 1965, which continues today and will continue for years to come.

It was as far back as 1961 that McDonnell began the first of a series of in-house studies, motivated by conviction within the company that at some time or other—in the not-too-foreseeable future, national defense would need a new fighter able to out-perform not only the alien threats but the McDonnell Douglas *Phantom*. As is so often the case with the inception of successful aircraft designs, a need not completely defined was anticipated with considerable accuracy. Simultaneously, conceptual studies were carried out by government teams.

In December 1965, the Air Force issued initial requests for concept formulation proposals. The intensity of design effort increased, and in December 1968 awards for contract definition were made to McDonnell Douglas, North American Rockwell and Fairchild Hiller, thus narrowing the F-15 contestants to three.

It is probably understood that the manufacturing of any modern aircraft is very exacting, but few outside the aerospace industry are aware of the tremendous labor entailed in preparing a proposal for a modern aircraft design, seeking at large cost a contract which a company may or may not win.

The stark facts are that some 2,500,000 man hours of grueling, night-and-day, seven-day-a-week effort by a team which ranged from 200 to 1000 men and women went into the F-15 design that culminated in the winning of the contract and the manufacturing now in orderly progress at the McDonnell Aircraft Company division of McDonnell Douglas.

By June 1969, design proposals required much more detail. Specifically, the proposal which led to the winning of the F-15 contract was 37,500 pages long, bound into 308 separate, printed books.

According to Don Malvern, F-15 team manager: "It was an evolutionary process stemming from many channels of contributory creation both within the government and within the company. It is not possible to assign the F-15 idea to any specific group or individual. Starting about 1962, there were a series of in-house studies by both government

and contractors, and in 1963 we started to intensify our efforts toward developing a next generation airplane to follow the *Phantom*.

"Some were company funded and some were done under contract with the government to find the answers to questions about potential application of new technology. I would say the crucial time period was the three years between 1965 and 1967 because then, various alternative applications of technology, developed since 1955, began to come together and these were matched against the foreseeable requirements for air superiority. The interaction between the requirements and the available technology considered several alternate designs with the winning concept leading to the F-15 as we know it today."

THE F-15 *Eagle* is a high performance, extremely maneuverable, single place fighter capable of gaining and maintaining air superiority for Air Force tactical air forces. Designed to achieve this air supremacy against enemy fighters in all types of aerial combat, the F-15 has the radar and defensive systems to detect, acquire, track and attack the threat when operating in friendly or enemy controlled airspace. The new advanced tactical fighter has the fuel for expanded combat radius and increased time in the combat area as well as the proper mix of aerial weapons to enable the pilot to aggressively engage and defeat the threat on any terms.

The McDonnell Aircraft Company of St. Louis is prime contractor for the F-15. Pratt & Whitney Aircraft Company manufactures the F-100 advanced technology turbofan engines that power the F-15.

The F-15 is an advanced, twin-engine fighter designed specifically for high maneuverability in air-to-air combat. Its low wing loading and high thrust-to-weight ratio provides unprecedented maneuverability.

The F-15 is the first U.S. fighter aircraft to possess a thrust-to-weight ratio greater than 1 to 1. Its two Pratt & Whitney F-100 turbine engines each generate thrust in the 25,000 lb. class. The F-15, with full internal fuel and missile complement, weighs about 40,000 lbs.

A clean wing, with inboard flaps and outboard ailerons, was selected for the aircraft after extensive tests and analyses of more than 100 wing designs. This wing provides the most efficient low-drag configuration at high lift in

Eagle displays array of various weapons it can carry. Strike power consists of bombs, rockets, rapid fire cannon, depending upon mission. Top speed is in excess of Mach 2.5 with high degree of maneuverability.

F-15 *Eagles,* the world's finest air superiority fighter, is operational with USAF squadrons within the continental US and overseas. In 1975, the *Eagle* set eight time-to-climb records. It can climb to 50,000 feet quicker than the rocket that boosted our astronauts toward the moon.

The USAF F-15 *Eagle,* said to be the world's finest air superiority fighter, is the first U.S. fighter aircraft with a thrust to weight ratio greater than one to one. First flown in 1972, the *Eagle* entered operational service with the Tactical Air Command at Langley AFB in January 1976. *Eagles* have also been ordered by Japan, Israel, and Saudi Arabia.

the Mach 1 speed range, but permits top speed in excess of Mach 2.5.

A low wing loading and an excellent thrust-to-weight ratio provide the F-15 with unprecedented maneuverability. Combined with an advanced electronic system to sort out and identify targets and to evade enemy defenses, these features enable the F-15 to find, identify, engage, and destroy any aircraft expected to be a threat through the 1980s.

F-15 *Eagles* have downed simulated MiG-25 *Foxbats* in tests over Eglin AFB, Florida.

Bomarc drones simulated high-performance MiGs. The first encounter saw an *Eagle* launch an AIM-7F Sparrow missile at a Bomarc traveling at Mach 2.7 at 71,000 feet—performance similar to that of a Foxbat. The missile, armed with a dummy warhead, passed within lethal distance of the target.

In a second engagement, the *Eagle* carried live Sparrow missiles. With the Bomarc at 68,000 feet and again at Mach 2.7, one Sparrow launched by the F-15 found and destroyed the simulated MiG-25.

During other tests at the China Lake Naval Weapons Test Center, California, two unarmed AIM-7F Sparrows launched by an F-15 scored direct hits on aircraft drones flying at about 500 feet altitude—an area normally obscured by ground clutter in previous fighter and missile radar.

A third Sparrow shot in the China Lake tests was equipped with an armed warhead. Launched by the F-15 at a range well beyond normal visual contact, the missile destroyed an F-86 fighter drone performing severe

evasive maneuvers.

In other mock air battles against simulated hostile aircraft, the *Eagle* won 176 of 178 encounters.

The first production *Eagle* aircraft No. 21 was delivered to the Tactical Air Command in November 1974, almost four years after the first preliminary design review was held between the Air Force and McDonnell Douglas people. First TAC unit to receive the *Eagles* was the 555th Tactical Training Command Squadron at Luke Air Force Base, Arizona.

In January 1976, *Eagles* became operational fighters with the 27th Tactical Fighter Squadron at Langley Air Force Base, Virginia. Today the F-15s are in service overseas with NATO forces.

Over the next five years the USAF is committed to buy almost 800 of the F-15s for its service squadrons. In addition to being an "air superiority" fighter aircraft, the *Eagle* can be used as an attack aircraft, for air-to-ground strafing and as a bomber. It can carry A-weapons.

Perhaps the greatest tribute of all for the *Eagle* is in the words of General Robert Dixon, head of the USAF Tactical Command when the first F-15 was delivered. After he flew the aircraft, General Dixon said—"There is no air superiority fighter in existence that can match its combat capability. This aircraft, let there be no doubt, gives us a decided edge . . ."

Then there's the story told by James McCartney of the *Detroit Free Press.* McCartney, upon a visit to Langley Air Force base, said he saw an F-15 parked out on the ramp with a

Eagle double-the-speed of sound fighter can slow down to 130-mph landing speed. Production F-15s have been in service with Tactical Service Squadrons as operational fighters since 1976.

F-15 *Eagle* production line in St. Louis probably will run well into the 1990s. Orders for the vaunted fighter plane total more than $1-Billion! And more are likely to be sold to other Free World nations when political clouds disappear.

267

A U.S. Air Force F-15 *Eagle* fighter taxiing prior to takeoff with a full load of missiles and bombs.

slogan on the fuselage that says it all.

It read—THE MEANEST MAN.

DESIGN AND BUILD a fighter that will outperform the fabulous *Phantom II*, that can outfly the vaunted A-7 *Corsair* and the versatile A-4 *Skyhawk* . Make it fast, and quick, easily maintainable, and rugged. Make it suitable for carrier takeoffs and landings and also for land-based operations. The U.S. Navy and the U.S. Marine Corps want it YESTERDAY. And it must be able to serve as a front line aircraft through the 1990s.

Such was the challenge that McDonnell Douglas accepted back in 1975. At the time some people called it impossible. Today it is called *Hornet* the F-18 strike fighter.

The F-18 *Hornet* is a single-seat, twin-engine strike fighter designed for use by the U.S. Navy and Marine Corps. It is being developed in two slightly different versions: An F-18 fighter escort to replace the F-4, and an A-18 light attack aircraft to replace the A-7. Larger and heavier than the A-7 but smaller and lighter than the F-4, the *Hornet* is superior to both in the performance of their respective missions. The F-18 and A-18 are 99 percent common, so each can do the other's job if necessary.

The F-18 *Hornet* is being developed by McDonnell Douglas Corporation, the prime contractor, and Northrop Corporation, which will do 30 per cent of airframe development and 40 per cent of airframe production work. It is an adaptation of the YF-17 air combat fighter prototype, which was developed by Northrop for an Air Force lightweight fighter competition.

When armed for air-to-air combat, the F-18 carries two Sidewinder missiles on its wing tips, two Advanced Sparrow missiles on the lower corners of its fuselage, and an M61 six-barrel 20-millimeter gun mounted in its nose. Three external fuel tanks are carried on the centerline and the inboard wing stations. For attack missions, the A-18 carries air-to-ground ordnance on center, inboard and outboard wing stations.

Its two General Electric F404 turbofan engines, each in the 16,000-pound thrust class, give the *Hornet* a thrust-to-weight ratio of approximately one-to-one, a top speed of more than 1.8 times the speed of sound, and a range of more than 400 nautical miles on internally carried fuel alone. The aircraft can fly at the speed of sound on intermediate power without engaging its afterburners.

Built to withstand the punishment of carrier launchings and landings, the *Hornet* combines a high level of reliability with excellent maintainability. Together, these attributes make it an available aircraft—one ready to perform its missions when needed.

Fully armed, the *Hornet* has a fighter escort range greater than that of the F-4J. It can also accelerate from Mach .8 to Mach 1.6 considerably quicker, turn in a much tighter cir-

McDonnell Douglas F-18 *Hornet* Strike Fighter. Navy and Marines have F-18 for escort duty and A-18 as light attack aircraft. *Hornet* would replace F-4 and A-6 *Corsair*.

The F-18, armed for air-to-air combat, carries two Sidewinder missiles on its wingtips, two Sparrow missiles on the lower corner of its fuselage, and mounts an M61 six-barrel 20-millimeter gun in its nose.

F-18 NAVY AIR COMBAT FIGHTER

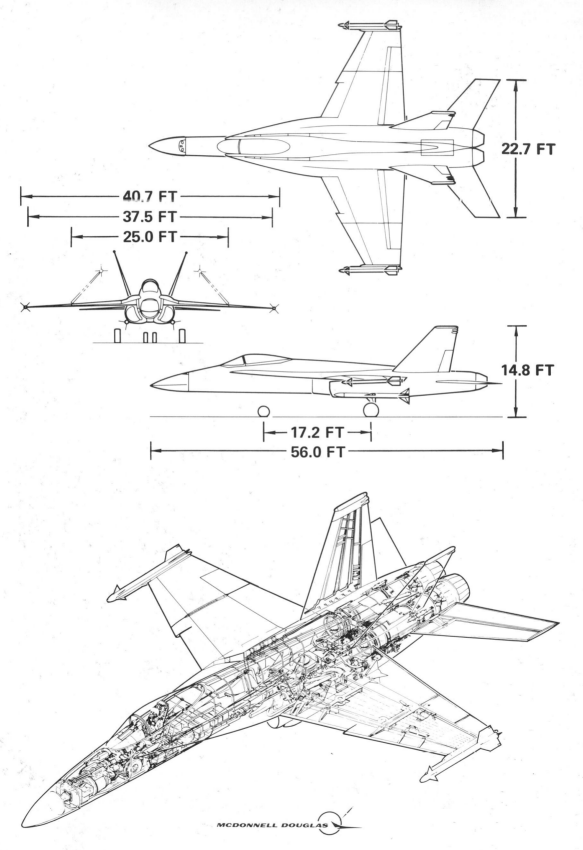

22.7 FT

40.7 FT

37.5 FT

25.0 FT

14.8 FT

17.2 FT

56.0 FT

MCDONNELL DOUGLAS

cle, and detect enemy aircraft significantly better. The F-18's tail-on detection range is greatly improved over the F-4J's.

In its role as a light attack aircraft, the A-18 offers accuracy as good as or better than that of any existing system. In comparison with the light attack system it will replace, the A-18's agility and power provide greater speed over target, a significantly improved loaded turn capability, and a considerable loaded thrust-to-weight ratio improvement. And because the attack *Hornet* is armed with a nose gun and Sidewinder missiles and can be cleared of its air-to-ground ordnance, it has a fighter capability of its own. The *Hornet's* combat ceiling is approximately 50,000 feet.

Systems used include an airborne weapons control system, an inertial navigation system more accurate than those currently in use, communication and weapons systems, an avionics system with all modes required for air-to-air and air-to-ground missions, and a control-by-wire system with a mechanical stabilator backup.

On September 13, 1978, America's newest strike fighter, the prototype F-18 *Hornet,* rolled out of the McDonnell Aircraft Company's plant in St. Louis. Among those watching the debut were Adm. Thomas Hayward, chief of naval operations, and Lt.

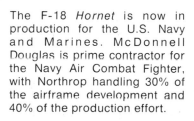

The F-18 *Hornet* is now in production for the U.S. Navy and Marines. McDonnell Douglas is prime contractor for the Navy Air Combat Fighter, with Northrop handling 30% of the airframe development and 40% of the production effort.

The U.S. Navy and Marine Corps F-18 *Hornet* strike fighter, refueling during a test flight by a Navy KA-3 tanker.

271

Gen. Lawrence Snowden, chief of staff of the Marine Corps.

Painted in Navy markings on one side and Marine markings on the other, the *Hornet* taxied into view as a crowd of about 900 watched and the U.S. Marine Corps Band from Quantico, Va. played.

The first flight on November 18, 1978 marked the opening of an extensive flight test program for the *Hornet*.

The first production models are scheduled for completion in 1980. Approximately 10 per cent of all F-18s produced will be two-seaters for training purposes; their back seats will duplicate all controls and displays except the head-up display mechanism.

Production of the *Hornet* is expected to reach a peak of nine aircraft monthly in October 1983.

The Navy said it intends to procure 1377 *Hornets,* with production building to a peak of 11 aircraft per month by 1985.

DURING ONE OF our many talks Mr. Mac was saying, "Where folks in the rest of the world have done a fine job, it is good for us to sit down and talk things over with them. Maybe that way we can all learn something. That's the way it was with us and the start of the development of our AV-8 Advanced *Harrier* VTOL (Vertical Take Off Landing) fighter.

"We didn't design this aircraft. The people at Hawker Siddeley Aviation, Ltd. (now part of British Aerospace) in England developed the original *Harrier.* But as you know, we had done a lot of work with STOL and VTOL machines, so we decided to get together with the British and exchange ideas. It started out as simple as that, and we both learned a lot.

"It so turned out that we are now going to produce an advanced *Harrier,* incorporating many of our ideas which make it a much better aircraft. We are proud that the Hawker Siddeley people are our new 'teammates' as a major contractor to the McDonnell Douglas AV-8B program.

"I honestly believe that this sort of togetherness has got to come and to a much greater degree. I think this will be the trend in this business, and we are doing all we can to promote it . . ."

The aircraft Mr. Mac was referring to is officially designated the AV-8B, an advanced, high performance version of the AV-8A *Harrier* (bought from the British) now in service with the Marines. McDonnell Douglas engineers, working with a design team from Hawker Siddeley, developed this prototype version. The advanced AV-8B will meet

Advanced AV-8B *Harrier* is planned as replacement for the A-4 *Skyhawk* with Marine Corps squadrons.

Making its first flight, the McDonnell Douglas YAV-8B vertical takeoff and landing aircraft hovers above the runway at Lambert-St. Louis International Airport. The YAV-8B later made its first forward flight. The Marine Corps has announced its intention to purchase about 350 AV-8Bs.

Marine mission requirements at a total development cost about one-third that of a modern non-V/STOL aircraft.

Features of the advanced technology to be incorporated in the AV-8B are: A new wing having a supercritical airfoil for better lift and cruise characteristics. Use of graphite epoxy composite materials for the new wing and for the ailerons, flaps and outrigger fairings to save weight. A new engine inlet designed to provide more thrust for vertical and short takeoff, and more efficient cruise. (The AV-8B will use the same Rolls Royce Pegasus 11 engine as the original *Harrier*.) Addition of aerodynamic devices underneath the fuselage

to improve vertical takeoff capability.

Changes to the highly successful original *Harrier* were made only when they improved performance, weight, reliability, and maintainability, or when they saved money.

The first YAV-8B advanced *Harrier* was flown on November 9, 1978. With test pilot C. A. Plummer at the controls, the AV-8B prototype lifted off the Lambert-St. Louis International Airport runway and hovered an estimated 130 feet above the pavement for seven minutes. In that brief time, it clearly demonstrated its VTOL capability.

The vertical and short takeoff and landing feature of the AV-8B is described thusly: The

They never leave the ground. McDonnell Douglas Manned Air Combat Simulator (MACS) is fixed base simulation device system which features computer input and visual presentations to train combat pilots. Pilots can fly variety of missions over and over again to maintain proficiency. Here, pilot in cockpit of simulator sees "enemy" image on screen.

single Pegasus 11 engine has four rotating exhaust nozzles, two on each side, which can direct the thrust vertically for VTOL or to an intermediate position for STOL. Aircraft attitude control during V/STOL and hover is provided by reaction controls located at the wing tips, nose and tail. Power for these reaction controls is provided by the Pegasus 11 engine. In normal flight, engine thrust is directed to the rear and the aircraft is flown like any other turbo-powered aircraft.

The AV-8B will have more than double the payload or range capability of the earlier *Harrier.* Full-scale production is scheduled to start in 1983, squadron service to begin in 1983-84. The AV-8B will fulfill Marine Corps requirement for a *Harrier* follow-on and will replace the ageless A-4 *Skyhawk.*

Approximately 350 AV-8B aircraft will be required by the Marine Corps during the 1980s. By the end of the 1980s, the Marines would like an all AV-8B light attack force that will significantly increase the Corps' ability to accomplish its mission.

MCDONNELL DOUGLAS doesn't just design and build commercial and military aircraft, but it also is engaged in design and development of related systems and devices to train air crews to fly its planes (and others) and provide new safety features. Some examples of these additional products are the new VITAL IV visual system for flight simulators, MACS, a Manned Air Combat Simulator and ACES II ejection seats for the new generation of high performance fighter aircraft.

VITAL IV being built in St. Charles, Missouri, at the McDonnell Douglas Electronics Company there, presents day, night and twilight scenes to simulate visual takeoff and landing, terminal docking and taxi, air refueling, formation flying, aircraft carrier and helicopter operations and weapons delivery images.

The high-resolution color scenes can include airports, cities, ground targets, ships, moving vehicles, or even other aircraft. Digital computer techniques are used to generate the visual image. The use of computers to produce a visual scene for pilot training is now in its seventh year.

In that time, according to Gordon Handberg of MDEC, writing in the ICAO bulletin, "computer-generated image (CGI) visuals for flight simulators have almost completely supplanted every other type of equipment being ordered by the airlines" and are now being chosen for military simulation.

"The visual equipment responsible for this dramatic change comes from a technology usually identified as calligraphic—a convenient yet forgivable extension of the word more commonly associated with penmanship . . . In computer graphics, the word calligraphic applies to the equipment which makes line drawings on the face of a cathode ray tube; it does this in order to communicate the contents of the computer to the person who is operating it. Calligraphic visual simulation does this in a manner disguised to delude the operator into forgetting that a computer had anything to do with it.

"The operator here, of course, is the pilot of a flight simulator. The delusion is deliberate because the value of the equipment resides in the illusion it creates. The real-world illusion achieved by a calligraphic visual is in fact quite good, producing scenes outside the simulator windshield that are very realistic in appearance and geometrically accurate."

Pilots accept the illusion enthusiastically. The result is that approximately 40 of the world's airlines have incorporated systems of this general type and are relying on them heavily for present and future pilot training needs.

MACS, Manned Air Combat Simulator, is a versatile, fixed-base simulator for air-to-air combat pilot training in all types of combat maneuvers. MACS permits development of air tactics to the very edge of aircraft performance, without risk. It provides repeated realistic practice while saving in maintenance, logistics and fuel.

MACS is an outgrowth of McDonnell Douglas simulator applications in spacecraft and aircraft development which began with the use of analog simulators to evaluate handling qualities, avionics and pilot procedures during aircraft design evaluation. Digital computers were later incorporated into hybrid systems, along with mathematical models, software and visual displays.

Primarily a visual air-to-air combat trainer, MACS has a variety of selectable modes of operation and a range of aircraft and armament models for both within and beyond visual range air combat. It can be easily modified to accommodate new armament, new threat capability, aircraft performance changes, new aircraft, and even proposed improvements for assessment of design changes. The cockpits are removable from trainee stations, enabling a change in aircraft type in less than two hours.

MACS is a cost-effective aid to develop and maintain combat skills and insure most productive use of actual flying time. One MACS system can fly many complete "missions" each hour, any hour of the day or night, regardless of weather or other flight considerations. Since MACS establishes combat scenarios at the touch of a switch, no "cruise out-cruise back" time is lost. MACS even supplies the adversaries.

McDonnell Douglas was awarded an ACES II High Technology Ejection Seat production contract in 1977 for F-15, F-16 and A-10 fighter and attack aircraft following a "fly-before-buy" competition. ACES II is the latest development in a 30-year program of escape systems that has led to production of more than 6800 ejection seats for combat aircraft.

ACES II gives fighter crews who must "bail-out" a far better chance of landing safely, being rescued or evading capture. A high speed drogue chute and a self-contained gyro controlled vernier rocket pitch control system yield unmatched stability, and help significantly reduce crew member limb flailing during the ejection sequence.

Sensing altitude and airspeed, the ACES II electronic sequencer selects the appropriate actions to stabilize, slow and recover the crew member from any point within its performance envelope—zero-zero to 600 knots. So effective is the system, it permits escape when inverted only 155 feet off the ground and safe escape from ground level to 50,000 feet!

In addition to such programs as the above, McDonnell Douglas is engaged in many diversified activities which many people never hear about or associate with the aerospace manufacturer.

Aces II ejection seat is "life saver" for high-speed bailout.

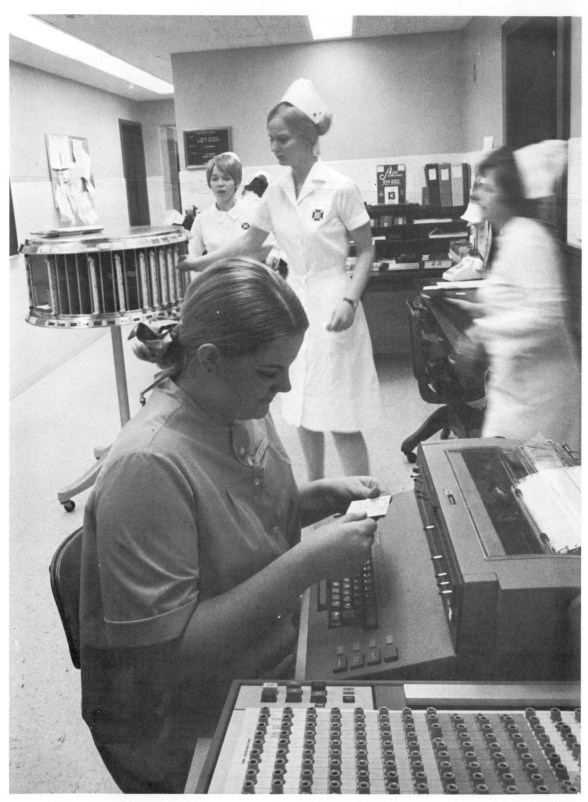

Nurses make use of McDonnell Douglas Automation Company's Physicians' Data Service.

Chapter
Twenty-one

Flight
And Life

MENTION THE NAME McDonnell Douglas and almost instinctively one envisions great silvery fleets of airliners carrying the world's commerce across the skies; sleek, supersonic fighters emblazoned with the ensigns of most of the Free World's nations, symbolic sentinels in times of change and strife; giant needle-nosed rockets pushing orbital payloads into the dark unknown regions of space. Perhaps, too, one sees unfolding the greatest venture of all—man on his way to the stars.

Think of this! All of these things Mr. Mac and Don Douglas and their thousands of "teammates" have helped make possible—turning fantasies into fact. Indeed, this is the world that McDonnell Douglas helped fashion, and it is just the beginning. For out of these efforts have come so many other things which have changed the way we think and act, work and play, make war and make peace, and have learned to survive on this whirling dervish, the Planet Earth.

In the process, each step in the long, long journey to touch a star, has produced not just things with wings and spacecraft, but many new inventions, new technologies, new services, new philosophies in virtually every field of endeavor. Perhaps no other industry—only the aerospace industry with McDonnell Douglas as a leader—has reached into so many corners of our daily lives.

There are so many things that McDonnell Douglas does besides build airplanes. Here, for example, are just a few of the many diversified activities.

In 1960 Mr. Mac founded a new company as part of a goal to become engaged in more diversified activities. "I decided," he told the author, "that it was time to blossom out beyond hardware products. It seemed to me that the trend in the years ahead will be toward new scientific and technical services."

MCAUTO was born, McDonnell Automation Company, which has grown into one of the largest data processing service firms in the world. Today, known as the McDonnell Douglas Automation Company, a division of McDonnell Douglas Corporation, the service organization has more than 150 sophisticated computers and associated supporting equipment valued at more than a quarter of a billion dollars! MCAUTO "teammates" total more than 5000 personnel and it has offices in major cities throughout the U.S., in London, Paris, and Stockholm. Data processing services are performed for more than 2400 clients.

With a variety of systems and vast computer power, MCAUTO offers a complete data service—consulting, programming, systems design, data conversion, training and documentation, software, hardware and teleprocessing.

Included among these services are:

MCAUTO's Health Services Division provides almost 850 hospitals throughout the United States with medical records processing, financial systems, data collection and computer-assisted EKG analysis via teleprocessing. It also provides medical groups and clinics with patient billing systems.

McDonnell Douglas Automation Company also provides data processing services to more than 30 clinics and Medical Group Practices. The system called PDS—Physician Data Services— is an interactive, on-line financial system that automates procedures to help handle accounts receivable and collections for medical groups and clinics. Although PDS is one of the most complete and sophisticated systems available today, it is extremely easy to use and its flexibility enables it to be adapted to the existing operating procedures established by most medical groups.

To help businessmen and scientists grasp important information quickly, MCAUTO computer specialists have devised a way to change tabular data instantly into pie charts, bar graphs and other visual aids on a graphics terminal or a pen and ink plotter.

This transformation is accomplished through computer logic called VIVIDATA, which MCAUTO's data processing customers can include within their computer programs.

The computer-drawn charts and graphs are more quickly available, more accurate and less expensive than illustrations drawn by artists and draftsmen.

VIVIDATA has few limitations. Basically, it converts any numerical data into equivalent graphs with appropriate annotations and labels. It also produces an assortment of pattern shadings for highlighting data, as for instance, in illustrating different mineral deposits at various levels below the earth's surface.

The user also can define his own symbols. Even foreign language characters could be produced. Other capabilities include producing a plot, and producing multiple graphs on the same video terminal screen to show the same information in different graphic forms.

MCAUTO, the Automation Company is a leader in the application of NC (numerical control) technology. Numerical control means machine tools are being governed by a computer. Information in the form of numerically-coded data guides the tool as it cuts the surfaces of a part. Today, more and more

manufacturing plants are milling parts this way. By means of terminals in the plant, data is fed to MCAUTO computers for processing into directions needed to drive the machine tools.

MCAUTO offers Computer Aided Design and Drafting, a totally new concept in computer processing services for the design engineer. By conversing or interacting with the computer, the engineer rapidly and accurately designs a product in a three-dimensional data base. Previously created geometry can be easily and quickly retrieved. The computer performs all the geometrical and repetitive tasks, allowing the engineer to focus his creative talents on designing. The overall result is significantly improved product design cost and schedule performance.

In 1979, McDonnell Douglas began construction of a new seven-building headquarters complex in St. Louis to house its expanding MCAUTO computer services division.

At its Monrovia, California, division, the McDonnell Douglas Astronautics Company builds Actrion III microcomputer numerical control systems for machine tools. Actrion III incorporates multiple microcomputers to provide an expandable and powerful system of management and guidance.

Machine servo performance is continuously monitored to minimize parts scrappage. Programmable machine interface substantially lowers interface costs. Electromechanical relays are virtually eliminated and interface electronics are at a minimum.

Actrion III adapts to diverse machine tool types, facilitating standardization of machine controls as well as spare parts. The company has recently announced the addition of several new features and improvements aimed at increasing productivity, with the further benefit of simplifying control programming and operating procedures.

In St. Louis, Missouri, an improved process for applying aluminum corrosion-protection coating to metallic parts has been developed and the equipment introduced by McDonnell Douglas. Called ivadizing, the process provides cost-competitive corrosion protection without the ecological disadvantages of alternative systems.

The patented McDonnell Douglas ion vapor deposition process is similar to conventional vacuum coating, except that during plating the parts are held at a high negative charge potential. This causes a "glow discharge" around the part, which results in continuous cleaning of the part by charged ion bombardment. It also causes a portion of the aluminum vapor to be ionized and accelerated toward the surface of the part. The resulting coating has superior adhesion and uniformity of thickness.

Two types of ivadizing equipment are being produced—one a large Ivadizer coater suitable for production speed rack-plating of detail parts; the other a system for coating small parts, such as fasteners.

Ivadizer deposited aluminum is a multipurpose coating, applicable to aluminum, steel or titanium and for a broad range of products. It offers significant advantages over more commonly used coatings. It can be applied to complex shapes and application of a half-mil coating takes about five minutes. *Neither the coating nor the coating process leaves any toxic or environmental waste.*

McDonnell Douglas is applying its advanced technology experience successfully in the promising new field of solar energy.

A conceptual design has been chosen by the U.S. Department of Energy (DOE) for the nation's first experimental solar "power tower," a 10,000 kilowatt electrical generating plant to be built near Barstow, California. The design is based upon the cylindrical "inside out" boiler (receiver), metal-glass mirrors (heliostats), and oil/rock thermal storage subsystems developed by a team headed by McDonnell Douglas Astronautics Company as part of a two-year development program.

The experimental plant at Barstow will generate electric power in the same way that a fossil or nuclear plant does, except that the energy which drives the turbine/generator will be produced from the heat of the sun. The chief solar components are the heliostats (sun-tracking mirrors) that concentrate sunlight, the receiver (boiler) that converts water into high-pressure steam, and a heat storage

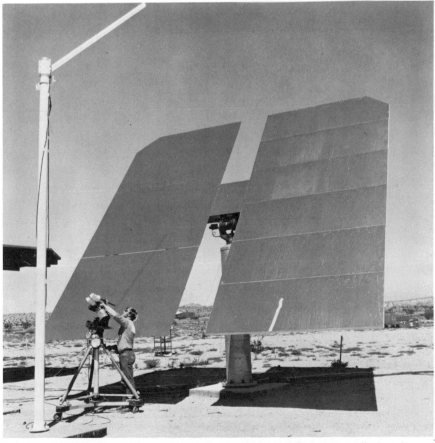

McDonnell Douglas is developing ways to concentrate and apply the vitally needed, non-polluting, inexhaustible energy of the sun to generate electricity for use in homes and industries. These include design concepts for experimental solar-powered electric generating plants at Daggett, California and Reno, Nevada.

system that permits steam to be produced when there is no sunlight.

In the concept chosen, a cylindrical configuration of boiler-tubes sits atop a 213 foot tower and absorbs sunlight reflected from approximately 2,000 mirrors surrounding the tower. Each heliostat will include multifaceted glass mirrors of approximately 400 square feet supported by a metal structure mounted on a concrete foundation. The field of heliostats will be computer controlled to continuously reflect the sun's energy onto the receiver.

Steam from the receiver passes through a turbine and generator on the ground, generating more than 10,000 kilowatts of electrical power. Additional steam can be produced from the storage system to continue generating about 7,000 kilowatts for four hours without sunlight.

DOE expects to place the plant in operation in late 1981. The plant will be built and operated under an arrangement with the Southern California Edison Company cooperative, the Los Angeles Department of Water and Power, and the California Energy Resources Conservation Commission. Southern California Edison will provide the non-solar generating equipment.

After developing the conceptual design for the Barstow plant, MDAC was awarded a follow-on contract for final design of the collector subsystem, including fabrication and testing of pre-production heliostats.

Under a separate contract, MDAC holds the key role of providing design integration services on the Barstow facility, which DOE has named "Solar One." Solar One will provide engineering data and operating experience leading toward the development of commer-

Solar Energy is absorbed using a refracting type fresnel lens in this McDonnell Douglas concept of a collector field subsystem under design study. Concentration is produced by focusing the fresnel lens on a black chrome plated steel pipe absorber through which the heat transfer fluid flows at variable rates to correspond with variations in solar insolation. The lens and absorber are housed in an array, which is rotated in azimuth and elevated by a solar tracking servo system.

cial solar-powered electric plants with capacities ranging from 1,000 to 100,000 kilowatts, or more.

According to program manager Ray Hallet, the pilot plant will be capable of serving the needs of a community of 8,000 to 10,000 people when developing rated power.

In addition to its effort on the Central Receiver System, McDonnell Douglas is working on other programs in the solar energy field.

One of these is a study for Sandia Laboratories, Albuquerque, N.M., in the type of solar energy generation known as the distributed field collector system. This involves the use of linear concentrators which focus the sun's rays on a field of liquid-filled pipes to develop heat for industrial use.

Also, under a DOE contract, McDonnell Douglas Astronautics Company is conducting studies to define solar total energy systems that are technically and economically feasible and can satisfy selected industry demands. Primary emphasis is on systems where industrial process heat, electrical demands, and space heating and cooling requirements are met at maximum possible efficiency. Over 500 industries including canneries, potash, paint, sodium sulfate, asphalt paving materials, prestressed concrete, and concrete block have been surveyed in this study.

NOT ONLY is McDonnell Douglas pioneering in the use of solar power to help in our country's growing energy crisis, but the company also is involved in programs that help keep vital fuels flowing.

A McDonnell Douglas Astronautics Company developed Cryo-Anchor®, based on heat pipe technology, is used along the Alaskan pipeline to stabilize foundation structures in

McDonnell Douglas developed Cryo-Anchor® arctic soil stabilizers installed along the trans-Alaska oil pipeline refrigerate pipeline structural supports on sections of the line constructed above ground.

the Arctic soil. More than 150,000 units have been installed along the oil-bearing artery.

Cryo-Anchor prevents permafrost degradation and active-layer "heaving" due to freeze and thaw conditions. When air temperature is lower than ground temperature, the unit senses this variation and extracts heat from the ground. The reaction maintains a low temperature in the soil the year around, eliminating the possible "sinking" of pipeline supports which could snap the line and cut off the oil flow until costly repairs could be made.

Cryo-Anchor can conduct heat more than 500 times as effectively as copper. The unit is totally automatic, requires no power, has no moving parts.

In another area McDonnell Douglas has joined with Gaz-Transport Company of France in the development of an advanced containment system that lowers the cost of tanker transport of liquefied natural gas. LNG Sea shipment from remote gas fields to large population centers is considered a major factor in helping relieve energy shortages.

McDonnell Douglas has a contract to provide insulation containment systems for two 900-foot tankers being built by Sun Shipbuilding and Dry Dock Company to carry LNG from Alaska to California.

The system is comprised of "logs"—3D planks—of polyurethane foam reinforced with strands of fiber glass, bonded directly to the inner hull of the tanker in brick-layer fashion. Welded to this is an invar membrane, a thin sheet of nickel and iron alloy manufactured by Gaz-Transport, completing the lining of the hull of the tankers.

The combined McDonnell Douglas and Gaz-Transport system permits an increased cargo load of LNG for established hull designs, or the same volume to be carried in smaller hulls.

At the McDonnell Douglas Astronautics Company facility in Huntington Beach, an MDAC designed machine for large scale manufacturing of the polyurethane-fiber glass ship lining has been installed in a new 30,000 square foot building. The machine is a 271-foot long automated production line that will turn out the "logs" at the rate of three feet per minute.

The product from the machine is an adaptation of the lightweight, high-strength insulation developed by MDAC to line the liquid hydrogen tanks of Saturn S-1V and S-1VB

rocket stages in the Apollo lunar program. Like hydrogen, LNG must be kept at cryogenic (extremely cold) temperatures— about −260 degrees F (−162 degrees C)—to maintain its liquid state.

The new facility for mass production of the Saturn-type insulation is a central part of the effort by MDAC's Cryogenic Insulation Program (CIP) division directed by Dr. Joseph Waisman.

Another outgrowth of the company's aerospace experience is MIVAC, a microwave vacuum crop dryer for agricultural products.

MIVAC, the world's first microwave vacuum system for drying crops, is being tested at the U.S. Department of Agriculture's Coastal Plains Station in Tifton, Georgia.

Developed under a U.S. Department of Energy contract, this small-scale experimental facility applies space-age technology to the drying of a wide range of agricultural products.

Aeroglide Corporation of Raleigh, North Carolina, a designer and fabricator of grain dryers, was subcontractor to McDonnell Douglas on the project.

In addition to lowering electric energy bills for crop drying, MIVAC also does a better job of drying delicate crops such as peanuts and rice. Microwaves heat the product from the inside out, thus minimizing heat damage, and the vacuum lowers the boiling point of water to speed the process.

Compared to conventional crop drying equipment, MIVAC is faster, quieter, cleaner, more efficient, simpler and safer.

McDonnell Douglas began considering applications for vacuum chambers and microwaves beyond space program uses following a 1973 fire at the Government Records Center in St. Louis.

The company's large vacuum chamber facilities, built to test spacecraft, were used to dry millions of water-soaked records after that blaze.

ALL OF THESE things and more, some of which can't be talked about for security reasons, and others still in "the discovery stage," are part of McDonnell Douglas' purpose and mission to better serve mankind.

Admittedly, a prime defense contractor, McDonnell Douglas can point with pride to the many by-products that have and are coming out of its aerospace programs.

McDonnell Douglas has acquired the Crow-Irvine interest in Douglas Plaza, a 43.7-acre commercial development adjacent to Orange County airport in Irvine, California. Through a subsidiary, McDonnell Douglas had been a partner with Crow-Irvine since development began in 1973.

Advanced supersonic transport (AST) concept under study at McDonnell Douglas Corporation in Long Beach, California, is illustrated in this artwork. As now envisioned, the AST would travel at a cruising speed of Mach 2.2, which would be nine percent faster than today's *Concorde* supersonic transport. Passenger capacity would be about 250, and range would be 5100 nautical miles, compared to 100 passengers and 3350 nautical miles for the *Concorde*. With more efficient engines and improved performance, the AST would be an economically sound and environmentally satisfactory transport for the mid-1980s and beyond, McDonnell Douglas engineers contend.

Chapter Twenty-two

Day After Tomorrow

ELEVEN YEARS AFTER the merger, the McDonnell Douglas Corporation was hale and hearty, an industrial giant with a firm backlog of $6,038,133,000 according to the 1978 corporate Annual Report. At that same time, Mr. McDonnell reported to his stockholders . . .

"Total backlog, enhanced by growth in commercial aircraft orders and the success of military programs, increased 22% during the year and was $8.5 billion on 31 December . . . we made substantial progress toward our goal of an even balance between commercial and government business. Commercial business was fully 50% of our firm backlog at year-end."

McDonnell Douglas had climbed to the No. 1 position in prime defense contracts awarded. It had 70,547 employees working in 72 communities in 29 states, the District of Columbia, the island of Kwajalein, in the Pacific, and 11 nations. Their payroll, during the year, totaled $1,292,998,063 contributing to the economic lifeblood of the communities in which they lived.

Physical properties of the corporation were widespread, with a total of more than 25,000,000 square feet of factory and office space. These properties represented a complex of companies.

These included McDonnell Aircraft Company, Douglas Aircraft Company, McDonnell Douglas Astronautics Company, McDonnell Douglas Automation Company, McDonnell Douglas-Tulsa, McDonnell Douglas Electronics Company, and wholly-owned subsidiaries, McDonnell Douglas Finance Corporation, McDonnell Douglas Canada Ltd., McDonnell Douglas Realty Company, and Vitek Systems, Inc. As we have pointed out in preceding chapters, these various divisions are engaged in everything from the building of huge jetliners like the DC-10 and faster than sound fighters to missiles and spacecraft that have helped put man on the moon. Moreover, they have produced new materials and services which have helped better our daily lives.

What lies ahead? What are some of the plans for this business (aerospace) as far as McDonnell Douglas is concerned in the twilight years of the 20th century?

When I talked with Mr. Mac about the future, he had some salient remarks . . .

"I certainly see no case for pessimism. There will always be a demand for multiplying diversity of aircraft as long as there is air, and there will always be a demand for spacecraft as long as there is space . . .

"Some of our new developments will surely include new and improved subsonic transport planes. In addition, we will see the beginning of mass transportation between centers of major cities by means of vertical and short takeoff aircraft. And we will, of course, see the beginning of supersonic transportation between major cities throughout the world. Hypersonic transports will be common place. The ballistic rocket transport may carry passengers halfway around the world in less than one hour . . . "

Such are some of the challenges that lie ahead.

ADVANCED SUPERSONIC TRANSPORT. During the past five years, McDonnell Douglas, working closely with a NASA sponsored program, has accomplished much model testing with a supersonic airliner design. It is far from an aircraft in being, but it reflects technology in existence today that can produce a viable SST for tomorrow, say, in the 1990s. By that time, surveys indicate that the traveling public will be ready to accept and pay the price for supersonic transportation.

Listen to Richard D. FitzSimmons, Director of Advanced Supersonic Transports, Douglas Aircraft Company—"Today, the supersonic era is a reality. The French/British *Concorde* is making history. For the first time in twenty-

five years on the major airline routes of the world, the domination by U.S. manufactured aircraft is seriously being challenged. The flooding of the media with stories of uneconomical costs for supersonic transport operations has done much to undermine interest in developing an advanced U.S. supersonic transport for the emerging market. This is now having an adverse impact worldwide on U.S. leadership in civil aviation.

"Unfortunately, some of the leaders of U.S. civilian aerospace, both in the manufacturing community and in the airlines, have found it convenient to believe that supersonic transportation always must be uneconomical. *Such is not the case.* Product research studies at McDonnell Douglas show that an Advanced Supersonic Transport (AST) system can be provided for full economy fare passengers at load factors equivalent to today's subsonic operations, and be profitable.

"A supersonic transport can be designed using technology in hand today. It would be environmentally sound. It could meet noise and

Richard D. Fitzsimmons, Director Advanced Program Planning Engineering Department, Douglas Aircraft Company division in Long Beach, with model of the McDonnell Douglas concept of an Advanced Supersonic Transport.

MCDONNELL DOUGLAS AST

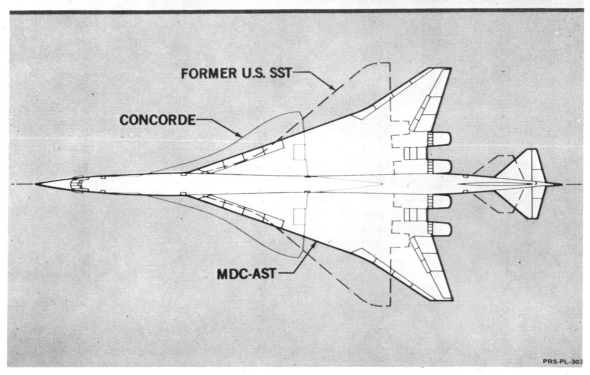

A McDonnell Douglas concept for an Advanced Supersonic Transport. The Douglas division has been investigating technologies for building an AST since 1972.

pollution standards, something which over 84 per cent of today's subsonic airline aircraft cannot accomplish. Even more important, a significant part of the traveling public, those who presently pay full economy fare and, of course, the first class passenger, would select supersonic transportation over subsonic flights. For the same fare as on subsonic flights they could arrive at their destination, in half the time.''

The NASA-sponsored SST studies program, Dick FitzSimmons pointed out, provided important seed money and technology information that motivated Mc-Donnell Douglas to initiate significant Company-funded efforts to accomplish important tests and undertake a detailed preliminary design of an Advanced Super-sonic Transport, unencumbered by preconceived notions of what should be the proper Advanced Supersonic Transport design. The configuration which evolved is a 273-passenger, 4590-nautical-mile range, Mach 2.2 transport incorporating titanium primary structure and aluminum for lightly loaded primary structure and secondary structure.

The proposed McDonnell Douglas Advanced Supersonic Transport (AST) would have a gross weight of 750,000 pounds. It would have a wing span of 123.5 feet, an arrow wing planform, like the paper sailplanes youngsters fold in school. The fuselage (310 feet in overall length) would be longer than a football field. Its huge vertical tail would tower 54.8 feet, higher than a four story building.

Propulsion would come from four mini-bypass turbojet engines each developing about 74,000-pound thrust and equipped with after-burners. Such engines are now being proposed by Pratt & Whitney, General Electric and Rolls-Royce.

How much would it cost?

Dick FitzSimmons' answer—Billions! No one company could afford it. "But at McDonnell Douglas today," he explained, "we are pursuing discussions that could lead to inter-

Advanced Supersonic Transport wind tunnel model.

national collaboration, on a much larger scale than any past or present program."

What would be the ultimate benefits?

Dick FitzSimmons had this to say—"An international advanced supersonic transport, developed jointly between the U.S. and foreign governments could do much to bring the free world closer.

"Supersonic travel is a major step forward, as no country in the world need be more than a day's travel away. Over 50 per cent of the world would be less than four hours away, allowing person to person contact the same day.

"The social advantages of bringing the peoples of the world closer is almost reason enough for supersonic transportation. The civil jet transport era, since 1952, may well go down in history as one of the great contributions to world peace. The supersonic era can do likewise."

Toward such a goal McDonnell Douglas is dedicated.

Beyond the AST, FitzSimmons said that by the year 2000 the world's fleets of transport vehicles may include the hypersonic aircraft. A proposed McDonnell Douglas concept, he pointed out, is the "DC-2000" which would be powered by four hydrogen-burning turbojets and four ramjets. The turbojets would be used for takeoff, transonic acceleration and cruise up to Mach 3.5. Above that speed, the ramjets would power the aircraft.

The DC-2000 would have a wing span of 170 feet with an arrow-like fuselage 475 feet in length. It would have a gross takeoff weight of 875,000 pounds and would be capable of carrying 500 passengers at a cruise speed six times the speed of sound. The hypersonic aircraft would have a range of more than 5,000 miles.

THE ERA OF SKY GIANTS. The author remembers boarding an American Airlines' DST (Douglas Sleeper Transport, one of the first to go into service) and he recalls the remark made by an elderly lady as she walked out to the silvery skyship. "My, oh my!" she exclaimed. "What a large airplane. They'll never build anything any bigger and make it fly . . ."

My fellow passenger would have a heart attack if she could see some of the futuristic designs "on paper" at McDonnell Douglas today. Let's take a peek...

THE NATION BUILDER—Takeoff gross weight 976,260 pounds, twice that of a 747! Payload, 340,000 pounds—170 tons. A wingspan of 269.5 feet, fuselage length of 218.2

288

J. P. (Jack) Hammil, design engineer, with model of McDonnell Douglas concept of *Nationbuilder* cargo transport.

By the year 2000, the world's fleets of transport vehicles may include hypersonic aircraft. A proposed McDonnell Douglas concept, designated "DC-2000," would be powered by four hydrogen-burning turbojets and four ramjets. Turbojets would be used for takeoff, transonic acceleration, and cruise up to Mach 3.5. Above that speed, the ramjets would power the 475-foot-long aircraft

feet, the length of four boxcars.

COMMERCIAL PASSENGER TRANSPORT—A wingspan of 187 feet, fuselage length, 237 feet, a gross weight of 894,800 pounds, capable of carrying 600 passengers!

SPANLOADER CARGO AIRCRAFT—A six-engined freighter capable of carrying a payload of 618,240 pounds—over 300 tons! Wingspan 285.4 feet, fuselage length 202.5 feet. Capable of 3,000 mile range at .65 Mach Number cruise speed.

Now, IMAGINE THIS: From Los Angeles to Honolulu in 18 minutes; to Tokyo in half an hour; to the most distant point on the globe in just 45 minutes!

That's a McDonnell Douglas concept of air travel at some future date *via PEGASUS,* a proposed passenger ballistic transport.

Pegasus, according to one McDonnell Douglas engineer, is a reusable one-stage rocket ship capable of vertical takeoff and of setting down on land rather than splashing into the ocean for recovery. The spacecraft could whisk 170 passengers and 18 tons of cargo high above the atmosphere from continent to continent at 17,000 mph!

Pegasus would have a bell shape configuration, 114 feet high (one-third as tall as Saturn V) and 49 feet wide at its greatest diameter. The upper end would contain a four-decked passenger area, each level fitted with 43 individual couches, on which travelers would ride during their brief flight through space.

The sister ship for orbital flights is distinguished by its taller payload section. It would carry only a limited number of passengers, but its performance characteristics

Front view of *Nation-builder* model. Aircraft would gross out at nearly 1,000,000 pounds.

woud parallel those of the *Pegasus*.

A freighter version of the global transport would carry 37 tons of cargo while an all-passenger version of *Pegasus* would transport a total of 260 persons and baggage.

Pegasus initially would be developed as a one-stage-to-orbit vehicle for maximum reliability, utilizing liquid oxygen and liquid hydrogen as propellants and an annular plug-nozzle engine. It would be controlled by a two-man crew. The vehicle would develop 3,210,000 pounds of thrust at liftoff, about half the thrust of the *Saturn V*.

Pegasus could be launched from spaceports which, by the time the vehicle would be operational, could be established near most key cities throughout the world. If un-populated areas were not available for spaceports, off-shore landing and launching facilities might be considered.

As an example of a typical mission, *Pegasus* could cover the 7500 miles between the California coast and Singapore in 39 minutes. In this typical trans-Pacific flight, passengers would be subjected to no more than three Gs during ascent or re-entry. Booster burnout would occur about six minutes after liftoff, at an altitude of 70 miles.

By then, *Pegasus* would be traveling at a speed of 17,000 mph and, during the next 12 minutes, would coast out of the atmosphere in a graceful arc, attaining an apogee of 125 miles. The greater part of the trip would take place above the atmosphere, where drag is

Six-engined *Spanloader* model. The aircraft is designed to carry more than 300 tons! payload!

The not too distant future might see this scene (artist's concept) at spaceport where passengers could board PBM—Passenger Ballistic Missile—for trip to other planets. *Pegasus* would make space travel possible.

non-existent—well above the "thermal thicket" in which the SST must fly.

The vehicle, following a gentle downward curve, would enter the atmosphere where it could be maneuvered. It then would be re-oriented so its blunt base would come in for a soft landing, in a manner similar to an Apollo moon landing. The base of the vehicle would be cooled by circulation of liquid hydrogen during atmosphere entry.

After re-entry, four engine modules would be ignited to provide retrothrust for terminal velocity cancellation. Within sight of the spaceport, *Pegasus* would hover overhead as landing legs were extended in preparation for the vertical touchdown.

Sound too fantastic?

Not according to Phil Bono, project manager, who more than 15 years ago described the *Pegasus* spacecraft.

"Certainly," Bono says, "if passengers can be rocketed the 240,000 miles to the moon, they can be rocketed much more easily and safely for only 12,400 miles, or halfway around the globe, by using techniques developed during the lunar program.

"This vehicle might tap an entirely new commercial market," Bono projected. "Just as today's 'jet set' hops over to the Riviera for the weekend, the well-heeled tourist of the 1980s might catch a *Pegasus* orbit express for rendezvous with a space station and a sojourn with companions 300 miles above the cares of the world."

With this kind of forward thinking and planning, it seems apparent that McDonnell Douglas *today* is in the middle of *tomorrow!*

Index

INDEX

A

B

C

Carr, Gerald P. (Astronaut), 245
Carroll, Frank O., 73
Chamberlain, John D., 194, 195, 198
Chance Vought (Co.), 105, 109
Chandler, Harry B., 21
Chidlaw, B.W., Gen., 73
Churchill, Prime Minister, 65, 73
Clover Field, 20, 21, 23, 46-48
"Cloudster," 19-22, 27
Collbohm, Franklin R., 44
Collier Trophy, 14, 28, 50, 100 104
Commercial Passenger Transport (new aircraft), 289
Concorde, SST, 69, 200, 284
Connecticut Aircraft Company, 16
Conrad, Charles "Pete" (Astronaut), 245
Continental Airlines, 189, 207
Cooper, Gordon L. (Astronaut), 240
Cover, Carl A., 48
Cowling, James C., 34
Crossfield, Scott, 96
Curtiss, Glenn, 15
Curtiss Condor, 52
Curtiss Field, 20
Curtiss "Tanager," 37, 85

D

Davidson, James T., 86, 87
Davis, David R., 19-21
Davis-Douglas Company, 19, 21, 217
DC-2000 (Hypersonic Aircraft), 288, 289
DeHavilland, 93
DeHavilland (Comet I, II), 93, 129
Delta Airlines, 167, 168
Dixon, Robert, Gen., 266
Doodlebug (Flying Flivver), 34-38, 90, 143, 251
Douglas Aircraft Co., 20, 21, 23, 26, 27, 29, 42, 44-46, 49, 50, 52, 53, 58, 59, 64, 69, 75, 76, 78, 94, 96, 97, 100, 111, 113, 117, 119, 122-125, 137, 144, 154-161, 165, 168, 172-174, 179, 183, 189, 195, 199, 211, 215, 218, 220-222, 231, 242, 285
Douglas Aircraft Co. (Canada), 160, 285
Douglas Aircraft Co. (Japan), 160
Douglas Aircraft (Long Beach), 132, 133, 138, 158, 166, 167, 171, 172, 180, 186, 189, 193, 194
Douglas Aircraft (Torrence), 185
Dolphin (Amphibian), 49, 51
Douglas, Donald W., Jr. 120, 154, 157, 159, 161
Douglas, Donald Wills, Sr., 14-19, 21, 23, 25, 26, 29, 30, 44-46, 48, 50, 52, 53, 57, 59, 64, 75, 115, 117, 118, 120-22, 124, 125, 131, 154-157, 161, 188, 189, 205
Douglas, Dorothy (Locker), 15
Douglas EL Segunda, 62, 94
Douglas Finance Corporation, 160
Douglas, Harold, 15
Douglas Realty Co., 160

N

Northrop, John K., 46
Northwest Orient (Airlines), 50, 167, 168, 189, 207

O

Oleson, M. K., 119
Orthwein, William R., 68, 69
Osborn, Bob, 85
Osborne, Stanley de Jong, 157, 158
Oswald, W. Bailey, 44

P

Pan American (Airways), 50, 115, 117, 126, 143, 171
Patterson, W. A. "Pat", 65, 117
Pearl Harbor, 60, 61, 68, 118, 218
Pegasus (passenger Ballistic Missile), 289-291
Perkins, Kendall, 67, 68, 84-86, 88
Platt-LePage Aircraft Corp., 251
Plummer, C. A., 273
Pogue, William P. (Astronaut), 245
Post Office Department, 23, 31, 50, 52
Pratt Whitney, 57, 101, 104, 113, 122, 141, 143, 156, 176, 206, 207,
    209, 211, 212, 252, 258, 264, 287
Princeton University, 30

R

Raymond, Arthur E., 44, 46, 50, 124-126
Rogers, F. H., (Buck), 143
Rolls-Royce, 128, 176, 211, 273, 287
Roosevelt, Franklin D., 40, 42, 49, 50, 53, 59, 65, 73, 86, 114, 230
Rockwell International Corp., 245, 246, 264
Ryan, T. Claude, 21

S

Shaffer, John H., 202
Shepard, Alan B. (Astronaut), 240
Sheppard, Irv., 86
Shogran, Ivar, 48, 125, 126, 131
Signal Corps, U.S. Army, 18, 24, 30
Signal Oil & Gas Company, 158
Sikorsky, Igor, 251
Smith, C. R., 52, 53, 124-126
SMS (Suspended Maneuvering System), 249, 250
Snowden, Lawrence, Gen., 272
Soviet Union (U.S.S.R.), 29
Spacecraft—see page 304
Spanloader Cargo Aircraft, 289, 290
Spradling, G. F., 179
Stanley, Robert M., 72
Stineman, Fred, 46
Stompl, George, 44, 46
Stout, Clifford L., 194-199
Stout, Raymond, 217, 218

Wright Field, 38, 41, 69, 73, 155, 217
Wright Flyer, 15, 118
Wright, Orville, (Wright Brothers), 15, 53, 54, 118, 176, 191

Y

Yakawa, Shojun, 194-197
Yeager, Charles E., 94, 96, 103
Young, John W. (Astronaut), 242

Z

Zakh, C. L., 37
Zakhartchenko, Leoyavich, 35, 251

AIRCRAFT

A-4 (Skyhawk I and II), 26, 77, 78, 100, 110, 111, 113, 157, 272
A-5D (Skyraider), 76
A-20 (Havoc), 26, 60, 62, 64, 77
A-4D (Skyhawk), 77
A-26 (Invader) (B-26), 26, 60, 77
AD-1 (Skyraider), 64, 76
Army O-2 (Observation Aircraft), 20, 24
AT-15 (Trainer), 69, 70
AT-21, 70, 71
B-17 (Flying Fortress), 43, 58-60, 62, 115
B-18 (Bomber), 43, 60, 61
B-23 (Dragon), 60, 61
B-24 (Liberator), 58-60, 62, 74
B-26 (Marauder), 17
B-29 (Superfortress), 90, 96, 97, 122
B-36 (Consolidated Bomber), 79, 80
B-52 (Stratofortress), 132, 182
B-66 (Destroyer), 77, 78
C-47 (Skytrain), 41, 42, 55, 56, 60, 64, 119
C-54 (Skymaster), 60, 63-65, 115, 118, 119, 122
C-74, 62, 63, 130
C-124 (Globemaster), 62, 63, 130, 131
C-133 (Turbo-prop), 130-132
D-558-1 (Skystreak), 94, 95, 97
D-558-2 (Skyrocket), 92, 95-97
DB-7 (French), 60, 64, 122
DC-1 ("Old 300"), 22, 44, 46-50, 100, 117, 125, 167, 177, 205
DC-2, 14, 46, 49-53, 117, 122, 205
DC-3 (Gooneybird), 26, 41, 42, 44, 46, 53-56, 60, 64, 69,115, 117-119,
    121, 122, 125, 126, 159, 167, 188, 192, 205, 211
DC-4, 26, 65, 68, 114, 116-119, 122, 205, 251
DC-5, 121, 122
DC-6, 26, 119, 122-127, 195
DC-7, 26, 125-127, 130, 195, 205
DC-8, 26, 27, 44, 58, 129-135, 137, 144, 157, 158, 162, 171, 173, 195,
    196, 205

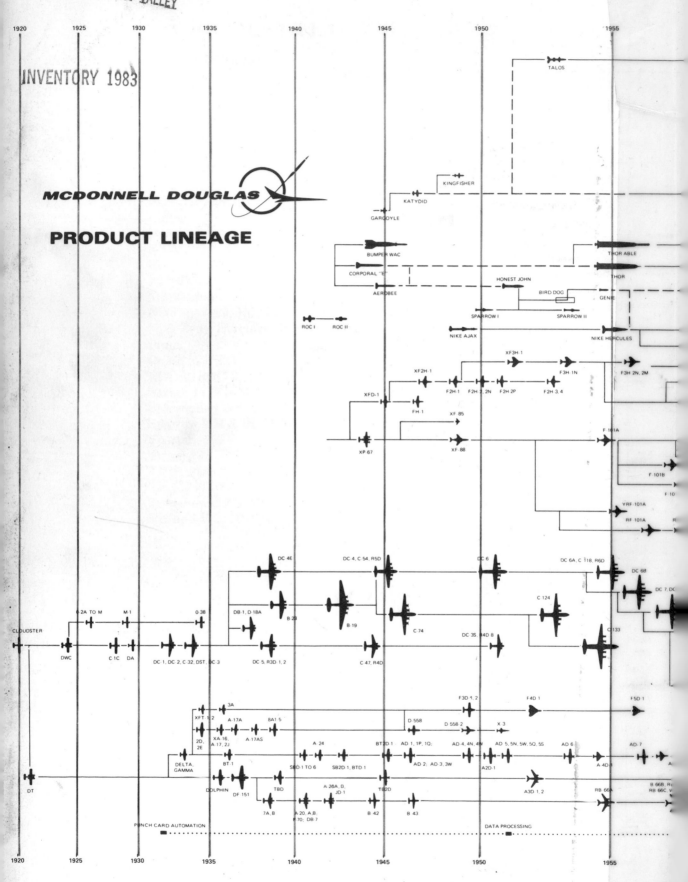

INVENTORY 1983

MCDONNELL DOUGLAS

PRODUCT LINEAGE